HORSE TACK

HORSE TACK

THE COMPLETE EQUIPMENT GUIDE FOR RIDING AND DRIVING

Edited by Julie Richardson

A London Editions Book

PELHAM BOOKS

Copyright © 1981 London Editions Limited

First published in Great Britain by Pelham Books Ltd,
44 Bedford Square, London WC1B 3DU
Copyright © 1982 London Editions Limited

Designed and produced by London Editions Ltd,
70 Old Compton Street, London W1V 5PA

ISBN 0 7207 1377 3

Printed in Italy

CONTRIBUTORS

Editor: Julie Richardson

Writers: Anne Alcock, Jennifer Baker,
John Bullock, Patricia A. Close, Chris Collins,
Anthony Crossley, Valerie Francis, Jane Fuller,
Elwyn Hartley-Edwards, Jane Holderness-Roddam,
Elizabeth Johnson, Pamela Macgregor-Morris, Tom Ryder,
Diana Tuke, Marylian Watney, Agnes Wilkie, Dorian Williams

Artist: Frederick St Ward

Photographer: Fred Spencer
except for photographs on pages 1, 122/123, 152/153,
180/181 by Mike Roberts, 2/3 by Sally Anne Thompson,
8/9 by Stuart Newsham

Editorial and Design Team: C. J. Tunney and Diane James

The Editor would like to thank the
following people for their help and advice:
Susan Bland; Davina Cockroft; Sgt Duker and
the North Yorkshire Constabulary, Mounted Branch;
Liz Kershaw; Jane Pontifex

Contents

INTRODUCTION

Introduction

This is not a book about how to ride. It is about equipment for the horse—what it is like and how it functions. Knowledge of these two things enables the horseman to use equipment to the greatest benefit of his horse and, therefore, of himself.

Great horsemen and horsewomen may or may not be born rather than made. But they all know an immense amount about the materials they have to work with and about how to use them. No one would expect a Formula One racing driver to be ignorant of the fittings of his car engine, or a painter to know nothing of the qualities of his paints and canvases. Yet a surprising number of those involved in the exacting art of horsemanship have little knowledge of the tools they use or should be able to use.

In the sphere of equestrian equipment, ignorance is not bliss. Knowledge can open a rider's way to greater understanding of what he is doing, and can help to bridge the gaps in communication between the rider and his horse.

In the modern equestrian world, there are few subjects that cause more discussion—often adamant to the point of heated argument—than equipment. Despite this, it is amazing how little most riders know of the range of equipment about which they speak with so much passion.

Much has been said, particularly in recent years, about 'gadgets'. Many new pieces of equipment have been categorized in this way at one time or another, from the draw rein to the drop noseband.

The merits or otherwise of 'gadgets' will always be a subject of discussion until the 'gadgets' become common and, hence, respectable. But in judging any new piece of equipment, it is useful to remember the well-known saying about 'the razor in the monkey's hands', a saying that refers to novice riders and the draw rein but which might equally well be applied to any potentially severe piece of equipment used by those with neither the skill nor the knowledge to do so.

Most items have been designed to meet a particular need. A man who once lived in Kineton, England, for example, owned a horse that pulled like a train. He invented the strong noseband that we still call the Kineton. When inventions are effective, they are widely adopted; and, often, their origins and their proper functions are ignored.

Although horsemen and horsewomen seem to be known collectively as conservative, the wide variety of tack and harness is proof of their continuing inventiveness. Much of the fruit of this inventiveness goes out of date. Some is so specific that it may suit just one horse in every million. But a lot remains as the solid, enduring basis of horsemanship.

This is just one of the reasons why a book such as this is necessary. There is very little written information about the subject of horse equipment. In early days, much was passed down by word of mouth: from parent to child, from trainer to groom. But a new breed of rider has been on the scene for a long time now—the first generation rider, the one who has no knowledgeable horseman at his elbow, the one who gleans his information where he can find it and has little help.

Few of us like to show our ignorance to those who are knowledgeable. A visit to the local saddlery shop can be an ordeal for those who are sure neither of what they want nor of what it will look like when they see it.

The welfare of the horse should be an over-riding concern for all riders and drivers. Welfare does not relate only to feeding and veterinary care, but also to every other aspect of the horse's life—whether work or pleasure. And at every point, equipment is involved.

Ignorance of the correct use of equipment militates against proper care and welfare: horses with saddle sores, girth galls and bruised or bleeding mouths are proof of this. But perhaps the blame should not lie solely with the obvious culprit, the owner, but also with those who are skilled enough to offer advice and information but fail to do so.

The writers of this book have had many years of practical experience in buying, using and caring for equipment for their horses. They are authorities in their fields. And they are anxious to share their knowledge: knowledge in one of the most neglected areas of the equestrian world.

The Scope of the Book

The book opens with a study of the materials used to make equipment for horses. Each type of material fulfils a different function in relation to the horse, his ability to perform and his personal comfort.

The first stage in using these materials is concerned with persuading the horse to accept man's authority: the breaking—or, better, making—equipment.

Then comes riding equipment—of necessity, the largest single section. In it, the theory and function of bridles and bitting act as preliminaries to the different types and their attachments. Information about how bits are made today gives an insight into buying them.

The saddle is covered from its construction and fitting to its design and use in specialist areas of equitation. A chapter on the general purpose saddle is followed by those on all other types of saddles, including showing, dressage, jumping, racing and cross-country saddles, and, of course, side-saddles. Special chapters deal with Western equipment and other types of equipment of particular interest.

An equestrian sport that is booming today is driving. The equipment used for all types of driving, from single turnouts to unicorns, teams and pairs, and harness racing equipment is explained in some detail.

A book on equipment for the horse would be incomplete without a comprehensive chapter on the horse in the stable: clothing, grooming tools and clippers, shoes and all that goes into caring for the horse's needs. It includes information about tack room and stable fittings, too, as well as vice prevention aids and veterinary aids for use by the horse owner.

Although correct dress for the rider is beyond the scope of a book devoted to horse equipment, there is one aspect of clothing that is vital: safety when mounted. Therefore, information about hats and boots is included. The horse is not the only one requiring protection in such an energetic sport as horsemanship.

History

It is surprising how little equipment for the horse has changed during the 24 or so centuries since man first decided to harness and ride the horse rather than to eat him.

Certain of the earliest pieces of equipment, such as the yoke, proved disastrous. The yoke almost garrotted the horse that wore it, and had to be changed. But what it was changed for—the collar—has stood the test of time to such an extent that it is still the basis of driving harness today.

Early man had far more successes than failures to his credit: such things as the straight bar and jointed snaffles, the curb bit, the saddle that incorporated a tree, and the stirrup. All these were known before the first century AD, and their appearance has not changed all that much over the centuries.

The story of saddlery and harness begins in about 4,000 BC, when the first harness was used in southwest Asia. Horses, unlike cattle and camels, were probably always bridled and bitted. The first bridles were rawhide halters looped either just round the nose—forerunners of the modern jumping

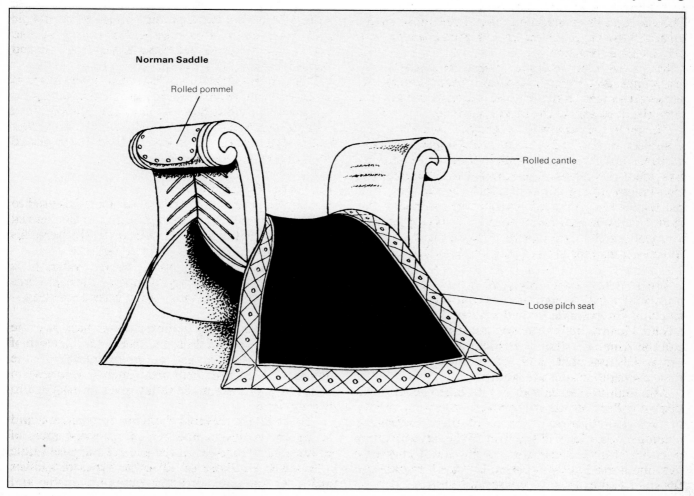

Norman Saddle

Rolled pommel

Rolled cantle

Loose pilch seat

Medieval French
side-saddle. It has
a horn and a planchette
for the feet.

hackamore—or through the mouth, a fashion later taken up by the American Indians.

Early bits were snaffles made of wood or horn. They had straight mouthpieces with rings at each side, to which were attached two reins and a headpiece. But by 1400 BC, somebody had invented a snaffle bit that was jointed in the middle to produce a nutcracker action in the horse's mouth, just as it does today.

For the next thousand years, this type of bit satisfied the horseman. He could control his horse with ease and, although his saddle was only a saddlecloth strapped on with a bellyband, he felt secure enough to hunt and to do battle with his neighbours. Later, he added cushions to the saddlecloth, but these simply helped him to stay more comfortably insecure.

As man discovered metals, the horse found metals in his mouth. Bronze bits came first, then iron, both of which must by definition have been more severe than wood.

Then came an invention that gave the horse even more to think about: the curb bit. This was probably first used by the Gauls before 500 BC. Certainly, the Greek horseman Xenophon knew of it by then, although neither he nor his contemporaries could claim the honour of having invented it.

Curbs promoted war. They enabled warriors to manhandle their horses with more dexterity than they ever could with a snaffle, and acted upon pressure points that the early horses had not realized they owned.

Three hundred years later, the first rigid tree saddles were being used in China. These saddles, although they still had no stirrups, were more stable and kinder to the horses' backs than anything that had gone before.

Ancient Cheek Snaffle Bit

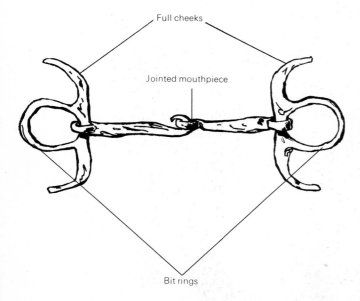

Full cheeks

Jointed mouthpiece

Bit rings

Tod Sloan-Style Race Exercise Saddle

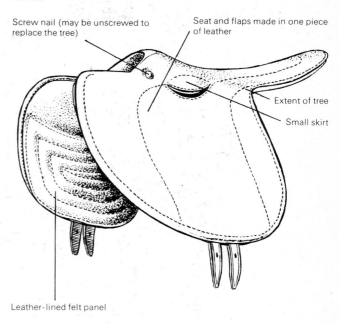

Screw nail (may be unscrewed to replace the tree)

Seat and flaps made in one piece of leather

Extent of tree

Small skirt

Leather-lined felt panel

Why man was capable of inventing all these immensely practical pieces of equipment—some of which we have hardly improved upon today—and yet took so long to devise a stirrup is a mystery. It is also rather a mystery who actually did invent it. According to some authorities, it was Attila the Hun in about AD 430; others say that it was the Indians, whose stirrups anchored the big toe only. Certainly, in AD 500 the Chinese had a stirrup arrangement into which the foot could be fitted.

Whoever produced the stirrup not only aided horsemanship, but made the most important advance in warfare until the invention of gunpowder. But that is yet another story.

There has been little pure invention in the last 15 centuries. Modern driving harness developed in Asia and came to Europe in about AD 800. By the twelfth century, it was being used in ploughing farmland in the whole of northern Europe. Just a hundred years later, large carriages with four wheels began to revolutionize land transport.

As harness was settling into a fairly fixed pattern, riding bits and saddles were becoming more and more complex and ornate. In the 1500s, curbs with cheeks as long as 380 mm (15 in.), twisted iron nosebands and saddles like huge chairs weighing around 18 kg (40 lb) were the norm. And such fighting people as the Saracens employed high port curbs with single reins, which acted fiercely on the roof of the mouth.

After the storm, came the calm. By the late 1700s, many saddles were of the English hunting type, and bits were of a more moderate length and action.

Materials

Equipment can only be as good as the materials from which it is made, the craftsmanship that fashions it and the care it receives when in use. The more the horseman knows about its production, how to recognize the best and how to keep it at its best, the better he will be served by it.

Hides

The first material to consider is leather. Most leather used in saddlery comes from cattle, and the best comes from young cattle and from certain breeds, such as the Aberdeen Angus.

In many countries, saddlers and harness makers have to use mainly

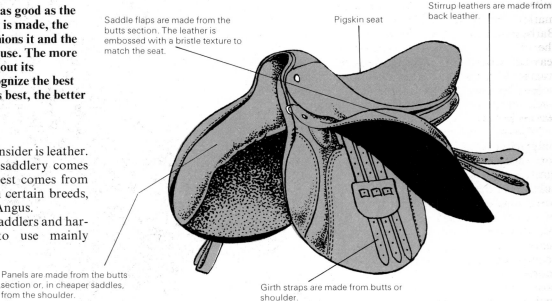

Saddle flaps are made from the butts section. The leather is embossed with a bristle texture to match the seat.

Pigskin seat

Stirrup leathers are made from back leather.

Panels are made from the butts section or, in cheaper saddles, from the shoulder.

Girth straps are made from butts or shoulder.

Sections of Cowhide

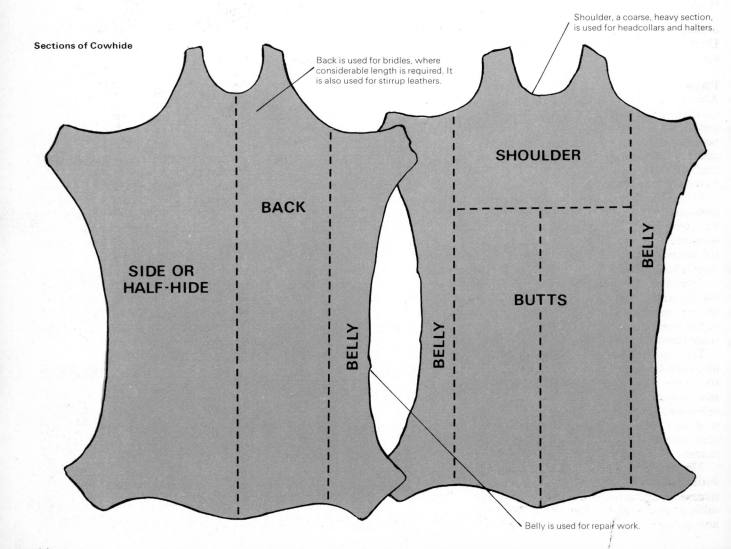

Shoulder, a coarse, heavy section, is used for headcollars and halters.

Back is used for bridles, where considerable length is required. It is also used for stirrup leathers.

SIDE OR HALF-HIDE

BACK

BELLY

SHOULDER

BELLY

BELLY

BUTTS

Belly is used for repair work.

imported hides, in order to obtain the necessary quality. In Britain, for instance, the hides used come chiefly from Argentina, although the USSR is beginning to break into this market. Many home-produced hides are un-suitable for use because they have been marked by barbed wire and warbles. Barbed wire used for fencing cuts into the hides when cattle rub against it, leaving scratch marks. The marks of warble flies, on the other hand, are holes. The flies lay eggs on an animal's back, and when the eggs hatch the larvae burrow through the hide.

Pigskin and sheepskin constitute only about a tenth of the leather used for saddlery. Pigskin is extremely elastic and light, but it has little substance (thickness). It is used, there-fore, mainly for saddle seats, the flaps of which are usually of cowhide im-printed with bristle marks to match the seats. It is also used for making light racing saddles, which must not weigh more than about 1 kg (40 oz), and to cover the flaps of some saddles, which makes them expensive and also extremely thick under the thigh.

Sheepskin is reserved for backing the linings and panels of cheaper saddles. Doeskin covers the flaps and skirts of expensive ones.

Preparing Leather

Animal hides are cleaned, tanned and curried before being made up by a saddler or harness maker. Briefly, the process begins when the hide is washed and soaked in milk of lime to loosen the hair, sweat glands and fat cells, and to separate the fibres.

Two roller machines remove the hair and loose flesh. The hides are then cut up (rounded) by hand before tanning proceeds, so that hides of the same substance receive the same length and type of treatment.

For saddlery, vegetable tanning is used. During this process, the hides lie in ever-strengthening solutions of tan liquor for up to nine months. They are then dried.

The next process, currying, takes about 20 days. First, the hide is soaked to remove scum, then a splitting machine reduces it to the required substance. Revolving drums clean it with acid and then water, and a hand-setting machine irons out any growth marks.

The leather is dried and then stained with a pad of dye. It is flattened with a plating machine before being sent to an oiling room, where tallow and cod oil are rubbed in to increase the finished

leather's tensile strength, flexibility and water-resistance.

Metals and Other Materials

As well as leather, various other materials are used in saddlery and harness making—chiefly the metals from which bits, stirrup irons and small fittings are made.

The most popular metal today is stainless steel, which has replaced the old-fashioned, hand-forged or drop-forged steel. Stainless steel is bright, rustless and almost unbreakable if it is of good quality. Because of production costs, only a limited number of patterns of stainless steel bits and irons is available, but they are usually of reliable design and material if manu-factured in Europe or in the United States. However, buyers must beware

Stainless steel bits of the German pattern, with a fixed-cheek curb and an eggbutt bridoon. Stainless steel is the most popular metal used in saddlery and harness today. It is not only bright, easy to maintain and almost unbreakable, but is also malleable which helps in bit manufacture.

of cheap mass-produced items, which are not up to standard.

Hand-forged stainless steel bits are now almost things of the past. But their finish and quality are so superior to anything else that if any can be found today they are worth paying a high price for. They last a lifetime.

Solid nickel is cheap and rustless, but it turns yellow. Because it bends and can break, it is often considered dangerous. Used with other metals as a nickel mixture, it is a lot more reliable and does not yellow.

Buying a Bit

- When buying a bit, great care must be taken to avoid flaws. They are not always easily seen.

- The surface of a bit should be smooth, with no irregularities, sharp edges or rough surfaces to irritate the horse's mouth.

- Quality is the aim: cheap bits are a bad investment.

For racing, aluminium has proved a suitable metal for bits and irons because of its lightness. Its major fault, particularly dangerous in steeple-chasing, is that it has been known to break under stress during a race.

Two other materials used in bit manufacture are rubber and vulcanized rubber (vulcanite). Both are softer than metal, rubber being the softest. The disadvantage of a plain rubber mouthpiece is that it can be chewed and torn. If it has a chain running through the centre for strength, this can be dangerous and can severely injure the horse's mouth. Vulcanized rubber—invented simultaneously in 1839 by an American and an Englishman—is tough and tear resistant.

Selecting Tack

Time taken choosing good tack is time well spent. Tack has to be lived with for a long time, and it is as well not to have to rely solely upon the maker's name to secure a good piece of equipment.

Judging Quality in Leather
Again, leather is of primary importance. The leather for normal saddlery should have plenty of substance: the more it has, the harder-wearing it will be, although obviously a bridle made for the show ground does not have to be as substantial as one for the hunting field. A light show bridle is not expected to stand up to the rigours of everyday hacking and hunting. Such articles as headcollars and rollers necessarily require extra substance if they are to do their job.

The flesh side (inside) of good leather is smooth and has no coarse fibres hanging from it, unless it is panel hide. The grain side (outside) is closely grained.

Inferior leather looks and feels dry and hard. The best leather has a re-assuringly greasy feel, and often a greyish tinge on the grain side, which is in fact surplus grease.

Good leather should also be firm to the touch. A flabby feel is a sure sign of poor quality. Such parts of the saddle as the flaps should submit to being rolled up in the hand without 'bubbling' on either side or giving the feeling that they may crack.

Colour
Colour is a matter of taste. Shades vary from manufacturer to manufacturer,

but the most usual is *London*, a light yellowish colour that tones down gradually but well. *Saffron* is a deeper shade of London colour.

Deeper brown is *Havana*, a rich shade that looks good from the outset and ages nicely. It is often a mark of quality. *Warwick* is darker still, and usually becomes black in time.

A relatively new fashion in saddlery is to buy black tack. Black is particularly common in the United States for showing, and in Britain for dressage. It is the most common colour for harness: harness makers were once distinguished from saddlers by being called 'black saddlers'.

Specialized Leathers
Certain varieties of leather have specific functions to which they are best suited. Rawhide and Helvetia leathers, for instance, are remarkably strong and are, therefore, sometimes used for stirrup leathers, headcollars, nosebands, martingales and the like. These two types of leather are some-times confused: rawhide is given a

special tannage that leaves the finished leather with a central strip of a lighter colour when viewed in section; Helvetia is yellow and very greasy.

For stirrup leathers, in particular, oak-bark tanned—a rich brown cow-hide that has been given a long treatment—is best. Buffalo, with its distinctive red colour and greasy feel, is also good and almost unbreakable.

Saddles are often made in what is known as *reversed hide*. This is ordinary cowhide buffed up to a rough finish. It should cost no more than ordinary leather and it gives the rider a good grip. The finish can be maintained for quite a long time with sandpaper.

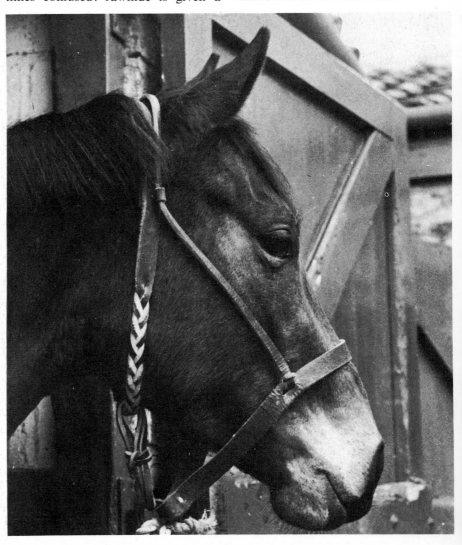

A rawhide halter, hand-fashioned for strength in the American style. This strong type of halter is a good investment for use on a horse that persistently pulls back and breaks headcollars made of weaker leather.

Taking Care of Equipment

Neglected equipment can significantly worsen the performance of horse and rider—and can be the cause of injury. Any faulty piece of saddlery or harness, whether it is a rein that needs restitching or simply a saddle in need of restuffing, should be discarded until it has been repaired. Keeping equipment in good repair simply means taking care of it and watching for signs of wear.

Caring for Leather Equipment

Caring for leather is an everyday task. Leather has a daily battle to keep supple against such opposition as water, heat and, of course, neglect. Unless it wins, it loses its fat, becomes dry and brittle and eventually cracks.

The grain side of leather is partially sealed but the flesh side is not, and leather loses fat from here each time it is used, because of the horse's heat and sweat. This means that it must be cleaned and the fat replaced daily. And not only the leather will benefit from this treatment: dirty tack causes all sorts of skin and hygiene problems for the horse.

The aim during cleaning is to wash off dried mud and sweat, which block the pores on the flesh side in particular. The tack is taken to pieces for cleaning and the washing is done with a well-wrung cloth. 'Jockeys', the small lumps of dirt and grease that accumulate in certain areas, are first removed with a blunt instrument. Glycerine saddle soap is then rubbed well in on both sides with a very slightly damp cloth or sponge. Aerosol foam soaps should not be used.

Once a week, a suppling preparation such as Kocholine, Flexalan or Harris's Saddle Paste should be rubbed by hand into the flesh side before soaking. Neatsfoot oil was once popular for this purpose, many people soaking new London colour tack in it for days. But treatment of this kind only makes leather soggy, lifeless and greasy, without benefit to the horse's skin, to the saddle stitching (which rots), or to the rider's breeches and gloves.

A final polish shines the leather before the tack is put away and covered, to prevent dust settling. Tack should be stored in a dry building at normal room temperature. Damp and too much heat are both bad for leather.

If tack has become wet, or has needed more vigorous washing, it should be wiped over with a dry cloth and left to finish drying naturally. Placing it near artificial heat will destroy its elasticity.

Storage of temporarily unused leather can be a problem. Leather can deteriorate rapidly. It should be cleaned and then liberally coated in Kocholine or Vaseline.

Some people clean show tack with boot polish. This does make it shine, but it also seals the pores and eventually cracks the leather.

Caring for Other Equipment

Girths and numnahs of materials other than leather and skin need washing and brushing regularly if they are not to gall the horse or rot. Articles that need washing but have some leather parts can cause problems. The leather will not respond well to the treatment needed by the other materials, nor vice versa.

Such articles as non-leather leg boots and saddle linings need to be brushed well when dry. Thick rugs that cannot be washed at home should be dry-cleaned before being stored, with mothballs, in a large, airy chest.

Little can be done to prolong the life of metals, although buckles benefit from a weekly coating of some sort of grease. Bits should be washed, dried and polished in the same way as stirrup irons and curb chains. Mouthpieces should not be cleaned with metal polish: no horse likes the taste.

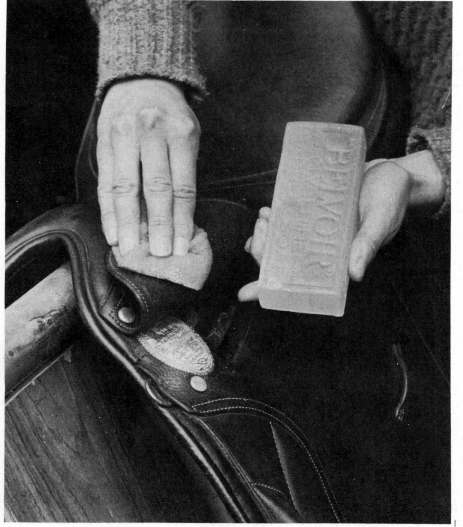

A daily cleaning routine is necessary to ensure the survival of expensive leather saddles. The best saddle soap is the glycerine block variety. After the leather has been washed and dried, the soap is rubbed well in on the flesh and grain sides using a well-wrung cloth. A cloth that is too wet causes soap suds, which lessen the benefit of the glycerine soap on the leather and stick in corners of the equipment causing unsightly dirt traps. If soap does stick in crevices, a matchstick is a useful tool to remove it.

BREAKING AND SCHOOLING

Breaking and Schooling

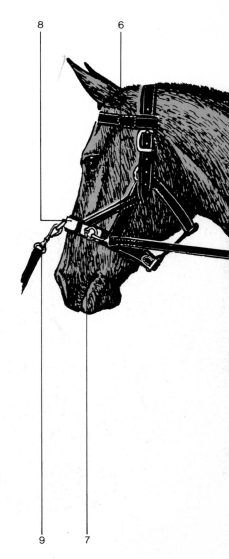

The term 'breaking' is unfortunate in relation to the training of a horse. Taken literally, it is gravely and dangerously misleading, though horses have been broken in spirit and flesh with appropriately-named breaking tackle for centuries.

Yet there is documentary proof that as early as 400 BC, the Greek cavalry used the humane methods of breaking horses from which modern practices are directly derived. These lapsed into oblivion in the Dark Ages and were not revived until the early eighteenth century in France.

But even today, methods that rely on force and restrictive tackle are still practised by a few horsemen with essentially conservative minds. They never produce the best results: but old habits, like old pieces of equipment, die hard.

Breaking today should simply mean the handling of the untamed horse, giving him confidence in human beings and in his enforced surroundings and circumstances. He needs to be educated to accept the benefits of elementary discipline and to live comfortably with people. And, of course, he has to be prepared physically and mentally to carry a rider.

It has been proved beyond question that these aims are best achieved by treating a young horse in much the same way as children are treated. Mutual trust should be the foundation of training.

Modern trends in breaking equipment reflect this. The young horse, surprised as he undoubtedly is by any tack at all, is laden with as little paraphernalia as possible. The few items that are used, however, must be of the right size and type, and must be made of high quality materials.

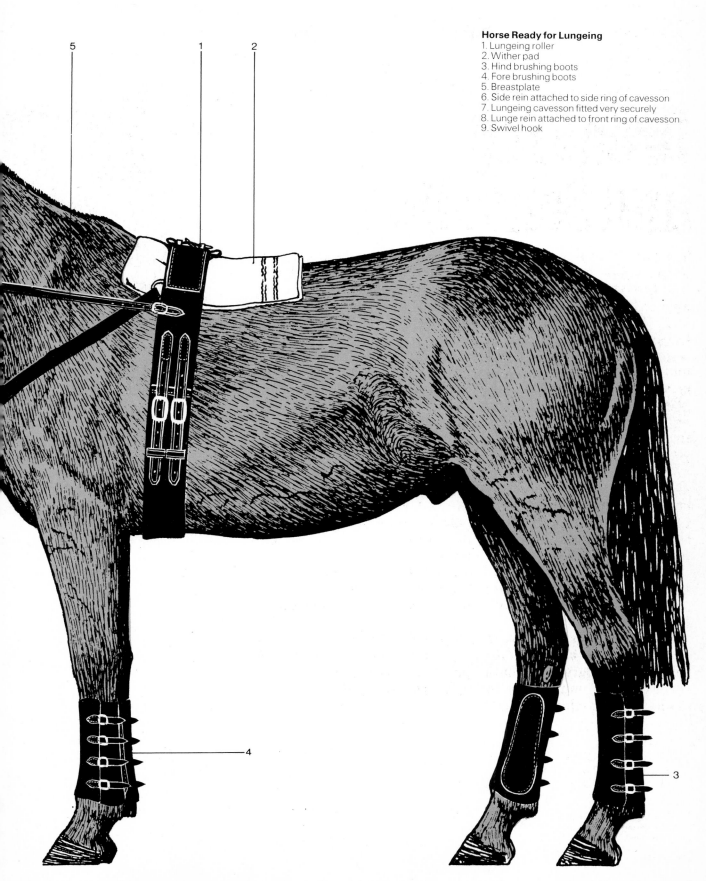

Horse Ready for Lungeing
1. Lungeing roller
2. Wither pad
3. Hind brushing boots
4. Fore brushing boots
5. Breastplate
6. Side rein attached to side ring of cavesson
7. Lungeing cavesson fitted very securely
8. Lunge rein attached to front ring of cavesson
9. Swivel hook

The Trainer's Aids

Cavesson Headcollar

The cavesson headcollar is the first essential piece of equipment required for the handling and training of a young horse and, most particularly, for lungeing. It is a simple but strongly-made bridle with a low-fitting noseband. The noseband is padded and is reinforced with a hinged steel band, to which a leading-rein or lunge-rein can be attached by a ring.

The overall strength of the leather and of the cavesson construction are vital. In no circumstances should anything break in the event of a horse putting on a trial of strength through playfulness or panic.

The reinforced noseband is fitted fairly low to give the handler greater leverage in an emergency. Many trainers prefer to fit it in the manner of a drop noseband when a snaffle is being used. The cavesson back-strap is pulled fairly tight so that the cheekpieces cannot slip forward over the horse's eye on the side farthest from the trainer.

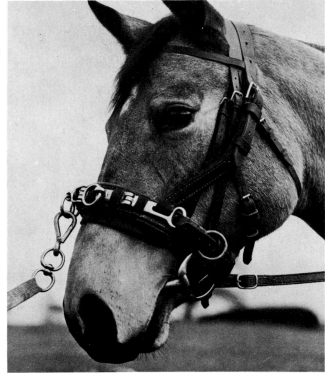

A stout Orssich-pattern lungeing cavesson. If the lunge-rein is fitted onto the central nosepiece attachment the horse may be lunged on either rein without further adjustment. The two rear attachments allow the cavesson to be used for long-reining. The cavesson nosepiece has been fitted over the cheekpieces of the bridle. Many trainers prefer the nosepiece to lie beneath the cheekpieces to obviate any danger of the horse's lips being pinched. The bridle noseband and browband are often removed to reduce bulk beneath the cavesson.

The cavesson is used on all occasions when the young horse is being led outside the stable. It is preferred to a snaffle or any other sort of bitted bridle because it eliminates the possibility of the mouth being pulled and damaged. Even at a late stage of training, when the tacked-up horse is being led from the stable to the place of work, a cavesson should be fitted over the snaffle bridle. No other form of headcollar should ever be used for lungeing or long-reining.

A popular modern cavesson is the Orssich pattern, which is a sturdy type. A projecting ring is swivel-mounted on the nose for lungeing or leading, and driving rings are fitted at both sides of the reinforced noseband. Some cavessons have a strap fitted from the centre of the noseband to the headpiece to prevent the noseband dropping lower than it is fitted.

Rollers

It is possible to buy rollers that are specially designed for lungeing, long-reining or otherwise 'breaking' a horse. These straps round the horse's girth introduce him to the feel of the saddle

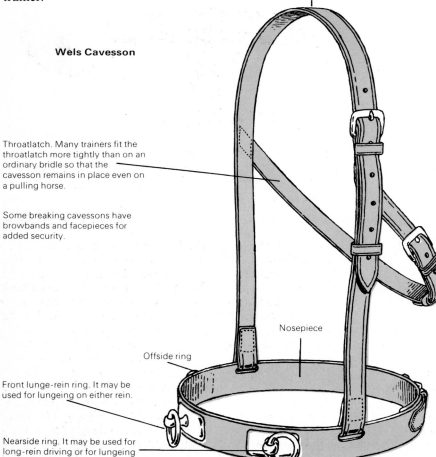

Wels Cavesson

Headpiece

Throatlatch. Many trainers fit the throatlatch more tightly than on an ordinary bridle so that the cavesson remains in place even on a pulling horse.

Some breaking cavessons have browbands and facepieces for added security.

Nosepiece

Offside ring

Front lunge-rein ring. It may be used for lungeing on either rein.

Nearside ring. It may be used for long-rein driving or for lungeing on the nearside.

and are fitted out with all essential, and some less essential, attachments in the form of brass D-rings and buckles.

Such specialist rollers, which are necessarily expensive, are virtually essential for efficient long-reining. But since it is now considered quite normal, and even usual, to employ only single-rein lungeing for working young horses from the ground, many people find it quite sufficient to use any suitable strong stable roller. It should have two or perhaps three D-rings attached to the front edge on each side to hold the side-reins, and a single D-ring at the back in case it should be thought necessary to use a crupper, although this is unusual.

Using a Saddle for Lungeing

It is possible, and perfectly sound, to use a saddle instead of a roller for lungeing, though it is then more difficult to stabilize the setting of the side-reins, which have to be passed through the girth straps. The roller is, and looks, more convenient and efficient, although it is desirable to use a saddle in the period immediately before a young horse is first backed.

Bridles and Bits in Breaking

There are no special bridles for breaking purposes, and the use of what are termed 'breaking' bits is questionable. The bridle used is the plain snaffle, worn under a cavesson headcollar throughout the lungeing phase of the horse's education. It is later used by itself and without the cavesson as soon as the horse is backed, and for at least the first six months of his mounted work.

It is convenient, when a bridle is used under a cavesson, to have the snaffle bit attached to a leather headpiece and cheekpieces only, dispensing with browband, noseband, throatlatch and reins. Using the snaffle in this way avoids much unnecessary clutter on a young horse's head—and also saves a lot of cleaning.

Only a simple snaffle bit should be used. All other bits, including those with keys, are injurious in one way or another in the early stages of training. The mouthpiece, whether the horse is on the lunge or mounted, should be thick and round, especially towards the outer ends. This renders it less aggressive and painful on the bars of the mouth.

Side-Reins

Side-reins should be used throughout the lungeing phase, with the exception

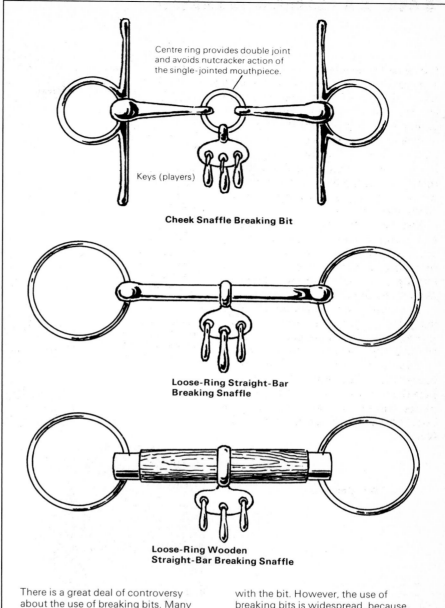

Centre ring provides double joint and avoids nutcracker action of the single-jointed mouthpiece.

Keys (players)

Cheek Snaffle Breaking Bit

Loose-Ring Straight-Bar Breaking Snaffle

Loose-Ring Wooden Straight-Bar Breaking Snaffle

There is a great deal of controversy about the use of breaking bits. Many trainers will not use them because of the danger of encouraging bad habits in the young horse by teaching him to play with the bit. However, the use of breaking bits is widespread, because some trainers hold firmly to the view that they give the horse a good mouth.

of the first one or two days. They are short leather reins, adjustable for length by means of a buckle in the middle or at the roller end. They are attached to the roller or saddle by means of a buckle, and to the snaffle bit by means of an easy-release clip.

The purpose of side-reins is five-fold. They exercise a mild degree of discipline by preventing the horse gazing around or throwing his head about excessively. They accustom him to the purely negative control of reins attached to the bit, which will not pull at him if he does not pull at them. They restrain the bit from moving about too much in the mouth and possibly starting off the bad habit of playing with

the bit. They encourage the horse to stretch his neck in order to find a contact with the bit as he works, and, finally, they provide the trainer with a means of adjusting the length of the frame within which he wants his pupil to work at any given time.

A plain leather side-rein has no harshness or force, because it is entirely passive. The horse can comfortably adapt himself to the set length, provided only that it is never fitted so short as to restrict the freedom of the action. It is the responsibility of the trainer to keep a constant watch on this aspect.

If a horse tends to carry his head too high, with a consequent restricted action of the back and loins, the side-reins should be fitted on a line more-or-less horizontal to the roller or saddle. If the head is consistently carried too low, with the horse making no effort to relieve the weight on the forehand, the side-reins should be fitted higher on the roller. To encourage a horse to stretch, the side-reins should be fitted long. If he is to be encouraged to collect himself, they should be fitted shorter. They will be too long if the horse cannot reach far enough to make a contact, and they will be too short if they appear to restrict the muscular freedom of the back and neck. Within those two limits, the side-reins should be adjusted according to the requirements of the moment.

Lunge-Reins

Lungeing means working a horse on a circle by means of a single long rein, normally attached by a buckle to the front ring on the noseband of a cavesson. This fastening usually swivels to allow freedom of movement. The end of the rein is held by the trainer, standing still in the centre of the circle.

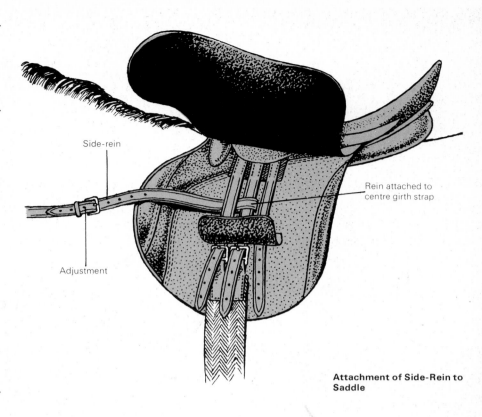

Side-rein

Adjustment

Rein attached to centre girth strap

Attachment of Side-Rein to Saddle

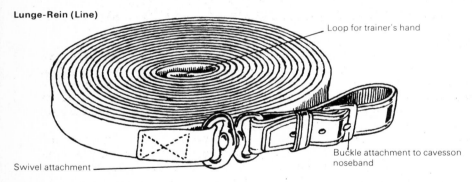

Lunge-Rein (Line)

Loop for trainer's hand

Swivel attachment

Buckle attachment to cavesson noseband

The lunge-rein should be made of webbing or cord, as light as possible but strong and rot-proof. In length, it should be between 7 and 10 m (23 and 33 ft), though some are shorter. It should have a loop at the trainer's end and it is helpful if the rein is marked with coloured paint at 1 m (3 ft) intervals from the buckle end, so that the trainer can tell at a glance the size of the circle on which the horse is working.

The rein is held in the trainer's left hand when the horse is circling to the left (anti-clockwise), and in the right hand when circling to the right.

Lunge-Whips

A lunge-whip is a vital piece of lungeing equipment. It is used to urge the horse forward with more energy than

he might otherwise offer, in the same way as the rider's legs will be doing in the later, mounted stage of training. It is also used to discourage the horse from creeping inwards on the circle, obliging him to track up and work on the full extent of the circle defined by the trainer.

For a lunge-whip to be effective, it is essential that it be long enough overall to enable the trainer to touch the horse with the lash. A whip soon becomes ineffective if the horse gets to know that he cannot be touched with it, and it must therefore be as long as the radius of the largest circle on which the trainer is likely to do much work.

The lunge-whip is never used to strike or alarm the horse. Indeed, the trainer's first concern must be to make the horse confident that the whip is

nothing to fear, and is more a friend than an enemy. Only then will he be able to obtain the sort of calm but conscientious response to the message of the whip that he requires.

The balance of the lunge-whip should be such that the trainer can use it with the precision of a dry-fly fisherman with his rod and fly. A crude, ill-balanced instrument will never produce that kind of result.

Most whips sold, though generally light and well-balanced, are too short overall and need to be fitted with an extension to the lash before they are used. An extension can easily be made from a length of nylon cord, about 6 mm ($\frac{1}{4}$ in.) thick.

Lunge-Whip

To be effective the whip must be long enough for the lash to touch the horse.

Long-reining a young horse from the rear nosepiece attachments of an Orssich-pattern lungeing cavesson. The trainer uses a leather breaking roller fitted with large D-rings to take the long-reins horizontally from the cavesson before they run to his hands. The legs of the horse are often protected by boots, and bandaging in front guards against strain on the ligaments.

Long-Reins

Long-reining a young horse means working him on circles, curves or straight lines by means of two long-reins, each equivalent to a lunge-rein. Both reins should normally be attached to the side-reins on the noseband of the cavesson and passed back to the trainer's hands, either through D-rings attached to the roller or direct in the case of the inside rein. Some trainers prefer to attach the long-reins to the bit, or to an ordinary cavesson noseband under a snaffle bridle.

Long-reining used to be very popular. It has several advantages; for instance, it enables an adult to train a pony to a more advanced stage without a child having to mount. But nowadays experienced and sophisticated trainers usually consider the practice unnecessary, as well as rather difficult and potentially harmful, preferring to school the horse either on the lunge or mounted.

That opinion is certainly held by the directorate of the Spanish Riding School in Vienna and by virtually all successful trainers of good dressage horses. The horsemen of the Spanish Riding School use long-reins only to give displays with old and fully-trained horses.

Boots and Bandages

Boots or bandages should always be worn on the forelegs when lungeing, and, if necessary, on the hindlegs also. Both types of protection should be fitted low enough to cover the fetlock joint.

The young horse, when weak and uncoordinated, can easily knock himself when working continuously on a circle, or when playing up at the end of a lunge-rein.

Ground Facilities

Good, all-weather ground facilities are as important as any other piece of equipment for lungeing a horse. Lungeing on grass is only practical in summer or on exceptionally well-drained land of a sand or gravel nature. Continuous circling on any one area will quickly poach the ground, so that the horse cannot work properly and becomes more subject to knocks and sprains: and the land will be spoilt for some time.

Intensive lungeing may continue for each horse for up to three months during breaking, and for some time after that at frequent intervals. The ground facilities must therefore not be neglected when the training programme is being formulated.

Riding

In the equestrian world there are many different styles of riding. Each country has its own unmistakable characteristics.

German riders, for instance, expect—and usually achieve—complete discipline from their horses. They do this by riding with very deep seat and long leg positions. So, too, do the great classical riders of the Spanish Riding School in Vienna.

French riders, on the other hand, prefer greater lightness of movement, and are therefore more reliant upon rein aids. The Italians, inventors of the forward-seat, use this style not only for jumping but also for flat work. Their style is characterized by the lower head carriages of their horses.

That not every rider conforms to his own or anyone else's national style is obvious. Many of the most effective horsemen in the world are individualists. But the fact remains that basic national styles have influenced the development of riding equipment in each country.

The basic German saddle, for example, is often heavy and has been designed with a very deep seat. The French patterns are lighter, often less bulky and flatter in the seat. In general, Italian saddles are also lighter, but they are more forward cut.

The general trend of mainstream equestrianism is, however, towards international forms of equipment. It is also towards simple equipment, particularly where bridles and bits are concerned. And what has become known generally as 'English' tack is accepted and used in most parts of the world.

Two major sections of the equestrian world prefer to use their own standard equipment. These are the military and the Western horsemen, whose tack has fulfilled its own highly individual function for generations.

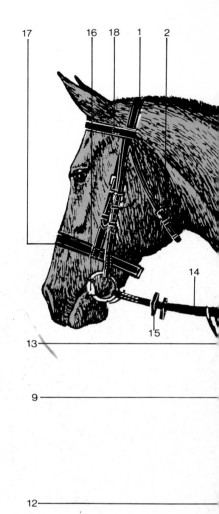

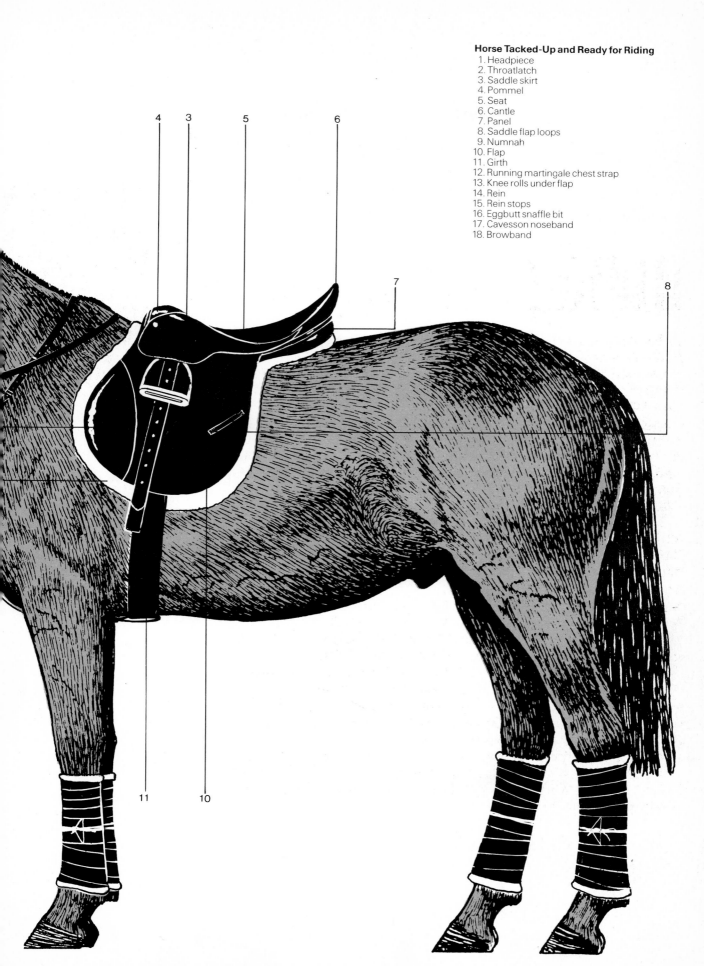

Horse Tacked-Up and Ready for Riding
 1. Headpiece
 2. Throatlatch
 3. Saddle skirt
 4. Pommel
 5. Seat
 6. Cantle
 7. Panel
 8. Saddle flap loops
 9. Numnah
10. Flap
11. Girth
12. Running martingale chest strap
13. Knee rolls under flap
14. Rein
15. Rein stops
16. Eggbutt snaffle bit
17. Cavesson noseband
18. Browband

The Theory of Bridles and Bitting

When a riderless horse is moving freely, the impulsion for forward movement comes naturally from the hindquarters. His direction is decreed by the movement of the head and neck.

However, when that same horse has a rider on his back, it should be the rider who creates the impulsion, by means of the legs and seat. It should also be the rider who controls the direction and speed by contact with the horse's mouth through the reins of the bridle.

Bridles have been in use in one form or another since man first made the horse his servant. In the early days, a bridle was little more than a thong of leather or rope passed round the head of the horse. But well before Roman times, a bit had been added and man was making use of the seven points of control.

These points of control are pressure points and are highly sensitive. They are easily hurt and damaged, which means that incorrect bridling can lead not only to excessive pain but to permanent injury.

If a horse is in pain, he cannot be properly controlled by inflicting more pain, although a degree of control may be achieved in this way for a while.

Before long, a badly-bitted horse will probably decide that he can stand no more and will bolt—and a horse running away from pain can only be expected to stop when the pain ceases.

Every rider must realize that the points of control he is using to convey his wishes to the horse can be abused—and, if abused, may cause the horse to rear, to bolt or to become unmanageable.

Rough riding or rough handling with any bit can cause untold damage to a horse's mouth; the sores that result may become so deep-seated that they affect even the bone structure of the lower jaw beneath the bars of the mouth. Old sore cavities deep in the bones of the jaw can be found in many horses with badly-damaged mouths. Bitting and riding such horses is always a problem, because they can pull extremely hard.

A dirty or ill-fitting bit can also give a horse a sore mouth. It may cause him to become head-shy or to refuse to accept the bit.

The Seven Control Points

When a horse is bridled, some or all of the following pressure points are immediately at the disposal of the rider, according to the bit or bridle adopted.

Within the mouth, there are four points: the lips, the tongue, the bars and the roof of the mouth. So far as the lips are concerned, the important factors are the length of the mouth and the sensitivity of the skin. The tongue may be neat and fit easily into the mouth, allowing the bit to rest correctly and to reach the bars. Or it may be 'coarse'—that is, it may be large and insensitive and prevent the bit acting correctly on the bars.

The bars are the skin covering the lower jaw bone directly in front of the molar teeth and above the corner incisors. They are easily damaged by bruising, especially if the skin is particularly sensitive.

The last of the pressure points inside the mouth is the roof, the ridged covering between the upper jaw bones. It is brought into play if a high-ported bit is used, the port jacking open the mouth by force.

Externally, there are three other pressure points: the nose, the chin groove (curb groove) and the poll.

Control Points

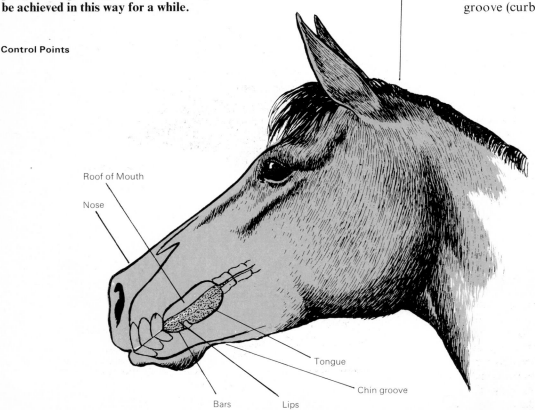

Poll

Roof of Mouth

Nose

Tongue

Chin groove

Bars

Lips

horse wearing a Fulmer cheek snaffle bit combined with a drop noseband. The horse is ot accepting the bit or the action of the oseband correctly. He is consequently stiff nd lying heavily on his rider's hands. A ange away from a single-jointed bit either a rubber mullen mouthpiece or to a ouble-jointed mouthpiece such as the ench snaffle could improve matters, as long these changes are coupled with a driving at and leg action from the rider.

The nose is the solid nasal bone ove the soft nostril. Pressure from a ridle should never be applied to the ostril in mistake for the nose. The in groove is the area directly above e point where the lower lip moves in meet the lower jaw bone behind the w. And lastly, and most vulnerable, the poll, which lies directly behind e ears and above the brain.

it Action
he snaffle family of bits acts on the ps, tongue and bars. However, when ch nosebands as the drop, Grakle or ash are used, the nose and chin oove are also affected, or the nose one if a Kineton noseband is worn.

The curbs, however, act on all the ints mentioned except the nose, and d the roof of the mouth if the port is gh, and the poll if the cheeks are ng enough to exert definite pressure ere.

The double, or Weymouth, bridle at mes doubles up the action in certain eas, such as the lips, by virtue of its o bits. The Pelham, being a hybrid the snaffle and curb, usually with a ngle mouthpiece, adopts the same essure points as they do.

The gag snaffle, however, acts prin-pally on the corners of the mouth d the poll. The cheeks of the bridle ss through holes in the bit ring, stening directly to the reins and not the bit. As a result, the rider can evate the bit in the horse's mouth wards the poll, exerting consider-le pressure and tension on both.

The bitless bridle, naturally, has no fect on the pressure points in the outh. It controls by acting on the se and the chin groove.

he Horse's Teeth
o matter what bridle and bits, and erefore pressure points, are used, omfort and control cannot be main-ined if the horse's teeth are not in der. All horses need to have their eth examined at least twice a year d filed (rasped or floated) as re-ired. Wolf teeth should be removed a veterinary surgeon, as they al-ost always interfere with the bit.

Position of the Bit

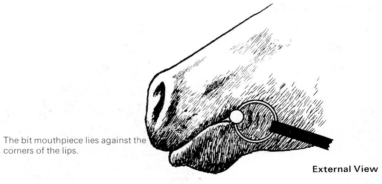

The bit mouthpiece lies against the corners of the lips.

External View

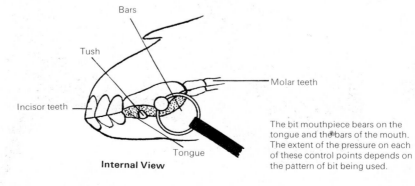

Bars

Tush

Incisor teeth

Molar teeth

Tongue

Internal View

The bit mouthpiece bears on the tongue and the bars of the mouth. The extent of the pressure on each of these control points depends on the pattern of bit being used.

The Snaffle Bridle

Though most snaffle bridles have the same basic design, there are many variations of pattern. Some of these variations result from the different uses to which bridles are put, others are attempts to achieve maximum efficiency, and others merely reflect differences in taste.

Every bridle that has the purpose of holding a bit in the horse's mouth has certain essential parts: a headpiece or crown, cheekpieces, a throatlatch, and a browband. To these may be added one of the many varieties of noseband.

Not all bridles are the same weight. Those used for showing and racing are usually lighter than those used for ordinary work. The type of leatherwork used in bridles varies, too. Flat straps are the more usual; but raised or rounded straps are popular with many people, especially for showing and racing.

Parts of the bridle

The weight of the bridle and the bit is distributed across the area of the poll, directly behind the ears, by means of the headpiece. In the basic English hunting bridle, this is a wide strap which, at the level of the lower edge of the ears, divides on both sides to form two straps: the front straps take the cheekpieces, and the rear ones are the throatlatch.

The purpose of the throatlatch is to prevent the bridle being pulled off over the ears in the case of a fall or some other accident. It is of sufficient length on the off-side to reach right under the horse's jowl and buckle on the near-side—without restricting movement of the animal's head and neck, or affecting his breathing and flexing. For correct adjustment there should be a width equivalent to four fingers on edge left between the throatlatch and the jawbone.

The cheekpieces are buckled to the front points of the headpiece. In some cases, they have keepers sewn on to hold a cheek snaffle, but most are plain. The cheekpieces determine the length of the bridle from the bit to the head-piece; it is advisable to have sufficient length available when the bridle is adjusted correctly and evenly—always match hole for hole on each side—for it

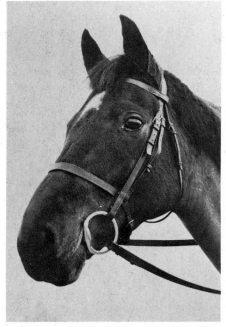

A well-fitted bridle: the browband is not too tight, the throatlatch is loose, and the bit is level in the mouth.

to be still possible to raise or lower one hole if necessary. In fact, it is better to have cheekpieces that allow two spare holes above the buckle. Otherwise there is a tendency for the buckles to sit level with the horse's eyes—a thing that should be avoided if possible.

Since the headpiece would, if worn alone, slip back down the horse's neck, a browband or front is fitted. This strap is often coloured, but many people fe that it should be of plain leather f ordinary riding. It lies across the for head directly below the ears, the hea piece passing through a loop at each e of it. The browband can be slid up down to fit comfortably below the ea Two fingers' width should be allow between it and the forehead.

If a noseband is used, its sliphead threaded under the headpiece to lie f over the poll. As the sliphead has on one buckle for lengthways adjustme and fastens on the near-side, it passed up through the off-side loop the browband, across the poll, a down through the near-side loop. T noseband should sit the width of fo fingers above the nostril and two bel the cheekbone.

Attaching the Bit

The bit can be attached to the chee pieces in various ways. It can be sev on—a method that has the advanta of neatness but means that the bit fixed and cannot be changed. Or it m be buckled: the buckles fasten on t outside of the cheekpieces and lo clumsy, but they are common racing bridles and are also used some pony bridles. Or the bit can secured with hook studs; these a probably the best for general use. simple but no longer very comm type of fastening is the 'monkey up stick'. This consists of a leather loop

Fastening the Bit

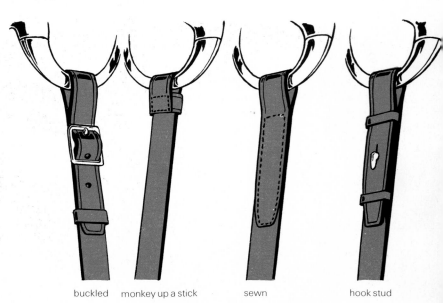

buckled   monkey up a stick   sewn   hook stud

one end of a strap, the other end being threaded through. There is also a special snap billet. This is neat, but probably not strong enough for general use.

Show and Race Bridles

The show type of bridle is lighter than the hunting type, and often has fancy leatherwork or stitching. Its aim is neatness and lightness. Flat-race bridles follow the same trend; but sometimes they are made in the same pattern as the dealer's or exercise bridle, having no side buckles but merely a single one at the poll. The single buckle makes adjustment easy.

American-Style Bridle

Sometimes, the American-style bridle, too, has only a single buckle, but more usually it is fitted with side buckles. Instead of having a combined headpiece and throatlatch, it has two separate straps. These straps pass through two loops on each side of the browband, and a short two-looped strap connects them between the horse's ears. This style of bridle is often double-stitched, and lined with rawhide for extra strength.

German Bridle

The German bridle is similar in pattern to the American; but it incorporates a noseband, and consequently uses triple loops. It is made of rolled (round) leather. The headpiece and the sliphead of the noseband have single buckles, and the throatlatch fastens behind the jaw, not on the side. These bridles are said to allow more adjustment.

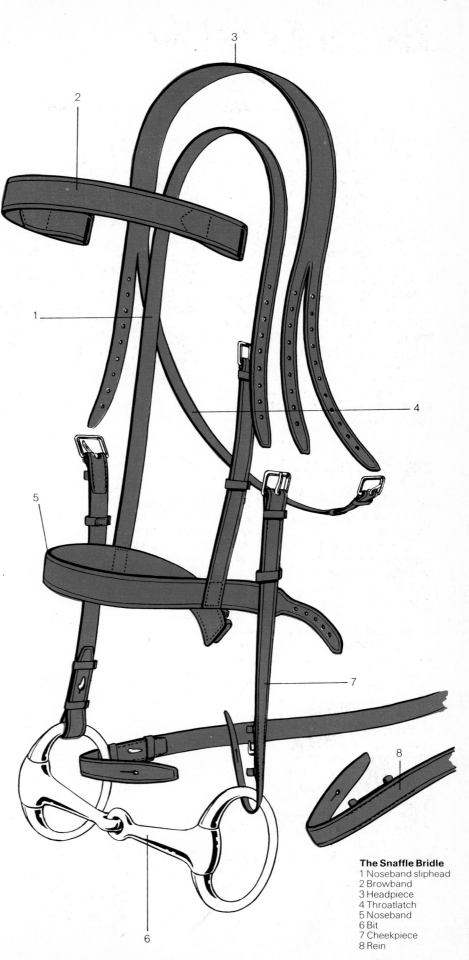

The Snaffle Bridle
1 Noseband sliphead
2 Browband
3 Headpiece
4 Throatlatch
5 Noseband
6 Bit
7 Cheekpiece
8 Rein

Snaffle Bits

Snaffles are probably the largest and most varied group of bits. A horse is often said to have a 'snaffle mouth', meaning that he will perform well in a snaffle. This still allows a wide range of choice in bitting, because snaffles include not only mild and kind bits, but also some of the most severe.

The mildness or severity of a bit depends on the design of the mouthpiece and the rings or cheeks. Generally, the thinner the mouthpiece the sharper the action and the more pain is inflicted directly on the horse's mouth. A thick mouthpiece is gentle and, provided that it is not too thick to be uncomfortable in the mouth, should be accepted happily and correctly by most horses. The amount of room available in a horse's mouth to accommodate a bit or combination of bits is the distance between the upper and lower jawbones when the mouth is closed.

Snaffle mouthpieces differ not only in thickness but also in shape and cross-section. They may be straight-bar, mullen (slightly curved), single jointed, double jointed (arms joined by links, plates or angled plates), plain, twisted, square, ported (with a central arched portion), hinged or hollow.

The cheeks vary too. Usually, they are circular or D-shaped rings, either loose or fixed, but some bits have a long full-cheek or half-cheek design.

Single-Jointed Eggbutt Snaffle

Single joints have a central nutcracker action on the tongue, and allow contact and pressure on the sides of the bars and on the top. The straighter the arms of a jointed bit, the sharper the action. Preferably, the arms should have a slight curve—similar to the curve of the mullen—and a fairly loose joint. If the joint is tight, the bit loses effectiveness because it has too little movement to encourage the horse to 'mouth' and therefore to maintain a soft mouth.

On the other hand, a joint that is too loose can result in a very sharp nutcracker action and may pinch the tongue. If this is coupled with a straight-arm mouthpiece, the pinching action will be severe.

The eggbutt cheek is kind because it cannot pinch. Its chief disadvantage is that it allows little movement of the mouthpiece and may therefore be rather wooden. It is commonly used with mullen and jointed mouthpieces.

The barrel-head cheek is a close relation to the eggbutt. It has a still wider cheek where it joins the mouthpiece, and makes pinching even less likely to occur.

Mullen Mouth Loose-Ring Snaffle

The mullen mouthpiece acts on the tongue, lips and bars, just as the straight-bar does. The pressure is taken first on the tongue and then—provided that the tongue is not too large and coarse—on the bars. If the tongue is so large that it overlays the bars of the mouth, the pressure on the bars is greatly reduced.

When the horse is at rest, the corners of the mouth—the junction of the lips—should take no pressure, but merely rest lightly against the bit. The corners of the mouth should react to the bit only when the mouthpiece is pulled onto them by increased rein contact.

Wire-ring cheeks are made of narrow tubular metal. Those used on racehorses are always large, but those seen elsewhere may be small. Flat rings are wide and therefore require larger mouthpiece holes. These tend to have rough edges that pinch and lead to sores.

Rubber Mullen Mouth Loose-Ring Snaffle

The rubber snaffle may be either flexible or hard. Usually, hard types have a metal core. Flexible patterns have a chain or cord centre.

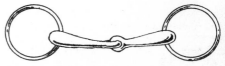

Mouthpiece may be all of rubber or have a metal core or chain.

This type of bit is softer than those with metal mouths. It may also be made of vulcanite or nylon.

German Snaffle

The German snaffle is popular with many riders, particularly for young horses, because it is kind but positive.

Hollow, jointed mouthpiece

The mouthpiece is usually hollow and consequently is light. Because it is also thick, it acts on a wide area of the tongue, lips and bars. Its thickness has the added advantage of comfort, and most horses are happy with it. Some German snaffles have wire rings; others have eggbutt cheeks.

The loose-ring cheeks pass through holes in the mouthpiece itself, therefore allowing movement not found with the eggbutt. They may be wire-ring or flat.

Fulmer Snaffle (Australian Loose-Ring Cheek Snaffle)

The Fulmer is one of the best of the full-cheek snaffles and is frequently used in training young horses. The long cheeks press against the sides of the muzzle during lateral movements, and they also prevent the bit being pulled through the mouth, causing the rider to lose control.

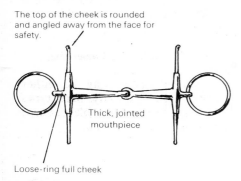

The top of the cheek is rounded and angled away from the face for safety.

Thick, jointed mouthpiece

Loose-ring full cheek

The cheeks can be left free, or they can be held in position by means of keepers attached to the cheekpieces. In the latter case, the bit acts not only on the corners of the mouth, the tongue and the top of the bars, but also on the sides of the bars, exerting more pressure.

The Fulmer has loose rings to allow movement of the mouthpiece, which is jointed. The bit's effectiveness is often increased by the use of a drop noseband. This provides control at two extra points: the curb groove and the nose.

D-Cheek Race Snaffle

The D-cheek race snaffle has large D-shaped rings to prevent the bit being pulled through the mouth and to stop

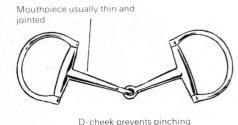

Mouthpiece usually thin and jointed

D-cheek prevents pinching

the lips being pinched. Usually, it has a jointed mouthpiece with rather thin, curved arms to provide the control necessary for use on racehorses or headstrong animals.

Half Spoon-Cheek Snaffle

The half spoon-cheek snaffle has half cheeks that hang below the mouthpiece to prevent the bit being pulled through the mouth. These are less

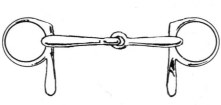

likely to become caught up in the horse's mouth or in equipment than the cheeks of some cheek snaffles. The bit is therefore used mainly in harness racing.

Dr Bristol Snaffle

Generally, double-jointed mouthpieces are joined in the centre by a smooth, flat plate. In the Dr Bristol family of bits, this plate lies at an angle to the tongue. When rein pressure is applied, one edge is brought into play against the tongue unless the horse flexes and bends his head to the correct position. The plate will then lie flat.

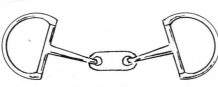

Centre plate slopes at about 45 degrees. This angling enables the bit to be used in a more severe position.

A severe but useful bit in the right hands, the Dr Bristol is accepted by many horses that prefer a double joint to the nutcracker action of a single joint. It may be fitted with any type of cheek. Most often it is seen with D-cheeks.

French Snaffle

The French snaffle also has a plate link, but this lies flat all the time and the bit is therefore milder than the Dr Bristol. Its spatula-shaped centre link makes it very comfortable for the horse's

tongue. Horses that fuss with other bits often accept the French snaffle more calmly. The bit is available as a

bridoon or a full snaffle; in the latter case some riders prefer it to have full cheeks.

Egg-Link Snaffle

The egg-link mouthpiece is a close relative of the French. It has an oval link in the centre which gives slightly more contact with, and pressure on, the tongue.

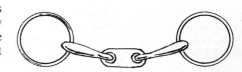

Dick Christian Snaffle

The Dick Christian snaffle is a double-jointed bit that seeks to eliminate

Ring joins two mouthpiece sections.

tongue pressure. It is therefore of particular value for horses with very sensitive mouths. It has a thick aluminium mouthpiece and a ring of steel that connects one arm to the other.

Fillis Snaffle

The Fillis snaffle, with its hinged low port, provides more room for the tongue and therefore is welcomed by the coarse-tongued horse. It is a hanging bit, which means that it is suspended in the mouth and does not rest directly on the tongue. Therefore,

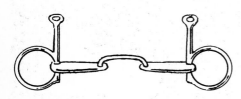

although the port is narrow across the top, the bit is not severe. It may help to dissuade a horse from putting his tongue over the bit, simply because it is comfortable.

A close relation of the Fillis is the Ostrich snaffle, a suspended bit used mainly for racing. It has a mouthpiece similar to that of the French snaffle.

Chain Snaffle

The chain snaffle family of bits have chain links to replace the normal bit mouthpiece. The basic chain snaffle has either single or double links and is fitted in such a way that it lies flat in the mouth. It is probably the mildest of the chain snaffles, all of which are classed as strong and should be used with consideration. In particular, they must never be 'sawed'—pulled from side to side.

Wellington and Waterford Snaffles

The Wellington snaffle is one of the better-known chain snaffles. Its hinged mouthpiece contains five large and rounded chain links that fold themselves around the bars of the mouth and are severe.

The Waterford snaffle is similar, but is heavier. It has solid metal balls inside the links.

Twisted Snaffle

Twisted snaffles are very severe, the thinnest patterns being the sharpest. Some have corrugations on one side only (as in the stallion straight-bar snaffle) and are therefore reversible. Others have twisting ridges winding around the mouthpiece. Of these, the moderately severe have rounded, smooth twists, and the most severe

have sharp and well-defined ridges. Twisted jointed snaffles dig into the tongue unmercifully because of their nutcracker action.

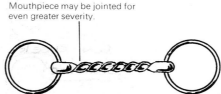

Mouthpiece may be jointed for even greater severity.

In the thin, twisted wire patterns, the sharpness is acute. These bits are made of twin strands of wire, twisted together to form the mouthpiece.

The cheeks of twisted snaffles may be loose-ring, eggbutt or D-cheek.

Magenis Roller-Mouth Snaffle

The Magenis is one of the better-known patterns of roller-mouth snaffle. It has a square, jointed mouthpiece with the rollers set inside it. Because the rollers are placed horizontally inside the mouthpiece arms, the bit has some sideways play. It is designed to stop a horse crossing his jaws and therefore evading the bit.

A well-schooled horse should have a moist mouth with a normal bit, but some require the help that a roller-

Lateral rollers set inside jointed mouthpiece

mouth gives. An added advantage of these mouths is that horses cannot easily take hold of them in their teeth— a means of bit evasion practised by horses that are frightened of their bits.

Cherry Roller-Mouth Snaffle

The cherry roller snaffle has rollers set right round the mouthpiece arms. The horse can play with them and mouth more easily than with the rollers of the

Magenis snaffle, but they do not allow the lateral play of the Magenis.

The cherry roller snaffle is sometimes jointed or ported, and some patterns have differing sizes of rollers. Any of the snaffle ring cheeks may be used.

Wilson Snaffle

There are several variations of the Wilson snaffle, all of which have cheeks

Cheekpiece rings fit round the mouthpiece, which is usually plain and jointed

consisting of two rings on each side of the mouth. These cheeks are severe because they exert an extreme pinching action on the sides of the mouth and lower jaw. The two inner, loose rings are free, and take the bridle headpiece. The rings on the mouthpiece take the reins. The rings may be wire or flat. Often, the bit has a twisted mouthpiece.

Scorrier Snaffle (Cornish Snaffle)

The Scorrier is also a four-ring snaffle, but instead of the headpiece rings being

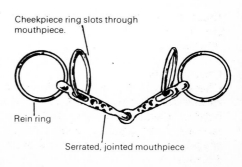

Cheekpiece ring slots through mouthpiece.

Rein ring

Serrated, jointed mouthpiece

free—as in the Wilson snaffle—they are slotted into the mouthpiece. The mouthpiece, too, varies from the Wilson design: it is square and one side of it is plain, the other twisted.

The Scorrier is very severe and must be used carefully. The unusual design of the mouthpiece results in extremely sharp action and this is increased by the way the rings operate when pressure is applied to the reins: the two headpiece rings press hard against the horse's cheeks and jaw bones.

W-Mouth Snaffle (Y-Mouth Snaffle)

The W-mouth has twin jointed mouthpieces. These are set at different sides of the horse's mouth and take up strong

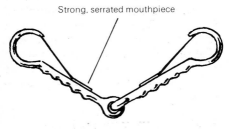

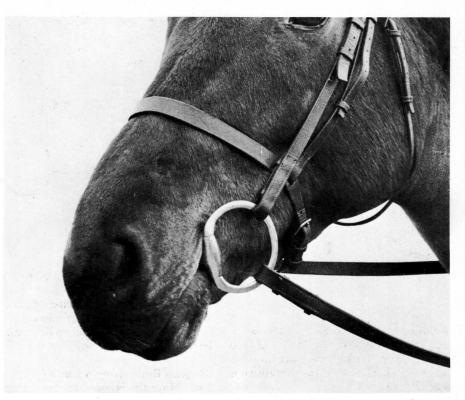

Most horses perform well in a snaffle. Generally, snaffles are mild in action though there is some controversy about the severity of the 'nutcracker' action of jointed mouthpieces.

double V formations when pressure is exerted from the reins. This type of mouthpiece pinches the tongue severely.

Spring Mouth (Butterfly Mouth)

The spring mouth is a clip-on mouthpiece attachment for snaffle bits. Some-

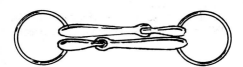
Strong, serrated mouthpiece

Spring hook attachment to bit rings

times it is a plain straight-bar, but it may be jointed or twisted. It is always strong.

Cheek Guards

Cheek guards are circular pieces of rubber or leather designed to fit between the bit cheeks and the horse's face to guard against chafing. Pear-shaped cheek guards are used with Pelham bits.

Tattersall Bit (Colt Bit)

The Tattersall is a circular ring bit that straps onto a headcollar and circles round behind the horse's chin. Sometimes, it has keys. It is used for unbroken yearlings and foals to allow them to become accustomed to a bit. Because of its shape, it fits any size of mouth, and it helps to prevent a young animal learning to put his tongue over the bit.

Bit Variations

- The mild rubber mouthpiece is kind to young horses who have not yet taken to the bit. Some authorities also recommend it for a horse that pulls: since it rests easily in his mouth, there is nothing for him to pull against.

- As a general rule, the thinner the mouthpiece the more severe the bit.

- A strong bit should never be used by an inexperienced or heavy-handed rider.

- In a jointed bit, the shape of the arms and the amount of free play in the joint determine the sharpness of the nutcracker action. Curved arms with a firm joint are less severe than straight arms with a loose joint.

The Double Bridle

The action of the snaffle bit is to raise the horse's head. It is not possible, other than in exceptional circumstances, to obtain any marked degree of real flexion without the use of a curb bit.

The action of the curb is to obtain flexion by applying pressure to the poll—the degree of pressure depending on the severity of the bit used—at the same time as applying pressure to the chin groove by means of the curb chain. In practice, no curb bit has the actions of a curb unless a curb chain is used. Without a chain, the bit reverts to a form of snaffle, its severity being governed only by the design of the mouthpiece and cheeks.

As the name implies, a double bridle is composed of two separate bits: a curb and a snaffle, called a *bridoon* or *bradoon* when used in this way. The bridoon rings are much smaller than those of an ordinary snaffle and are therefore more direct in their action. Also, the mouthpiece of a bridoon is not as thick as that of the normal snaffle—chiefly so that it may be accommodated in the horse's mouth with the mouthpiece of the curb and also because it gives direct action.

The bridoon raises and places the horse's head, while the curb produces flexion to give greater and more accurate control. The rider should control the bits independently.

A curb bit used alone tends to produce overbending, the term used to describe a head bent at such an angle as to be behind the vertical. Consequently, the horse loses his power of free forward movement and the rider loses control. A horse must go up into the bridle, and not draw back from the bit or bits. He should bend his head at the poll to such a degree that the nasal bone down the front of the face is vertical. With a snaffle alone, the horse tends to carry his head in advance of this angle and to be unwilling to relax his lower jaw. A point to note, however, is that if some form of noseband fastening across the chin groove is employed, the back strap of this then becomes a curb strap and has an effect similar to that of a curb chain.

Parts of the Double Bridle

A double bridle has three straps passing over the horse's poll: the bridle headpiece, from which the curb bit is suspended, the noseband sliphead and the bridoon sliphead. The last two are usually the same width. The bridoon sliphead is always narrower than the cheekpieces of the curb. The bridoon cheekpieces have a single buckle fastening on the offside, instead of on the nearside as with the noseband. As a result, there are two buckles on each side of the face, which is neat and uncluttered.

The bridoon sliphead is passed through the browband loops from the nearside to the offside. It lies between the noseband sliphead and the main headpiece.

There is another strap on a double bridle: the lip strap. This is a narrow strap—flat, or, preferably, round—fastening to small D-rings on the arms of the curb cheeks below the mouthpiece. It serves two purposes: preventing the curb chain riding up or becoming twisted, and restricting excessive movement of the lower cheeks of the curb, especially if the cheeks are of the revolving type. It is also a safeguard against the loss of the curb chain.

Types of Double Bridles

Double bridles are produced in various forms. Those made of strong, thick leather that will withstand hard wear are used for hunting and everyday hacking or other work; but for showing in hack or pony classes, a much lighter bridle is necessary.

Double bridles used for dressage are of medium weight. They are strong but also smart: the types of bridles that would be suitable also for showing hunters.

The only noseband considered permissible for use with a double bridle is a cavesson, fastened above the bit.

A German fixed-cheek curb bit, eggbutt bridoon and double-link curb chain make for a comfortable double bridle.

Bits and Chains

The bits for a double bridle are attached to the bridle cheekpieces and reins in the same way as are snaffles. The sewn, hook-studded or snap-billeted patterns are the neatest and most elegant for showing or dressage. In some countries, buckles are used, but these can be rather ugly.

When assembled, the double bridle bits should be adjusted to hang one above the other. The curb is the lower. The bridoon mouthpiece should lie just clear of the curb mouthpiece.

The bits should lie comfortably, without excessive wrinkling of the corners of the mouth. The bridoon just touches the mouth corners and the curb is suspended just below it.

The curb chain is then attached to the offside. The lip strap is threaded through the fly link in the back of the curb chain and fastened loosely, also on the nearside. The double bridle should always take two reins.

Double Bridle
1. Headpiece
2. Bridoon sliphead
3. Noseband sliphead
4. Keeper
5. Bridoon rein
6. Fly link
7. Curb rein
8. Lip strap
9. Single-link curb chain
10. Low-ported fixed-cheek curb bit
11. Curb rein ring
12. Lip strap ring
13. Plain curb hook
14. Loose-ring jointed bridoon bit
15. Nosepiece
16. Cheekpiece
17. Throatlatch
18. Browband

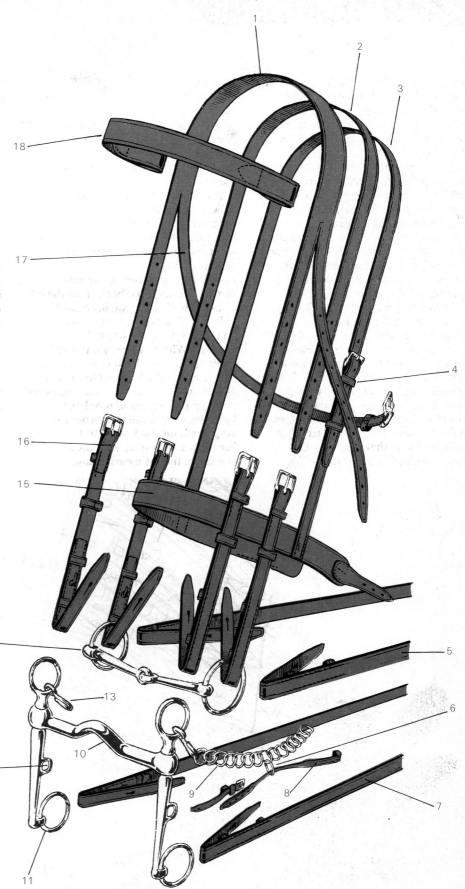

Curb Bits

As with snaffles, there are many curb bits to choose from. Some are relatively mild; others are extremely severe. In former days, when bits were hand forged, there were many weird and wonderful bit patterns. Today, the making of bits from moulds has reduced the range considerably.

Long-Cheek Weymouth Curb
The longer the arms (bars) of a curb bit below the mouthpiece, the greater the leverage on the horse's mouth available to the rider. And the longer the cheek between the eye and the mouthpiece, the greater the pressure available to act upon the poll; great force used in this way can damage the poll and brain and even fracture the lower jaw.

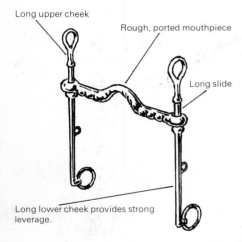

Long upper cheek

Rough, ported mouthpiece

Long slide

Long lower cheek provides strong leverage.

The long-cheek curb bit is not, therefore, a bit for common use. It should be reserved for those with extreme tact and brilliant hands.

Tom Thumb Curb
At the other end of the scale from the long-cheek curb is the mildest of the curbs, the Tom Thumb. This is a pleasant, short-cheek bit that gives good control of any well-schooled horse or pony without causing pain and damage.

Short-Cheek Weymouth Curb (Slide-Cheek)
A slightly longer version of the Tom Thumb curb is the short-cheek Weymouth. This is an ideal bit for many horses, giving more control than the Tom Thumb but without causing discomfort.

The slide-cheek Weymouth is the most common type of double bridle curb, and is the one normally associated with a double bridle. The severity of its action is governed by the length of slide movement possible, which is usually about 13 mm ($\frac{1}{2}$ in.). The longer

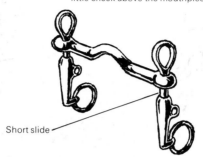

The bit is mild partly because there is little cheek above the mouthpiece.

Short slide

the slide, the more action is available upon the poll, for the mouthpiece rides up in the mouth in the same way as it does in the gag snaffle, forcing the headpiece of the bridle to apply pressure upon the poll. Slide cheeks not only allow movement of the mouthpiece, but are themselves reversible.

Gated Port Bits
Gated ports are also found in some curbs, the Bentinck being one pattern that is fitted with a gated port in addition to the normal mouthpiece. Most ports are open to allow the tongue to slide up into them, but closed ports can be found in such bits as the Tom Bass and the Mameluke (Turkey). The latter has a large ring attached to the port centre. It is rarely seen today.

Western Weymouth Curb
In some patterns of curb, such as the Lowther or the Arkwright, the rings for the curb rein are suspended from the ends of the cheeks. Others, including the Western Weymouth, have eyes that are part of the curved cheeks. These are flat, rather than round, as is usual in the English Weymouth. Many of them are loose-jawed (revolving) in the same way as the Banbury bit and for the same reasons.

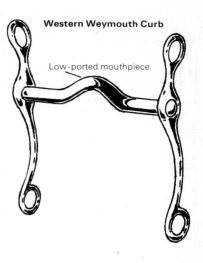

Western Weymouth Curb

Low-ported mouthpiece

Segundo Curb
From low ports, curbs move up through many stages to those with very high ports, the highest of which may even act upon the roof of the mouth. But such bits are now quite rare.

One pattern of mouthpiece that holds the tongue in an arch of the port

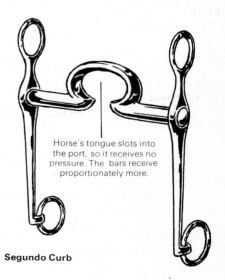

Horse's tongue slots into the port, so it receives no pressure. The bars receive proportionately more.

Segundo Curb

is the Segundo. It allows direct contact on the bars and is therefore strong—especially if it has revolving cheeks—because they may be used to give a high degree of leverage.

Fixed-Cheek Portsmouth Show Curb
Fixed-cheek (fast-cheek) curbs have a mouthpiece that is welded to the cheek so that it cannot move. This allows less

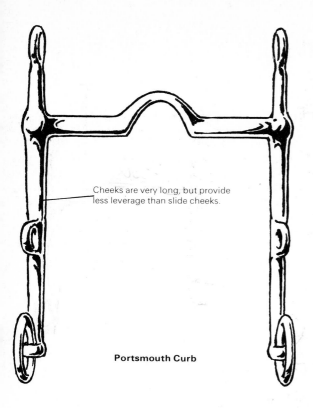

Cheeks are very long, but provide less leverage than slide cheeks.

Portsmouth Curb

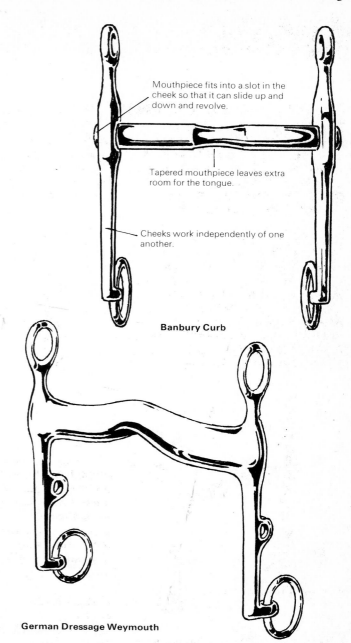

Mouthpiece fits into a slot in the cheek so that it can slide up and down and revolve.

Tapered mouthpiece leaves extra room for the tongue.

Cheeks work independently of one another.

Banbury Curb

German Dressage Weymouth

German Dressage Weymouth

leverage than is available with the slide-cheek. The Portsmouth show curb is an example of a fixed-cheek bit with very long cheeks.

If possible, when a fixed- or a slide-cheek curb is being selected, the one chosen should have the eye angled slightly away from the face, as this will prevent chafing. The bit is then attached to the bridle so that the curve points away from the face. Bits without a curve will fit either way round.

German Dressage Weymouth

The German dressage Weymouth has a hollow mouthpiece, usually with a Cambridge port, and fixed cheeks. The mouthpiece is broad, but horses find it delightfully comfortable and most will perform very well in it.

All dressage Weymouths have a medium length of fixed cheek. They are now compulsory for three-day event dressage tests.

Banbury Curb

The revolving type of curb has cheeks that circle round the mouthpiece independently of one another. An example of this is the Banbury pattern; its mouthpiece slots through the cheeks, as opposed to the cheeks slotting through the mouthpiece. As a

result, the rider can operate the cheeks independently by using one rein at a time, which is useful on one-sided horses.

The mouthpiece of the Banbury curb is tapered, with an hourglass centre that rotates in the mouth. The object of the bit is to allow the horse to mouth freely, but to stop him from catching hold of the bit between his teeth. Pressure is greater upon the tongue than upon the bars.

Bit Mouthpieces

- Plain mullen-mouthed curbs act first on the tongue, then on the bars.

- Arch-mouth curbs allow varying amounts of tongue space, and the bars receive pressure mainly on their sides.

- The Cambridge mouth, with its low port or tongue groove, allows the tongue enough room to be comfortable. The sides of the mouthpiece apply even pressure on the bars.

Bridoons and Curb Chains

Although the curb is the principle bit used with a double bridle, the bridoon is very important too. Some patterns of bridoon are mild, others extremely severe. Usually, mild bridoons are employed.

As the bridoon is in fact a scaled-down version of an ordinary snaffle—with its much smaller rings giving a closer contact between the rider and the horse's mouth—many of the snaffle combinations of cheeks and mouthpieces are to be found in the bridoon family.

Types of Bridoons

On a basic double bridle, it is usual to adopt a smooth-mouth jointed bridoon of medium thickness to match the Weymouth. Commonly, a wire-ring bridoon is used with a slide-mouth curb, but eggbutt cheeks are just as acceptable, and with a fixed-cheek curb they make far better sense.

The German dressage bridoon is a hollow-mouth eggbutt that gives a fairly direct action on the tongue, lips and bars, and suits the curb. Sometimes, it is used alone, as a small-ring eggbutt snaffle.

Mullen-mouth bridoons are also used with Weymouths. The twisted patterns are seen, too, but these are particularly severe and should be used with care.

The French bridoon with its flat centre plate mouthpiece, and the Fillis with its hanging cheek and hinged mouth, are two of the more moderate. They act upon either side of the curb port. Provided that the plate or hinged port does not become trapped under the port of the curb, they should be comfortable for the big-tongued horse that dislikes a single joint.

Many riders favour gag bridoons, either of the small full-ring or the half-ring variety. They are smaller versions of the ordinary gag bits. As bridoons, gags are sharp and very strong, since their mouthpieces are thinner than those of ordinary gag snaffles.

Overcheck Bridoon

The overcheck bridoon is used in driving bridles for Hackney horses and ponies, and for trotters and pacers. It is similar in appearance to the normal bridoon, with very small loose-ring cheeks and a thin, rounded mullen mouthpiece. The bit rings are held high up in the mouth by the overhead bearing rein or overcheck. Its purpose is to keep the horse's head up.

Some overcheck bridoons are attached to normal driving bits, as, for example, the combination buggy bit. This is a thin overcheck bridoon attached by two rings on its mouthpiece to the mouthpiece of the main half-spoon cheek, jointed bit.

Another combination bit is the Benison anti-pulling device. The overcheck bridoon used here has a straight-bar mouthpiece riding higher above the main mouthpiece than the combination buggy bit. The bit, which has a main mullen mouthpiece, is rarely seen today.

Curb Chains and Hooks

Curb chains vary greatly in design and in materials. The main patterns are: single-link metal, double-link metal, leather (humane), elastic and jodhpur polo.

The ordinary style of curb chain is the same width all the way along. But some patterns have a swell centre, the links gradually becoming larger towards the middle. The object of this is to allow more bearing surface on the area behind the jaw.

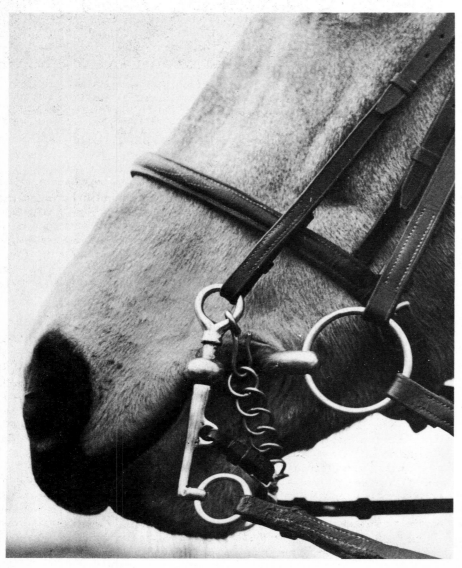

A Weymouth double bridle. The curb has a slide cheek and is fitted with a single-link curb chain. The matching bridoon has been pulled through the horse's mouth to show the loose-ring attachment to the thin mouthpiece. The Weymouth is probably the most widely-used double bridle today.

Single-Link Metal Curb Chains
The single-link metal curb chain may be either rounded or flat, but it is always twisted so that the links lie flat to each other in order to minimize chafing. Chains put on with the links twisted up incorrectly can cause injury in the horse's curb groove.

Single-Link

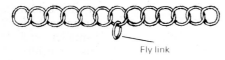

Fly link

Double-Link Metal Curb Chains
Double-link metal chains present a more uniform surface and are therefore less liable to pinch than the single-link types. They are the best of the metal chains and are the ones most in use.

Double-Link

Curb hook link Fly link

Leather Curb Chains
If a horse does not perform well in a metal curb chain, the softer action of a leather curb chain may solve the problem. It has metal links at each end to hook onto the curb hooks, and a centre section of double leather, with the fly link stitched to the centre on the outside. It gives a positive action without pinching, but must be kept clean and soft.

Leather (Humane)

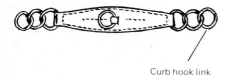

Curb hook link

Elastic Curb Chain
Elastic is another material used for curb chains. The stretch it allows is often acceptable to a sensitive horse that resents his jaw being gripped in an unyielding combination of bit and chain.

Jodhpur Polo Chain
The jodhpur polo curb chain differs in design from other chains by having a large, curved oval ring in its centre. This fits across the lower jaw bones and exerts considerable pressure.

Jodhpur Polo (Cap Curb)

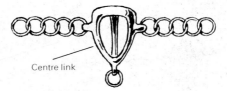

Centre link

Curb Guard
With all curb chains, chafing can be a problem. It may be resolved by the use of some form of curb guard.

A rubber guard is the most common type, but is clumsy. Therefore, the alternative of sheepskin is worth considering. Sheepskin curb guards are not often available ready-made, but must be either commissioned or made at home. All that is required is a piece of fine sheepskin cut to length and stitched, allowing room for the fly link to be brought through to the outside.

Correctly fitted, the double-link curb chain suits most horses. It should be twisted-up clockwise until flat, with the fly link at the bottom to take the lip strap. Then it is twisted a further half-turn and looped from underneath onto the nearside curb hook.

Curb Hooks
Curb hooks are available in three types. The most common is the Melton pattern, but there are also circle and stubby patterns. The circle pattern is good because the hook is fitted inside the circle and is unable to cause chafing. Curb hooks vary in size between 32 and 64 mm ($1\frac{1}{4}$ and $2\frac{1}{2}$ in.). They are sold in pairs.

Fitting of Curb Chains
To fit a curb chain correctly, the offside link should first be attached to its hook and the chain passed behind the jaw. It should be twisted clockwise so that it lies flat, with the fly link on the outside and to the bottom. If the chain is then given one extra half-turn and the bottom of the link slipped onto the nearside hook, it will remain correctly twisted.

Once fitted, the angle of the curb cheek should be 45 degrees to the mouth when the curb chain is in action. If the angle is less, the curb chain is too tight. If it is more, the chain is ineffective.

Pelham Bits

Many riders dislike using two bits, yet they find a snaffle insufficient for their requirements. For them, the vast family of Pelham bits probably has something to offer.

The Pelham is a hybrid bit resulting from the crossing of a snaffle with a curb to form a single mouthpiece. It is designed to give the action of both. But in practice it gives no definite action from either.

The Pelham bears a distinct resemblance to the curb. All the cheeks and features found on the various curbs are found on the different patterns of Pelham, but with the addition of many of the mouthpieces used on snaffles. The principal difference between a true curb and a Pelham lies in the fact that, since the Pelham incorporates the snaffle, an extra D-cheek is attached on either side of the mouthpiece.

The rider is supposed first to use the top (snaffle or bridoon) rein to raise the head and then, by twisting the wrist downwards and inwards, the curb. But, in fact, both reins come into play at the same time, owing to the usually moderate length of the cheeks. This confuses the horse, causing him to open his mouth and hollow his neck at a point somewhere between the poll and withers, instead of bending his head correctly at the poll.

The effect of this is a shortening of the horse's top line (which should be long) and a strengthening of the lower line (which should be short). The horse is therefore given a ewe neck, making control and true flexion hard to obtain.

Horses are, however, great individuals, and some not only like a Pelham, but perform better in this bit than in any other. In such cases, of course, there is no argument against the use of the Pelham.

Pelham cheeks and mouthpieces vary greatly in design. Among the types of mouthpieces seen are mullen, straight-bar, jointed, eggbutt, loose-ring, fixed-cheek, slide-cheek and angled patterns, as well as those with rollers and ports, double joints and links.

The majority of Pelham bits have metal mouths, but popular patterns are available in nylon, rubber and vulcanite. It is these last three types that make the Pelham bits useful, since they are very acceptable to horses that hate cold metal bits and welcome the comfort of thick, soft ones.

Mullen-Mouth Pelham

Probably the most common of the Pelhams is that known as the half-moon or mullen-mouth. It is made with metal—including copper—rubber, nylon or vulcanite mouth-pieces, and with various lengths of cheek. The Tom Thumb has the shortest cheek, but some have cheeks up to about 180 mm (7 in.) in length.

Sometimes, mullen-mouth Pelhams have eggbutt sides. And they may have turning cheeks—cheeks that will turn to face either backwards or forwards, but will not slide up or down.

Rugby Pelham

The Rugby pattern is fitted with a fixed cheek and its bridoon ring is linked to the cheek to give it the appearance of a double when it is fitted on the horse. It has a well-defined action upon the poll and curb groove.

Berkley Pelham

The Berkley Pelham is a close relation of the Rugby. It has rings attached to the existing top ring, and a mullen mouth.

Kimblewick Pelham (Kimbelwicke or Kimberwick)

Of the Pelhams with a Cambridge (ported) mouthpiece, the Kimblewick is probably the most valuable. It is a useful bit for a horse that requires something strong yet not over-severe. The Kimblewick differs from the ordinary run of Pelhams in that it has only one rein. When the reins are held normally, it is a snaffle with a Cambridge mouth, but when the hands are lowered, or a running martingale is used, the action is that of the curb. Snaffle and curb cannot work simultaneously, and in this lies the secret of the bit's success.

There are five patterns of Kimblewick.

The true Kimblewick has a square eye and a D-ring running the full length of the short cheek. It is found with either metal or rubber-type mouths.

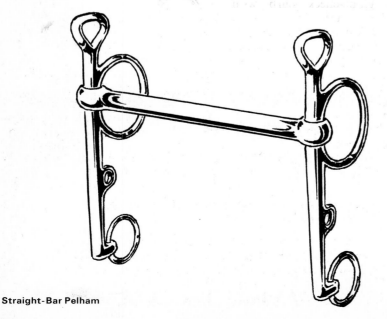

Straight-Bar Pelham

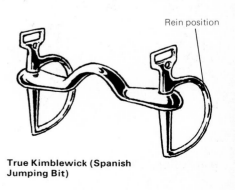

Rein position

True Kimblewick (Spanish Jumping Bit)

In the Uxeter Kimblewick, the D-rings are flat. They have two slots so that the reins can be fixed by the mouthpiece or lower down the cheek.

The Whitmore is similar to the true Kimblewick but with the addition of a curb ring directly below the large D-ring. If the rider uses two reins, this pattern of bit may subject the horse to the action of two curb bits through the one mouthpiece: a true Kimblewick has only one rein, and consequently the snaffle and curb cannot be used together. Designs that cater for more than one position of the reins, or for two reins, can badly confuse and upset a horse.

The fourth pattern of Kimblewick has a mullen mouth. The fifth has a single-jointed mouth. As in all jointed Pelhams, the curb chain here largely loses effect, since the joint allows the cheeks to move back and therefore slides the chain out of the curb groove.

Jointed Pelhams
It is possible to find an ordinary Pelham bit with a jointed mouthpiece. Such bits are known either simply as jointed Pelhams or as Dexter mouths (not to be confused with the Dexter ring bit, which is a snaffle with a single large ring attached to each cheek). The difference between these two Pelhams is the size of the D-ring, the Dexter's being smaller, and the shape of the mouth, the Dexter's being more tapered.

Hartwell Pelham
The Hartwell is the Pelham that is most like the Weymouth curb. It has a slide cheek and a normal port, allowing the bit to lie across the bars of the mouth.

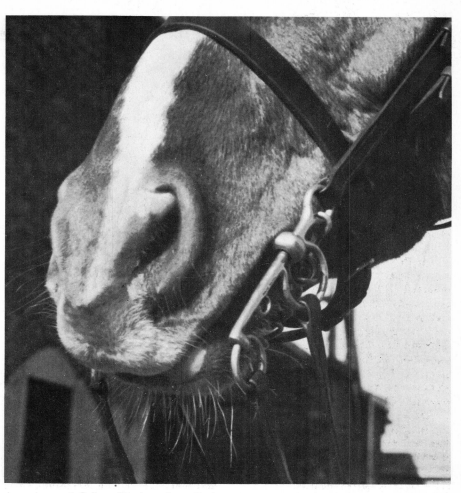

An arch-mouth Pelham fitted on a horse that goes better in this than in other bits. The long cheek helps to give some difference in action between the top rein and the bottom rein. However, many riders and horses dislike Pelhams.

Globe-Cheek Pelham

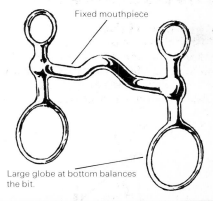

Globe-Cheek Pelham
Fixed mouthpiece
Large globe at bottom balances the bit.

Globe-Cheek Pelham
Globe-cheek Pelhams usually have short cheeks, and some are found with a high port or jointed mouthpiece. The fixed globe-cheek curb with a Cambridge mouth—known as a Pelham but taking only one rein—is the best of these designs, as the cheeks are so short that two reins would simply cancel one another out.

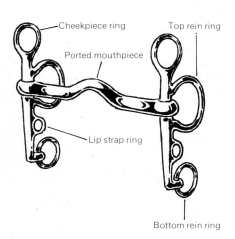

Cheekpiece ring
Top rein ring
Ported mouthpiece
Lip strap ring
Bottom rein ring

Hartwell Pelham

Loose-Ring Pelham
The loose-ring Pelham rings are fixed directly to the cheeks. The bit has a Cambridge mouth.

The Pelham and the Curb Chain

- The Pelham comes into its own on horses with thick tongues and short mouths. On such horses, the curb chain remains in the correct position.

- On long-mouthed horses, the Pelham rides too high in the mouth, taking the curb chain with it.

- If the chain is not in the correct position, it acts across the solid bones of the lower jaw instead of working properly in the curb groove. This can cause the bones to become calloused.

Scamperdale Pelham

The Scamperdale Pelham has a straight-bar mouthpiece with the ends angled back to take the cheeks right away from the face of the horse. Should the horse have a sore mouth, the

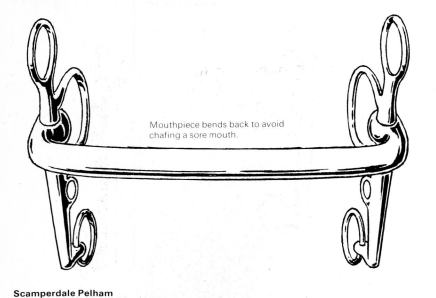

Mouthpiece bends back to avoid chafing a sore mouth.

Scamperdale Pelham

Scamperdale will not aggravate this as much as other bits. However, because the curb chain seldom acts in the correct place, this bit is well suited for use as a snaffle without a curb chain. It is named after Sam Marsh's old equestrian establishment at Edenbridge, in Kent, England.

Arch-Mouth Pelham

The arch-mouth Pelham is a well-known pattern. It is a moderate bit, its upward curve allowing enough room for the tongue so that the bit lies across the bars.

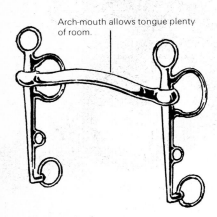

Arch-mouth allows tongue plenty of room.

Arch-Mouth Pelham

Reverse Arch-Mouth Pelham

The reverse arch-mouth Pelham is also well-known. It is severe and presses into the tongue. This bit's only redeeming feature is that it leaves the bars of the mouth alone to a certain extent.

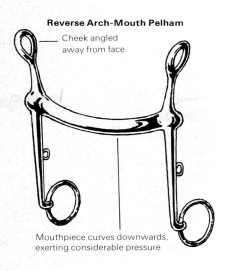

Reverse Arch-Mouth Pelham

Cheek angled away from face.

Mouthpiece curves downwards, exerting considerable pressure.

Ramsey Pelham

The Ramsey Pelham has a mouthpiece that hinges onto the bit cheek. The mouthpiece is held in a tiny D-ring inside the larger bridoon ring.

SM Pelham

The SM Pelham is a fairly well-known pattern. Its mouthpiece is a wide plate bent into an arch in the centre, rather like a port. The mouth never changes position, as it works on a swivel. It has a wide bearing on the bars of the mouth.

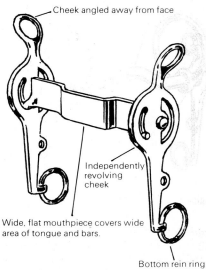

Cheek angled away from face

Independently revolving cheek

Wide, flat mouthpiece covers wide area of tongue and bars.

Bottom rein ring

S M Pelham

Banbury Pelham

The Banbury Pelham is the counterpart of the Banbury curb. Again, it encourages the horse to mouth and discourages him from catching hold of his bit. It may have either plain or fancy cheeks. It is one of the two main military bits.

Angle-Cheek Reversible Pelham

The other main military bit is the angle-cheek reversible Pelham. It has a Cambridge or arch-mouth that is rough on one side and plain on the other, and has two slots for a high or low curb rein. It is therefore expected to suit horses and riders of many types. It is used generally with the smooth side of the mouthpiece in contact with the horse's tongue and bars.

IX Lancer Pelham

One of the traditional strong polo bits is the IX Lancer Pelham. It is made on the Wilson principle, with two flat Wilson rings round a Cambridge mouth. These rings press together and allow considerable leverage to the bit, which is not suspended in the mouth in the usual way.

Swales 3-in-1 Pelham

Another strong polo Pelham is the Swales 3-in-1. It has wire rings round the mouthpiece, again in the Wilson style. Its cheeks have 'pigs' tails' instead of curb hooks for the chain, making its curb action very severe. There is little poll pressure, but the rings produce a severe squeezing action in the same way as the IX Lancer.

Hanoverian Pelham

The Hanoverian Pelham has long cheeks and a high, hinged port. Cherry rollers are set at each side of the port. The bit has long been used for ponies and also for polo ponies.

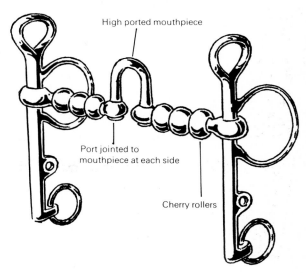

Hanoverian Pelham

High ported mouthpiece

Port jointed to mouthpiece at each side

Cherry rollers

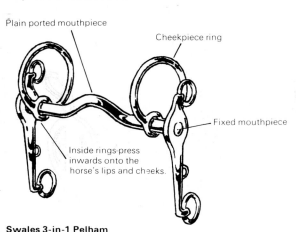

Plain ported mouthpiece

Cheekpiece ring

Fixed mouthpiece

Inside rings press inwards onto the horse's lips and cheeks.

Swales 3-in-1 Pelham

Segundo Pelham

The Segundo mouthpiece is also used in Pelhams, but such bits are not in general use today, though one is seen occasionally. The action relies upon bar pressure, different-shaped ports catering for different shapes of tongue.

Attachments

Pelham Roundings

Pelham roundings are attachments for riders who like to use a Pelham but dislike handling two reins. They are loops of rounded leather that fasten to both curb and snaffle rings on the same side of the bit. They then take a single rein. They nullify the action of the curb to a very great extent.

Mohawk Pelham Attachment

Another Pelham bit attachment is the Mohawk. This is a straight bar encircled with rubber ball washers, clipping onto the eyes of the bit above the mouthpiece and anchoring in the centre with a figure-of-eight rubber ring. It doubles the bearing surface of the bit and exerts greater pressure on the bars. Consequently its effect is severe.

A Pelham with short cheeks that are further nullified by the use of roundings—the curved leather straps joining the bridoon and curb bit rings. A snaffle is probably a better answer for a rider who cannot manage two reins.

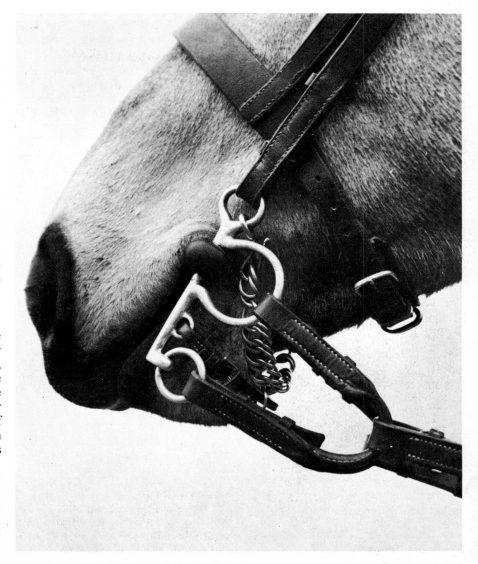

Gag Bits and Bridles

The gag bridle, in all its forms, has its origins in the various overchecks and pulley-operated reins used on driving horses to fix the head carriage in what was considered a desirable position. The use of such devices on harness horses reached its peak in the late nineteenth century. By this time gag bridles were also being used on riding horses.

Between the wars, gag bridles were relatively numerous in the hunting and polo fields and were also used for jumping. Later, as less emphasis was given to obtaining control and carriage by mechanical means and greater attention was paid to basic schooling in the snaffle and drop noseband, the gag decreased in popularity. It is, however, still in evidence as a means of restraint for a particularly strong horse.

Basically, the action of all gags is an upward one against the corners of the mouth. This is made possible by the cheekpieces of the bridle passing through holes in the top and bottom of the bit cheeks. The cheekpieces, which are specially constructed, slide through the holes in accordance with the pressure applied by the rein, and cause

Cheekpieces
Rounded leather cheekpieces are commonly used for gags. They are made by stitching the leather around a core of cord.

Plain rawhide is equally effective and is probably less likely to stick. All leather cheekpieces should be well greased so that they will slide easily through the pulleys or holes. Sometimes cord is used on its own to prevent the sticking problem.

Ideally, any gag cheek should be fitted with metal or leather stops to limit the upward action.

Gags Used With Curbs

Gags used with curbs have small cheeks so that the curb cheeks may also be accommodated. The mouthpiece is lighter, too, and is similar to that of the normal bridoon.

Gag bridoons are employed quite differently from the powerful gag snaffles used alone. Their purpose is to raise the head, whilst the curb bit assists in causing the nose to be retracted. In expert hands, this improves

the bit to rise upwards in the mouth and exert a strong action on the corners.

It is generally thought that the effect of the upward movement of the bit is the raising of the head. In certain instances, such as when a small gag bridoon is used with a curb, that certainly is the effect. But it would be an over-simplification to think of the action as always being of that kind. Some authorities point out that the gag also has an action on the poll, via the headpiece, and that this is a lowering, rather than a raising, action.

Most gags are used as a powerful means of controlling a strong horse. They are made even more severe by being used with a martingale. When a martingale is fitted, two directly opposing forces are brought into play: the upward pull of the bit and the downward pull of the martingale. The horse's head is therefore fixed between the two. This may appear to be illogical and in defiance of simple mechanics, but it achieves a result.

There are many varieties of gag bit, but the essential division is between those used with a curb and those used without any attachment.

the head carriage, if only by mechanical means.

Hack Overcheck
The gag mouthpiece is sometimes thin enough to be called a 'wire-mouth'. In the hack overcheck this mouth is twisted, jointed and fitted with very small ring cheeks. It gives an extremely sharp action.

Cheltenham Gag Snaffle

Shrewsbury
The Shrewsbury gag also has loose-ring cheeks, but these are slightly larger than those of the hack overcheck, and the jointed mouth is thicker and is usually plain. The bit is therefore milder.

Duncan
The Duncan cheek gag has evolved to accommodate the curb still better. It has no rings, but instead has two loops through which the cheekpieces slide.

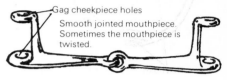
Gag cheekpiece holes
Smooth jointed mouthpiece. Sometimes the mouthpiece is twisted.

**Duncan Gag Snaffle
(Duncombe Gag)**

Single Mouthpiece Gags

Single mouthpiece gags may be used with only the gag rein. But it is recommended that an extra rein, fastened to the cheek in the normal way, be also used. With such an arrangement, the gag action can be brought into play only when necessary.

Single mouthpiece gags include the Cheltenham, Rodzianko's and the Balding.

Cheltenham
Any mouthpiece can, of course, be fitted with gag bit rings, either loose rings or fixed eggbutt types as in the Cheltenham. The advantage of the Cheltenham, it is claimed, is that it drops more easily when the gag rein is released.

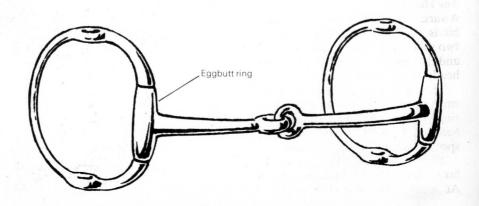
Eggbutt ring

Rodzianko's

Rodzianko's gag—named after the late Colonel Rodzianko, a famous jumping trainer—has a mouthpiece fitted with cherry rollers. It is thought to prevent a horse bearing heavily on the bit or setting his jaw against the mouthpiece.

Rodzianko's Gag (Roller Mouth Gag)

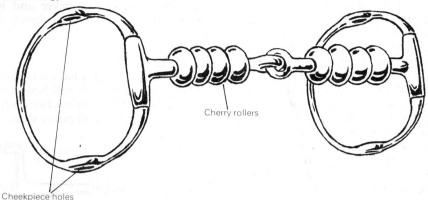

Cherry rollers

Cheekpiece holes

A Balding gag with a Grakle noseband—a popular combination particularly on the horse trials scene. The Balding gag is large and heavy, and as a result its action is less immediate and therefore not as sharp as many other gags. It was perfected by an English polo player called William Balding, who had stables at Rugby in Warwickshire.

Balding

The Balding gag is the largest of the loose-ring cheek gags. It is available also with only half of its cheeks, and is then known as the *half-Balding*.

Other Uses of the Gag

The gag has many other uses, of which the commonest are its use with the Pelham and the Hitchcock gag.

Gag Cheeks with Pelhams

In general, gags used as single bits are of the snaffle type; the mouthpiece can vary as much as in the usual snaffle range. However, gag ring cheeks have also been fitted to the top of Pelham bits, but these arrangements are usually restricted to the polo field.

The Hitchcock Gag

A variation on the basic gag bridle and bit is the Hitchcock gag. It employs two sets of pulleys, one on the bit rings and the other on each side of the bridle headpiece.

The cheekpieces, which are of rounded leather, pass through the bit ring pulleys and then through the headpiece pulleys. They attach to a special loop above the bit rings.

The Hitchcock gag can be used faster than the ordinary gag bridles. And it is more severe in its action.

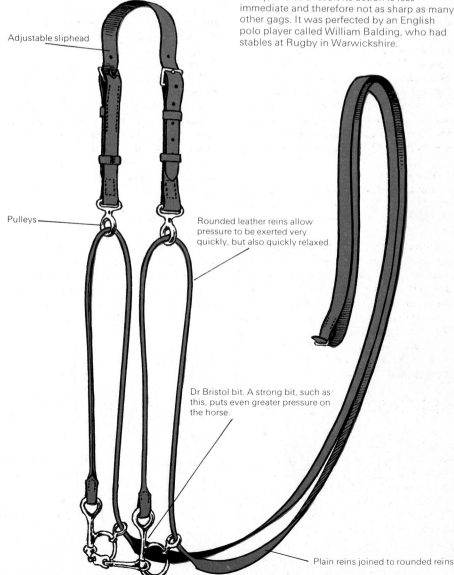

Adjustable sliphead

Pulleys

Rounded leather reins allow pressure to be exerted very quickly, but also quickly relaxed.

Dr Bristol bit. A strong bit, such as this, puts even greater pressure on the horse.

Plain reins joined to rounded reins

Bitless Bridles

An important group of bridles, often both misunderstood and mis-named in Europe, is that to which the hackamore belongs. Often, the name 'hackamore' tends to be given to any form of bridle that does not employ a bit, though this is by no means correct.

Hackamore

The hackamore (la jaquima) is of Spanish origin and belongs to a horse culture that today exists in its most advanced form all the way up the western coast of the United States and extends into Canada. The true basic hackamore, as it would be understood in California, comprises a *bosal*, which is a noseband of plaited rawhide, shaped like a tennis racquet with a weighty knot (*heel knot*) at the chin end; hair ropes (*mecate*) used as reins; and a simple *latigo* headstall that is kept in place by a single ear slot.

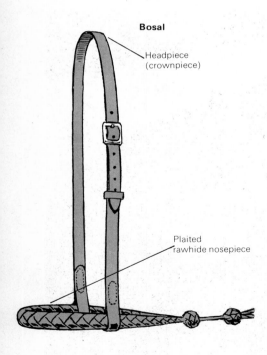

Bosal

Headpiece (crownpiece)

Plaited rawhide nosepiece

Of course, there are variations. The bosal itself varies in weight: a heavy noseband may be used in the initial stages of a horse's training, and a very lightweight one during the later stages.

Some trainers also include a cotton or hair *fiador* in the hackamore. This item of equipment fastens round the throat rather like a throatlatch and is attached to the knot at the rear of the bosal so that the knot is held a little clear of the chin and does not hit the horse continually in the course of schooling.

The knot, to which the mecate reins are attached, causes the noseband to lie at an angle of about 45 degrees, well clear of the nostrils and barely in contact with the nose proper. The knot and the hair ropes act as a counterbalance to the heavy noseband. The weight of the ropes varies according to the preference of the trainer.

The number of 'wraps' of the mecate over the knot determines the pressure that will be applied by the rider raising his hand. The raised hand acts as a restraint, through the pressure of the noseband, and is used also to teach the horse to flex (tuck) at the poll. Changes of direction are made by the shifting of the rider's body weight and the carrying of the acting hand outwards, whilst the supporting hand lays the rein on the horse's neck.

Blair's Pattern

The bitless bridle that is best known in Europe, possibly because of its use by show jumpers, is Blair's pattern. This, in common with other patterns of the same type, achieves control by combining pressure on the nose with pressure on the curb groove. The degree of leverage possible depends upon the length of the cheekpieces, which may be as long as 30 cm (12 in.) or more. A number of variations are produced with much shorter, and therefore less severe, cheeks.

The cheeks, as in a driving bit, are connected by a half-moon shaped bar (attached above the bit rings) to ensure that they cannot become caught up dangerously by a horse tossing his head or making some violent action. The bar also gives the necessary rigidity to the whole structure.

The nosepiece and the curb strap of this bridle have to be well padded to avoid chafing the horse. Also, because the straps encircling the nose need to be adjusted fairly tightly to be effective, it is prudent to alter the position of the noseband slightly up or down at frequent intervals to avoid callousing the nose.

Obviously, the noseband must never be fitted so low that it affects the breathing, and causes distress to the horse.

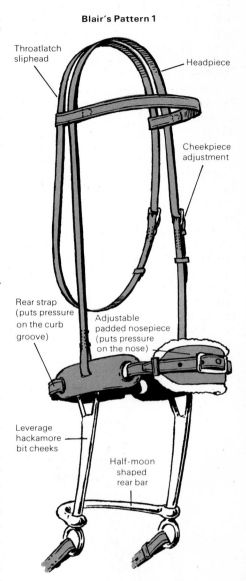

Blair's Pattern 1

Throatlatch sliphead

Headpiece

Cheekpiece adjustment

Rear strap (puts pressure on the curb groove)

Adjustable padded nosepiece (puts pressure on the nose)

Leverage hackamore bit cheeks

Half-moon shaped rear bar

Bitless Jumping Bridle

The bitless jumping bridle is often referred to as the *jumping hackamore*. It is a modern form of bridle now much used in Europe.

Usually, the bridle buckles only at the poll and its cheekpieces divide to meet the reinforced and padded noseband a little way apart. A thin leather strap joins the two rear cheekpiece straps and acts upon the curb groove. The noseband ends at the rear in two rings, which take the reins.

This bridle is ideal for jumping because it has no lever action. Again, its noseband should be moved frequently to avoid callousing.

Scawbrig

The English version of the American hackamore, and the one that conforms most nearly to the Western training system, is the bitless bridle known as the Scawbrig. This is a piece of equipment in the tradition of noseband control. Perfected by the Robinette family in Lincolnshire, it was once popular in Britain but is not now so much in evidence.

The features of the bridle include a broad nosepiece attached to rings that connect it with the bridle cheekpieces, a backstrap to maintain the position of the nosepiece and a rein that passes through the two rings and has a padded strap in its centre. When used in this form, control is obtained by pressure on the nose and on the curb groove.

Horses can learn to jump in such a bridle without fear of being jabbed in the mouth. Or the bridle can help in reschooling a horse that has lost confidence because of heavy hands on the reins. Additionally, it may be used successfully to teach novice riders how to jump.

In training a horse, a bit could in time be introduced to the bridle by the addition of a sliphead, the bit being suspended in the mouth without being fitted with a rein. Finally, with the addition of a rein, increasing emphasis could be given to the bit, whilst retaining the support of the nosepiece and the curb straps.

Simple bitless bridles can, of course, easily be made by the addition of a pair of rings to a strong drop noseband.

WS Bitless Pelham

The WS Bitless Pelham is an interesting type of bitless bridle, which has been copied extensively, although not always effectively. WS are the initials of William Stone, a bit-maker for many years for the firm of Matthew Harvey, of Walsall, England. The bridle was at one time known as the *Distas bridle*, taking the name of the English saddlery firm that manufactured and promoted the device.

This bridle employs a Pelham action and is thus used with two reins. The top rein puts pressure on the nose, and the lower rein operates the curb chain. The

cheeks are much shorter than those of the Blair's pattern bridle. They are also able to move independently and therefore allow a degree of finesse in the bridle's action that is not obtainable in other patterns.

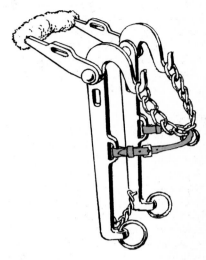

The bitless jumping bridle is designed to eliminate the strong lever action applied to the nose by other bitless bridles. It has been used with great success by such international riders as the American Kathy Kusner.

Blair's Pattern 2

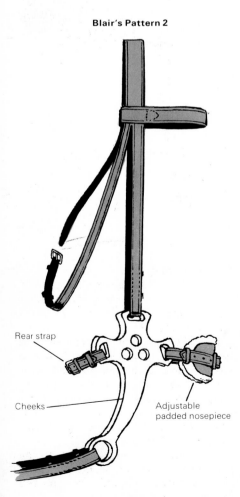

Rear strap

Cheeks

Adjustable padded nosepiece

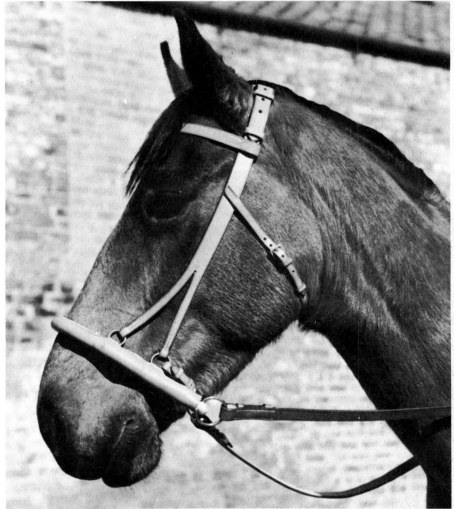

Other Bridles

Show Bridles

The standard bridle for showing in English classes is a double bridle. It has its own characteristics, however, one of which is the extreme narrowness of the cheeks—sometimes only 13 mm ($\frac{1}{2}$ in.) wide—and reins.

Some show people take this peculiarity to extremes, particularly for ponies. The result may look elegant but does not help the rider to maintain a light hand on the pony's mouth, because narrow reins induce tension.

The bit fastenings of show bridles are often of the snap-billet pattern for the sake of appearance. It is otherwise correct for the bridle cheekpieces and reins to be stitched to the bits.

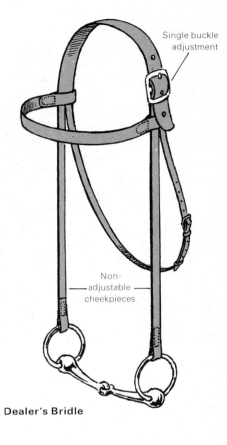

Single buckle adjustment

Non-adjustable cheekpieces

Dealer's Bridle

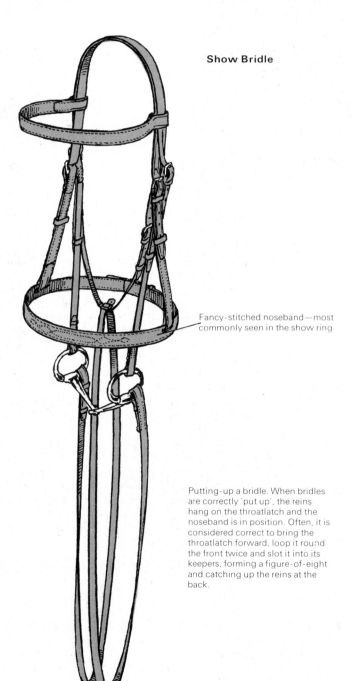

Show Bridle

Fancy-stitched noseband—most commonly seen in the show ring

Putting-up a bridle. When bridles are correctly 'put up', the reins hang on the throatlatch and the noseband is in position. Often, it is considered correct to bring the throatlatch forward, loop it round the front twice and slot it into its keepers, forming a figure-of-eight and catching up the reins at the back.

Dealer's Bridle

The dealer's bridle is a very practical form of exercise bridle for use on a variety of horses during a morning's work. It is a simple snaffle bridle, but instead of having buckles for adjustment on the cheekpieces, there is a single buckle to the left of the poll of the horse, above the browband loop. As a result, it is an easy bridle to adjust evenly and quickly.

Although the dealer's bridle is English in origin, its type of adjustment has been taken up all over the world, and is now seen more frequently outside England than inside.

Rockwell Bridle

The Rockwell is the best-known of a group of bridles that employs bits and nosebands in combination. These bridles are mostly of American origin and are connected with flat racing or, in some cases, with harness racing. Generally they are intended to control the head position of strong-pulling horses.

The Rockwell has a snaffle bit of medium weight fitted with metal

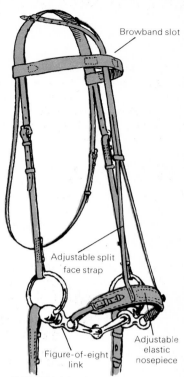

Rockwell Snaffle Bridle

Browband slot

Adjustable split face strap

Figure-of-eight link

Adjustable elastic nosepiece

Fairly thick jointed mouthpiece makes the Rockwell snaffle milder than the Norton Perfection, which has a double mouthpiece.

figure-of-eight loops round the mouth-piece. The top of these loops is attached to an adjustable noseband, usually made from strong elastic, which is held in place by a divided strap running up the face and fastening and adjusting at two points on the headpiece between the ears.

The action of the noseband can be controlled by sliding a tight leather loop up or down the bifurcated central strap to vary the pressure exerted. When the loop is moved up, the pressure is decreased; when moved down, it is increased.

Although the action is concerned largely with the effect of the relatively low-fitting noseband, a further—psychological—effect of restraint is supplied by the strap running up the face. The bit, noseband and divided central strap cause the horse to lower his head, allowing the bit to act on the bars of the mouth, and giving greater control to the rider.

Newmarket Bridle (Weedon Bridle)
A simple bridle of the same type as the Rockwell, but without the divided central strap running up the face, is the Newmarket bridle. Its alternative name of Weedon is that of the British Army cavalry school between World Wars I and II.

Essentially, the bridle makes use of a four-ring driving bit of the Wilson

A beautiful light double bridle for use in the show ring. The narrow leather used is perfect for the show ring but is not substantial enough for everyday use. The bridoon rein is laced to give extra grip and is wider than the curb rein, so that the rider can put more pressure on the bridoon than on the curb.

pattern, the mouthpiece being either jointed or mullen. Pressure on the rein is transmitted to the nose through the light noseband attached to the inner rings. Additionally, there is a squeezing action on the jaw that is relatively mild if a mullen mouthpiece is used and considerably stronger if a jointed snaffle is employed.

Again, the effect of the bridle is to cause the head to be lowered so that the bit acts effectively across the bars. Originally, the Newmarket bridle was used as a training device for a young horse before he was introduced to a full double bridle. It was also used frequently as a jumping bridle.

Norton Perfection Bridle (Citation Bridle)
A more complicated bridle is the Norton perfection, which employs the Rockwell-type loops on a secondary mouthpiece that is very thin and therefore very sharp. The squeezing action of the bridle is relatively severe; it may be considered as stronger than the Rockwell or Newmarket. Its alternative name *Citation* is that of an American racehorse that always ran in this bitting arrangement.

An attribute of both the Norton perfection and the Rockwell bridles is that their bit or bits may be raised high in the mouth by adjusting the facepieces. So fitted, they will discourage all but the most inveterate offenders from getting their tongues over the bit.

Special Bridles

● If a strong-pulling horse needs a high-control bridle whenever he goes out, the rider should not be afraid of using it all the time. But if such a bridle is needed only for events where the horse becomes excitable and hard to control, it should be reserved for those occasions.

Remedial Attachments

Various devices are made for attachment to the bridle in order to remedy common faults. These faults include evading the bit, pulling, refusing to turn, hanging to one side and rearing.

Evasion Devices

There are different reasons for horses evading the bit. Most evasions can be cured by careful training or by removing the cause of the trouble. But when an evasion persists, there are several pieces of equipment that may help.

One of the most common evasions occurs when the horse puts his tongue over the bit. If his bars are too low or too flat and he has a thick or sensitive tongue, the tongue will take more pressure than normal. As a result, he may try to evade the action of the bit by putting his tongue over it. Bits with mullen or ported mouthpieces sometimes help with this problem. If they do not, the following devices may help.

Tongue Strap

The tongue strap passes across the tongue, fastening under the lower jaw. It is quite painful, but is used in flat racing to stop the horse swallowing his tongue.

Tongue Grid (Australian Tongue Spoon)

The tongue grid is a thin metal serpentine suspended high in the mouth above the bit. The horse is scarcely aware of its presence, but he cannot physically bring up his tongue high enough to put it over the bit.

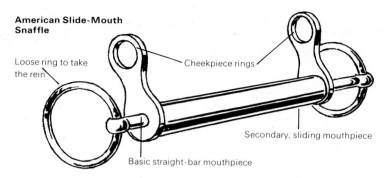

American Slide-Mouth Snaffle

Loose ring to take the rein

Cheekpiece rings

Basic straight-bar mouthpiece

Secondary, sliding mouthpiece

American Slide-Mouth Bit

Although called the American slide-mouth, the aim of this bit is to stop the bit sliding through the mouth and therefore to stop the horse evading its action. Its cheekpiece rings are set on a tube of metal around the mouthpiece itself, which is a straight bar. As the horse tries to slide the bit through his mouth, the mouthpiece slides with him.

Spoon Bit

The spoon bit has rounded plates extending at each side of the centre of the mouthpiece. It is effective, but it causes the horse to open his mouth because the spoon acts on the upper palate.

Circle and Strap

The circle and strap device consists of two circular pieces of leather placed round the ends of a mullen mouthpiece. They are connected by an adjustable strap which is attached to the noseband by a small strap in the middle. The device puts pressure on the horse's nose and raises the bit in his mouth, making it hard for him to get his tongue over the bit.

Rubber Tongue Port

The rubber tongue port is a small device that is fastened to the centre of a mullen mouthpiece. Its port lies flat on the tongue, facing to the rear, and its bulk discourages the horse from the evasion.

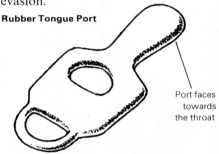

Rubber Tongue Port

Port faces towards the throat

Pulling Devices

There are also a number of devices to restrain a pulling horse, without having to resort to a very strong bit.

Nose Net

The nose net is a light cord muzzle designed to give greater control on a hard-pulling horse with little or no mouth. The net is placed over the nose and fastened tightly to the noseband. It does not inflict great pain, but the nose is so sensitive that the horse is always aware of it and will therefore hang back. Also, the horse is unable to evade the bit by opening his mouth. The nose net is used mostly by polo players.

Australian Cheeker (Australian Noseband)

The Australian cheeker is a flat rubber device shaped like an inverted Y. The two bottom arms end in disks, which have holes in them so that they can be pulled over the bit rings at each side of the mouth. The arms join on the nose, and the device runs straight up the face and fastens onto the headpiece. The

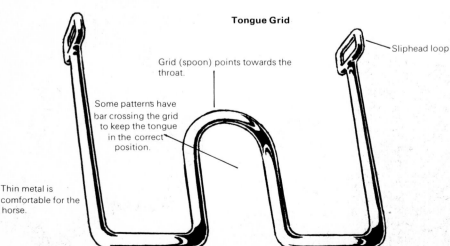

Tongue Grid

Sliphead loop

Grid (spoon) points towards the throat.

Some patterns have bar crossing the grid to keep the tongue in the correct position.

Thin metal is comfortable for the horse.

Australian cheeker keeps the bit up in the mouth and at the same time exerts slight restraining pressure on the nose, some of it psychological. Generally, it is used for racing.

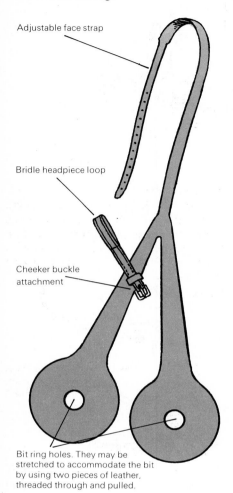

Adjustable face strap

Bridle headpiece loop

Cheeker buckle attachment

Bit ring holes. They may be stretched to accommodate the bit by using two pieces of leather, threaded through and pulled.

Turning Devices

Horses that refuse to turn to one side, or that hang to one side, present the rider with another problem. A running martingale may help by stopping the horse raising his head above the line of bit control. If not, one of the following devices may be the answer.

Brush Pricker

The brush pricker can be used only as a temporary answer because it becomes less effective when a horse gets used to it. It is a circular piece of leather studded with bristles, and fits round the side of the bit, bristle side inwards. The rein action pulls the bristles towards the nose and the horse reacts by turning away from the pain.

Slit allows the bit to pass through to the centre hole.

Anti-Lug Bit

The anti-lug bit is a jointed snaffle with one arm of the mouthpiece shorter and more curved than the other. The short side has a stronger action than the long and is therefore fitted on the opposite side from that to which the horse hangs.

A loose-ring racing snaffle mouthpiece passing through the rubber ring of an Australian cheeker. This device keeps the bit high in the horse's mouth during a race, helping to prevent him putting his tongue over the bit and getting out of control.

Circle-Cheek Snaffle

The circle-cheek snaffle has large ring cheeks similar to those of the Liverpool bit used for driving. Its rein attachment is in the centre of the cheek. It produces a squeezing action which, combined with the extra-large cheeks, helps to keep the horse straight.

Other Devices

Many other bridle attachments have been developed. Some remedy such faults as rearing, others add to the horse's comfort.

Blinkers

Racehorses that seem unable to keep their minds and eyes on the job in hand are often fitted with blinkers. Blinkers are a head covering of fabric, with leather eye shields. They allow the horse to see only to the front. Blinkers are available with full cups, half cups or very large cups known as 'wide-eyes'. The head covering is held in place by straps and buckles or by clip fastenings, which are neater and easier to fit.

Cheek Guards

These are designed to stop the bit cheeks from chafing the lips. They are simple flat rubber circles, with holes in the centre to accommodate the bit mouthpiece.

Chifney Anti-Rearing Bit

Rearing can be a problem when leading stallions and young stock, particularly colts. The Chifney bit is sometimes used to try to stop this, but without great success. It has three rings, two for the cheekpieces and one for the lead rein. The upper part of the cheek swivels on the mouthpiece independently of the lower section.

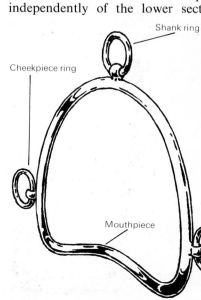

Shank ring

Cheekpiece ring

Mouthpiece

Nosebands

Nosebands can have a decorative effect but their principal purpose is to aid the action of the bit. They do this either by laying greater stress upon it or by actually altering it. There are many different types in common use.

Cavesson Noseband

The cavesson is the most common noseband and is the one most suitable for early training. No other type of noseband is ever worn with a double bridle for showing.

The cavesson noseband generally comprises an adjustable leather headpiece and a broad strap, the nosepiece, fitting round the nose. But some fashions, especially in the show ring, dictate the use of a very narrow nosepiece, perhaps rolled and stitched. This type does not suit the face of every horse. A plain nosepiece with a breadth of 25 mm (1 in.) at the front is a good standard fitting.

A well-made nosepiece hangs at a right-angle to its own cheekpieces, which should be hidden by the bridle cheekpieces. Some noseband cheekpieces are simply stitched to the nosepiece. A loop fastening is stronger— something that is particularly necessary if a standing martingale is to be fitted.

In badly-made nosebands, the front of the nosepiece is too short and the rear too long. This causes the noseband cheekpieces to fall in front of the true cheekpieces and the rear strap to fall too low, pinching the horse's skin between the bit cheeks and the nosepiece. When this happens, the horse tends to carry his head too high.

Drop Noseband (Dropped Noseband)

The drop noseband is a German invention and comes from the German Cavalry School in Hanover. It is used to prevent the horse opening his mouth or crossing his jaws, both of which actions slide the bit away from its correct position on the bars and tongue and enable the horse to evade the rider's control.

Also, when pressure is put on the bit by means of the reins, some pressure is exerted on the front of the nosepiece.

This helps the rider to keep the head below the angle of control, ensuring that the bit acts correctly on the bars and not simply on the corners of the mouth and lips.

The noseband, which is usually stitched and rolled at the front, should be broad enough to prevent too much localized pressure being put on the nose. Correctly fitted, it should be fastened below the bit, with its cheekpieces in front of the bridle cheekpieces. It lies about 50 mm (2 in.) above the nostrils, resting upon the bottom of the nasal bone at the front of the face.

If the noseband is too low, it will interfere with the horse's breathing, and skin will be trapped between the bit and the noseband. If it is too high, it will push the bit up in the mouth and pinch the corners of the lips.

The nosepiece is often fitted too tightly, preventing the horse from relaxing the lower jaw. There should be ample room to place two fingers between the nosepiece and the face.

A well-made drop noseband has a correctly-proportioned nosepiece, and has small leather loops connecting the nosepiece and cheekpieces at each side to prevent the nosepiece dropping too low. Some badly-made nosebands

When fitted correctly, the cavesson noseband does not restrict the horse unduly and allows the bit to move easily and without pinching the lips. It does, however, prevent the horse from crossing his jaw high up the jaw bone. The nosepiece should be adjusted so that it hangs the width of two fingers below the cheek bone; it is at the correct tightness when two fingers will fit between it and the horse's face.

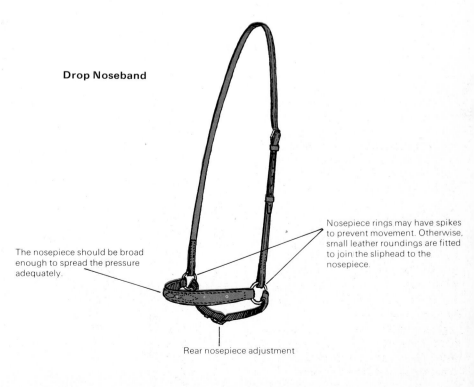

Drop Noseband

The nosepiece should be broad enough to spread the pressure adequately.

Nosepiece rings may have spikes to prevent movement. Otherwise, small leather roundings are fitted to join the sliphead to the nosepiece.

Rear nosepiece adjustment

A sheepskin-covered noseband teamed with blinkers on a nervous racehorse. This type of noseband is a favourite on the racecourse and is considered by many to be inappropriate when seen anywhere else. Some racing trainers believe it stops a horse shying and unbalancing himself in a race. It is particularly popular in the United States and in France.

bit and fasten at the rear in the same way as those of the drop noseband.

A way of achieving a flash noseband without actually buying one or spoiling a cavesson is to use two simple buckle and strap attachments, one very much longer than the other. The smaller of the two is buckled vertically round the nosepiece front. The larger is slotted through this so that it rests immediately below the nosepiece in the centre of the face and fastens at the rear.

One problem with the flash noseband is that the lower strap or straps tend to pull down the front of the cavesson. But the flash is the only correct way of combining the action of a drop noseband with that of a standing martingale, should this be thought necessary.

have a nosepiece that is too long in front and too short behind, allowing the front to drop too low and also pressing the bit tightly into the corners of the lips. If the front of the nosepiece is about 230 mm (9 in.) long, the rear straps should add up to about 410 mm (16 in.).

Very sensitive horses will appreciate a piece of soft sheepskin slotted round the rear of the nosepiece to prevent chafing. Hard-pulling horses may have the rear strap replaced entirely by a curb chain and rubber curb chain guard.

A standing martingale should never be used with a drop noseband because the pressure on the lower part of the nasal bone would be too great.

Flash Noseband

The flash noseband is a cavesson that incorporates, to a lesser degree, the action of the drop noseband. It is less severe than the drop noseband because its pressure point is slightly higher — but it does not push the bit into the corners of the mouth.

In the flash, the plain cavesson is fitted with two straps sewn at angles onto the front of the nosepiece and crossing immediately below it. The straps pass round the muzzle below the

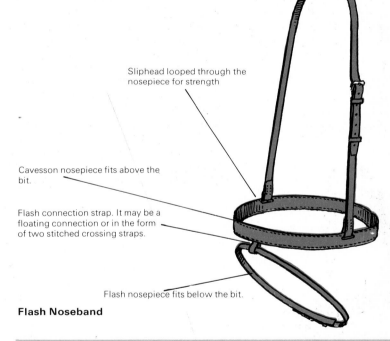

Sliphead looped through the nosepiece for strength

Cavesson nosepiece fits above the bit.

Flash connection strap. It may be a floating connection or in the form of two stitched crossing straps.

Flash nosepiece fits below the bit.

Flash Noseband

Noseband and Curb

- Jumping and event horses are often ridden in a drop noseband or a Grakle noseband in conjunction with a curb and curb chain. This is harsh and incorrect.

- A horse's curb groove can accommodate only one strap or chain.

- The curb bit requires a horse to open his mouth slightly and relax his lower jaw. He cannot do this when wearing a drop or Grakle noseband.

- With a double bridle, if any further restriction is necessary, it must be done from above the bit by fitting a cavesson slightly lower than normal.

Grakle Noseband (Cross-Over, Figure-of-Eight, or Mexican Noseband)

The Grakle noseband, named after the British Grand National winner, *Grakle*, is composed of three sets of fairly thin straps attached to a combined fitting of headpiece and cheekpieces that is shorter than usual. The front two straps extend from the ends of the cheekpieces, cross at the point on the nose where the cavesson is usually placed and then branch off under the bit, to be fastened at the rear. At the point where the two straps cross, a flat, round piece of leather or sheepskin is interposed next to the horse's skin for comfort and protection.

The Grakle should be fitted only as tightly as the normal cavesson and drop nosebands. Its top rear strap will then exert gentle pressure on the muscles that lie around the horse's cheeks, and its lower straps will act in the same way as those of the flash noseband. This combined action helps to prevent the horse opening his mouth, yawing and fighting the bit.

The Grakle is particularly safe in that it cannot drop any lower than it is fitted at the front. Consequently, it cannot obstruct the horse's breathing.

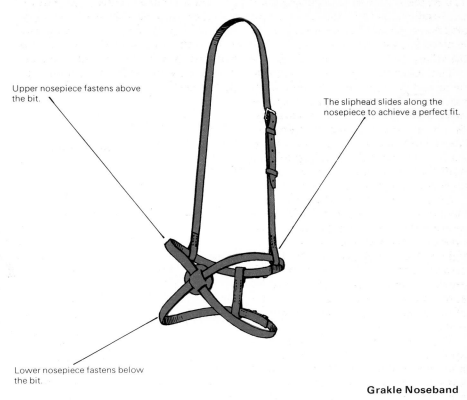

Upper nosepiece fastens above the bit.

The sliphead slides along the nosepiece to achieve a perfect fit.

Lower nosepiece fastens below the bit.

Grakle Noseband

Brinekind Noseband (Jobey or Bucephalus Noseband)

The Brinekind noseband, perfected by an English horseman named George Brine, is designed for use on a strong-pulling horse with a cavesson noseband and either a Pelham or a curb bit.

The front of the noseband is an oval or a scalloped padded strap tapering into two thin, flat straps with D-rings at the ends. In the centre of the nosepiece, a small strap and buckle attachment is fitted.

The strap and buckle fasten the nosepiece to the cavesson front. The two thin straps pass round behind the jaw, crossing and fastening to the curb hooks on the opposite sides.

This noseband exerts circular pressure around the nose when the curb rein is used. It must be made-to-measure for each horse because, usually, it has no adjustment other than on the cavesson attachment.

Anti-Pulling Cavesson Noseband

The anti-pulling cavesson has the same effect as the Brinekind noseband, but is rather stronger. Again, it can be used only with a Pelham or a curb bit.

The noseband has the ordinary cavesson headpiece, cheekpieces and nosepiece front. But the normal leather strap and buckle fitting at the rear is replaced by two long pieces of curb chain. As with the straps of the Brinekind noseband, these chains cross behind the jaw and are attached to the curb hooks on their opposite sides.

The anti-pulling cavesson exerts a great deal of pressure around the nose and can be extremely severe. It does, however, have more adjustment than the Brinekind.

Sheepskin-Covered Noseband (Shadow-Roll, Anti-Shadow or Anti-Shying Noseband)

The sheepskin-covered noseband is used mainly on the racecourse and racetrack. It has long been particularly popular in France and the United States.

It consists of an ordinary cavesson headpiece and nosepiece. The front of the nosepiece is covered with a thick roll of lamb's wool, padded to increase its bulk. This roll is designed to prevent the horse noticing fearsome things on the ground, such as his own shadow, and flinging up his head, thereby losing rhythm, balance and impulsion. To be of use, it must be fitted fairly high up the face.

The sheepskin-covered noseband has definite safety merits in harness and Thoroughbred racing. Its benefits for other activities and other types of horses are dubious. But some show hunter trainers believe that the device helps to make a timid horse stand off from his fences instead of getting too close and screwing over them.

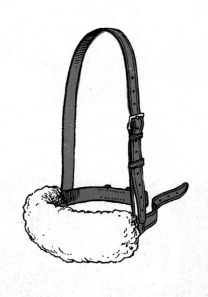

Kineton Noseband (Puckle Noseband)

The Kineton noseband is designed for hard-pulling horses and is a good alternative to the use of a strong bit. It is named for its inventor, who lived in the village of Kineton in England.

The Kineton has a normal head-piece and cheekpieces, but the cheekpieces are attached to two rounded metal loops that curve round inside the bit cheeks behind the mouthpiece. These loops are attached to a double leather nosepiece that is adjustable on both sides. The centre of the nosepiece is reinforced with a strip of light metal.

Correctly fitted, the Kineton loops should be in contact with the bit mouthpiece, but should not exert pressure until the reins are used. The tighter the nosepiece is fitted, the greater the pressure that will be exerted. The nosepiece should not be allowed to fall lower than the bottom of the nasal bone or it will be far too severe.

When the reins are used, pressure is applied to the bit and to the nose. The horse is forced to lower his head and, as a result, the bit can work correctly on the tongue and bars. The horse's awareness of the pain that can be inflicted on his nose by the metal in the nosepiece also tends to slow him up.

The Kineton noseband does not prevent the horse opening his mouth, something that he will almost certainly do. It can be of benefit to a young and weak rider on a hard-pulling pony. The rider has more control without ruining the pony's mouth by continuous pulling on the reins.

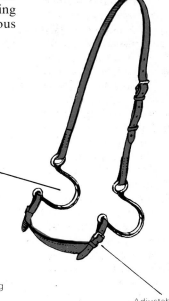

Kineton Noseband

Metal loops fit around the rear of the bit.

Adjustable metal reinforced mouthpiece

Kineton nosebands are regarded by some riders as a last resort on the hardest-pulling and most wooden-mouthed horses. The Kineton is sometimes used on the racecourse. Trainers fit the horse with an ordinary cavesson and put the Kineton on top. The jockey then has control cantering down to the start—a favourite time for horses to bolt with unwary jockeys. Once safely at the line, the jockey can whip off the Kineton and start the race.

Martingales

Most martingales consist of a strap or straps attached at one end to the girths and at the other end to the reins, noseband or bit cheeks. They are designed to stop the horse placing his head above the angle of control, thereby evading the action of the bit. There are many types of martingale, some more restrictive than others.

Standing Martingale (Fast or Tie-Down Martingale)

The basic standing martingale comprises an adjustable neck strap with a loop at the bottom through which a broad, flat chest strap is passed. This strap has a loop at one end and is adjusted by a buckle at the other.

A well-made standing martingale has the chest strap adjustment at the end that loops over the noseband. The plain loop is passed between the front legs and onto the girth.

The martingale is fitted in such a way that there is room for a hand between the neck strap and the neck, and so that the chest strap acts only when the horse raises his head too high. When correctly fitted it should act to balance the horse yet allow him adequate freedom of the head and neck, particularly over fences.

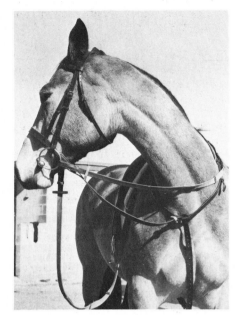

A correctly-fitted standing martingale. A rubber martingale stop should be used to prevent the chest strap slipping through the neck strap.

Grainger Martingale

The Grainger martingale is a variation of the standing martingale. Its chest strap divides at the top to attach to its own noseband, the nosepiece of which has no rear fastening and is fitted just below the normal cavesson noseband position.

This martingale puts a lot of pressure on the nose and also acts upon the poll through the cheekpieces and headpiece. It is more restrictive than the standing martingale.

Cheshire Martingale

Another form of standing martingale is the Cheshire. The chest strap, instead of fastening to the noseband, has a metal ring at the end, to which two metal chains are attached. These are fitted to the bit cheeks either by spring hooks or by buckles.

The action is therefore directly on the bit and, consequently, is severe. This is particularly so if a jointed bit is used because it accentuates the nutcracker action of the joint and puts pressure on the bars.

Whalley's Martingale

Whalley's martingale is a Cheshire martingale that adds a piece of rubber into one section of the chest strap. The purpose of this is to soften the action on the bit.

Running Martingale

The running martingale is probably the most widely used today. It passes from the girth in the same way as the standing martingale, but forks into two straps immediately after it has passed through the neck strap loop. The reins pass through a ring at the end of each strap.

As a result, the martingale acts upon the bit whenever the head goes up above the angle of control. Its action is particularly acute when used with a jointed bit. But so long as it is fitted in such a way that it has no effect when the head is in the correct position, it is a less restrictive aid than the standing martingale. Because its effect is removed as the reins are slackened, the rider need never interfere with the horse's head and neck over fences.

The two split straps of the running martingale may be of either flat or round leather.

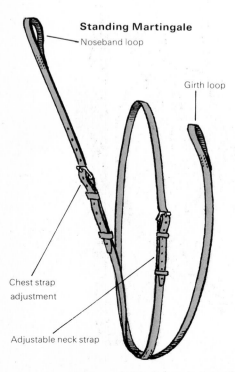

Standing Martingale
- Noseband loop
- Girth loop
- Chest strap adjustment
- Adjustable neck strap

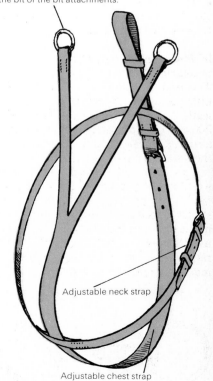

The rings should be smaller than the rein stops or they may catch on the bit or the bit attachments.

- Adjustable neck strap
- Adjustable chest strap

Running Martingale

Bib Martingale

The bib martingale is popular with some racehorse trainers. It is a running martingale, but the space between the two straps is filled in with a triangle of baghide.

Bib Martingale

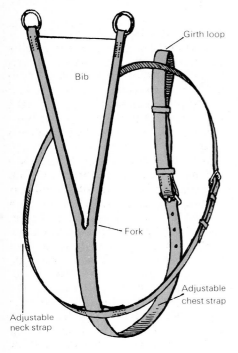

This martingale is safe for excitable young horses because it cannot become entangled in their corner teeth or round other pieces of equipment. It should be fitted at the same length as the normal running martingale.

Irish Martingale (Irish Rings or Spectacles)

The Irish martingale is a very useful little piece of equipment. It is a simple leather strap of between 125 and 200 mm (5 and 8 in.) in length, and has a ring sewn at each end through which the reins are passed.

This not only keeps the reins together and prevents them flying over the horse's head in a fall, but actually stops an excitable horse from throwing his head about. For these reasons, it is used almost without exception on racehorses, on which other sorts of martingales are dangerous.

Irish Martingale

Pugri Martingale

The pugri martingale is used on polo ponies. It is a standing martingale made of a length of coloured turban (pugri) cloth, tied at each end. The cloth is softer than leather and therefore neither chafes nor pinches the skin during the match.

Pulley Martingale

A refinement of the running martingale is the pulley. Instead of dividing, the chest strap ends in a small pulley. A cord with a ring at each end runs through the pulley and the reins pass through the rings.

This device gives the horse's head and neck more lateral flexibility than does the running martingale. It therefore helps in movements such as fast changes of direction.

Market Harborough Martingale

The Market Harborough martingale is similar to the running martingale, but the split straps are about twice as long and are made either of rawhide or round leather with clips or buckles at the ends. These straps thread through the bit cheeks and are attached to reins that have D-rings at equal points along their lengths.

The Market Harborough is operated by the horse himself. If he raises his head, the pressure on the bit forces him to lower it, when he instantly relieves himself of the action of the martingale.

Combined Martingale

The combined martingale is fitted with both the standing martingale chest strap and the running martingale split straps. It therefore combines the action of both.

Martingale Splits

Martingale splits are the working sections of running and standing martingales used with breastplates. They have buckles at the chest and to attach them to the breastplate chest rings.

Rein Stops

Rein stops are leather or rubber ovals fitted on the reins close to the bit. They prevent the martingale rings becoming caught on the rein attachments, bit cheeks or corner teeth.

Martingale Stops

Martingale stops are rubber rings fitted diagonally across the point where the neck strap joins the chest strap. They keep the chest strap up out of the way of the horse's forelegs.

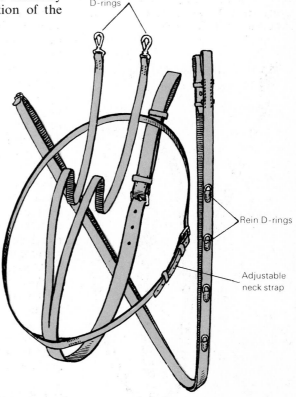

Market Harborough Martingale

Reins

The reins, the lines of communication between the rider's hands and the horse's mouth, vary in length from 1·25 to 1·5 m (4 ft to 5 ft) and in width from 13 to 25 mm ($\frac{1}{2}$ in. to 1 in.), depending on their function. Although very narrow reins are not as strong and hard-wearing as wider ones, they are more sensitive. Wide reins are preferred by many riders but can lead to less tactful rein aids. Too-long reins are a hazard to the safety of rider and horse. Too-short ones are obviously restrictive.

Most reins are made of leather, but other materials are used too. There are numerous variations on plain leather reins, all aimed to give the rider better grip.

Plain Leather Reins

Plain leather reins are attractive but they become slippery when wet. A well-made pair, as with all reins, is buckled in the middle rather than stitched.

Plain Leather Reins
Very wide reins may lead to insensitive hands. Narrow 'bootlace' reins may be dangerous.

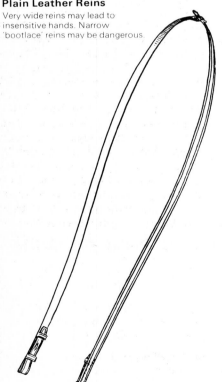

For double bridles, the curb rein is always narrower than the snaffle. This enables the rider to feel which is which. He will also put less pressure on the curb.

Laced Leather Reins

Laced reins are plain leather with thin, flat laces threaded through the hand-parts to form a series of Vs. They give the rider a good grip and are less likely to stretch than plaited reins.

Laced Leather Reins

Lacing gives at least as good a grip as plaiting, and does not stretch.

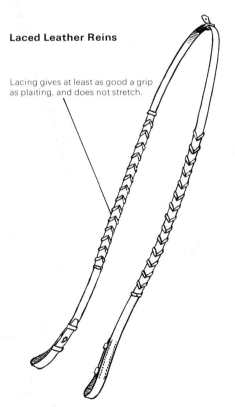

Dartnall Reins

The reins least likely to chafe the rider's hands and the horse's neck are the Dartnall. They are made of soft, plaited cotton, shaped to the rider's hands. They are excellent and very light.

Nylon Plaited Reins

Nylon plaited reins are not to be recommended. When dry, they are slippery, and when they have been wet they become hard and brittle and totally unsuitable for good riding.

Rubber-Covered Leather Reins

Rubber-covered reins give a good grip in all conditions. They are plain leather with cloth-backed pimpled rubber drawn over them and widely stitched, preferably by hand. Close machining weakens the rubber. Usually, the rubber begins approximately 250 mm (10 in.) from the bit attachments and is between 450 and 750 mm (18 and 30 in.) long. The shortest lengths of rubber are used in racing, where the jockey takes a closer contact on the mouth.

The rubber hand-parts can be replaced as they wear and lose their ability to grip.

Rubber Reins
Buckled reins are always preferable to sewn reins because running martingales may be fitted more easily and a single broken rein can be replaced.

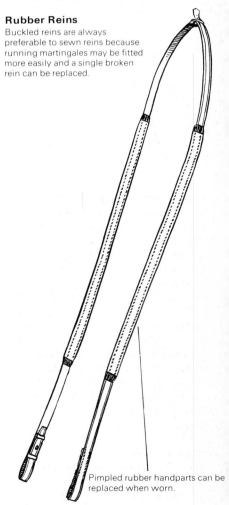

Pimpled rubber handparts can be replaced when worn.

Plaited Leather Reins

Plaited leather reins are plain leather cut into five strands about 250 mm (10 in.) from the bit attachments and plaited to provide extra grip. They are inclined to stretch.

Plaited Leather Reins

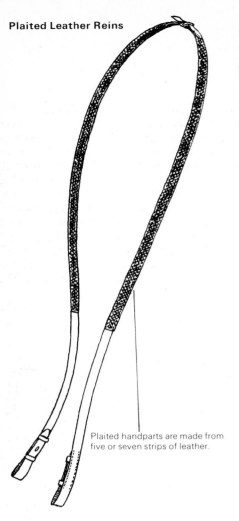

Plaited handparts are made from five or seven strips of leather.

Draw Reins (Running Reins)

Draw reins are long leather reins used with a normal bridle and reins. They are attached to the girth—either between the front legs or at the sides—or to the saddle as high up as the front D-rings. From here, they run through the bit cheeks and to the rider's hands.

Draw reins are used to compel a horse to assume a vertical head carriage. They are severe and should only be used by experienced riders who are able to co-ordinate leg, seat and hands, so that the horse's free forward movement is not inhibited. Used incorrectly, they have been called 'the razor in the monkey's hands'.

Show Lead Reins

Usually, show lead reins are made of white web or leather about 2·5 m (8 ft) in length. Most of them have a loop at one end and a short length of chain at the other, which is attached to Y-shaped couplings. The couplings are made of either chain or leather. The arms are attached to the bit cheeks by buckles or spring hooks to give the handler even control over the bit.

German Web Reins

German webs are very light reins with small leather grips sewn across the hand-parts. Usually, they are plain leather for about 450 mm (18 in.) to accommodate martingale rings. These reins are inexpensive and give excellent grip.

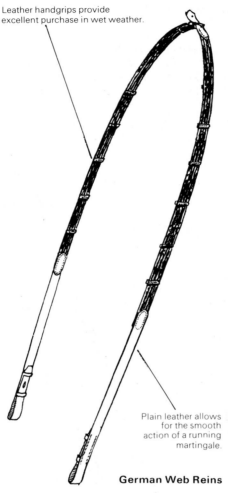

Leather handgrips provide excellent purchase in wet weather.

Plain leather allows for the smooth action of a running martingale.

German Web Reins

Chambon

The Chambon is used during lungeing to develop the muscles of the horse's back and quarters, and to supple and balance him. It is especially useful on a young horse.

The rein is French in origin and comes from the Army Equestrian School at Saumur. It consists of a special headpiece worn beneath a snaffle bridle. To the headpiece is fitted an extra strap with a ring at each end. A nylon string passes through the rings, and spring clips at each end are attached to the bit cheeks. A leather chest strap, with a loop at one end to pass over the girth, has a rubber ring at the other to take the nylon string.

The Chambon is fitted in such a way that the horse feels its effect only when he raises his head too high. When this happens, the bit moves up in the mouth and there is a slight pressure on the poll, encouraging the horse to lower his head. There is no backward pressure on the mouth, as there can be with draw reins.

Gogue

The Gogue reins are also used in training, but when employed on ridden horses are suitable for older animals. There are two patterns of Gogue: the independent and the command. Both have a double action, putting pressure on the poll and bars to induce correct head carriage.

The independent Gogue has a chest strap similar to that of the Chambon. Through its loop is threaded a cord approximately 2 m (7 ft) long. The cord passes through the headpiece rings and through the bit rings at each side of the head. It is clipped back to the chest ring by spring hooks. The rider has no control over the rein when mounted.

The command Gogue is the same, except that the cord is attached to a further pair of reins about 1·5 m (5 ft) in length instead of being clipped to the chest ring. The rider uses these reins in conjunction with the snaffle reins and can therefore control their action.

Reins and Hands

- Reins that are held or used incorrectly can damage a horse's mouth. The rider should use both hands to hold the reins and maintain a steady, even contact with the horse's head.

- Approximately 225 mm (9 in.) of rein should be left below the rider's hands. If there is more than this the rein may catch in the rider's foot.

- Plain leather reins are generally used with double bridles and Pelhams.

Saddle Design

A well-designed and correctly-fitted saddle is vital to the performance of both horse and rider. The actual shape of a saddle and the positioning of its attachments not only permit the rider to maintain a correct position for any type of equestrian activity, but assist him in a positive way.

A good saddle places the rider over the horse's centre of gravity in any situation. The centre of gravity moves forward towards the withers as the horse gallops and jumps, and slightly back for advanced dressage movements.

Therefore, a jumping saddle places the rider forward and brings the knees up higher than normal, and a dressage saddle places the rider slightly farther back and lets the knees fall naturally. It is said, however, that the test of a good dressage saddle is that it feels comfortable enough to be used for jumping.

Buying the right type of saddle for everyday use can be a problem. But unless the rider has a definite intention to specialize in a particular area of equestrianism, a modern spring-tree general purpose saddle is probably the best answer to most problems.

Whatever type of saddle is chosen, the main consideration is that it should fit both horse and rider. To check that it does so, not only must the rider sit on it, but it should be put on the horse and its fit studied before it is bought.

Often it is not possible to keep a saddle for use on one horse only, particularly in a busy yard where the horses are constantly changing. But it is still necessary to remember that a badly-fitted saddle not only causes discomfort to horse and rider, but can actually stop a horse moving properly.

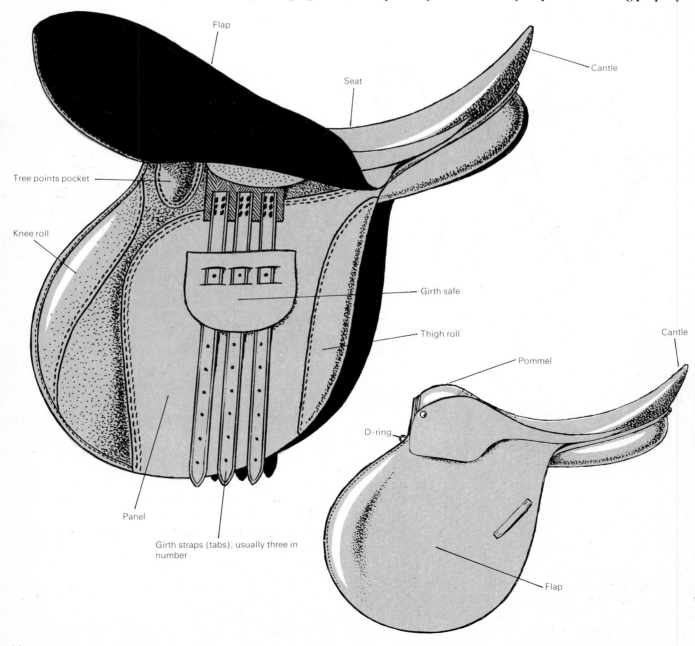

Flap

Seat

Cantle

Tree points pocket

Knee roll

Girth safe

Thigh roll

Cantle

Pommel

D-ring

Panel

Girth straps (tabs), usually three in number

Flap

Fitting the Tree

The fit of the tree is the first thing to check. English saddle trees are made in three basic widths: narrow, standard and broad. And although a good saddler can broaden a narrow tree to fit a wider horse, narrowing a broad tree is not usually successful.

Saddle Length

Saddle length is also important to the fitting. On a short-coupled horse, a long saddle can rest on the loins. If the rider then sits back—as can happen easily in the flat, old-fashioned types of saddle—the horse's sensitive loins and kidneys may be damaged, and the horse may react with such resistances as tail-swishing, moving badly behind, or bucking. A too-short saddle is equally bad. It does not distribute the weight of the rider over enough of the horse's back, and can cause soreness.

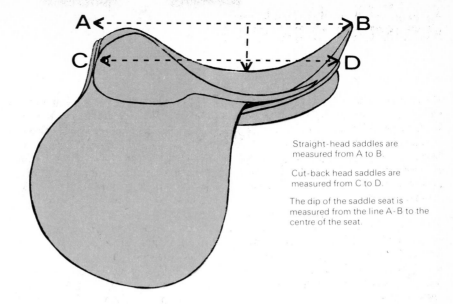

Straight-head saddles are measured from A to B.

Cut-back head saddles are measured from C to D.

The dip of the saddle seat is measured from the line A-B to the centre of the seat.

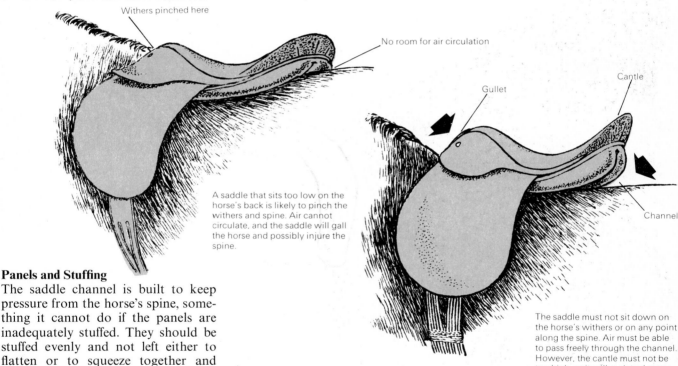

Withers pinched here

No room for air circulation

Cantle

Gullet

Channel

A saddle that sits too low on the horse's back is likely to pinch the withers and spine. Air cannot circulate, and the saddle will gall the horse and possibly injure the spine.

The saddle must not sit down on the horse's withers or on any point along the spine. Air must be able to pass freely through the channel. However, the cantle must not be too high, or it will rock and cause soreness.

Panels and Stuffing

The saddle channel is built to keep pressure from the horse's spine, something it cannot do if the panels are inadequately stuffed. They should be stuffed evenly and not left either to flatten or to squeeze together and therefore bear down on the spine. At the pommel, the forearch (head) must be at least three fingers in width above the withers when the rider is mounted.

It is not enough to buy a saddle that appears to have been well stuffed, and then to forget about it. The saddle must, of course, be evenly stuffed to begin with, or it cannot distribute the weight of the rider as it should. But daily use can cause irregularities in the stuffing.

Some riders, for instance, ride with one stirrup leather longer than the other, or simply sit most of their weight on one half of the saddle seat. If this happens, one side of the panel will be

Choosing a Saddle

- The tree and panels of a saddle should be chosen to fit the horse. The seat length should be chosen to fit the rider.
- The idea that a particular size of saddle will fit every horse of a particular size is erroneous.
- If a saddle is continually changed from one horse to another, it will not bed down to the shape of any one of them, and in the end will not fit any horse properly.

flattened long before the other; that side must then be frequently re-stuffed to compensate.

Horses can also affect the way the stuffing wears—particularly those that are young or green—because of un-evenly-developed backs. Usually, such horses are less well-developed on the nearside, and until they are schooled out of this one-sidedness, the problem must be solved by the saddle stuffing.

Another point to watch for is over-stuffing. Although an over-stuffed saddle will bed down in time, it may not do so before it has made the horse's back extremely sore by its constant, bouncing friction. If a saddle rises to meet the rider's seat at the rising trot, it needs attention.

Care of the saddle panels is of great importance in making sure that a saddle continues to fit well. The panels should be kept scrupulously clean and checked for cracks or even the smallest lump or ridge. Any defect of this kind may cause soreness, as will a leather panel that has not been kept supple.

Children's Saddles

Children's saddles have an added fitting problem—ponies. Ponies expand and contract with the changing seasons. What may fit a pony beautifully in summer may be hopelessly wrong in winter.

One answer to the problem is to buy a saddle that is never too narrow for the pony, and then to use cruppers, wither pads and numnahs as short-term remedies when the pony slims off a little.

If, in addition, the saddle tends to roll round the pony in his weighty days, a full-panel serge-lined saddle may help, with an added surcingle as a safety girth, a breastgirth or an extra girth which fits in front of the normal girth onto the extra girth strap known as a *point strap*.

It is worth remembering that a pad saddle will fit just about anything in just about any condition.

The Rider

A saddle that fits the horse, must also fit those who are going to sit on it. Saddles that are too big for the rider give no support and allow far too much movement. Those that are too small are painful for horse and rider alike.

Even a saddle of the correct size will not suit all riders. A saddle that gives absolute comfort to one may be extremely uncomfortable to another. The only answer to the problem is practical experiment.

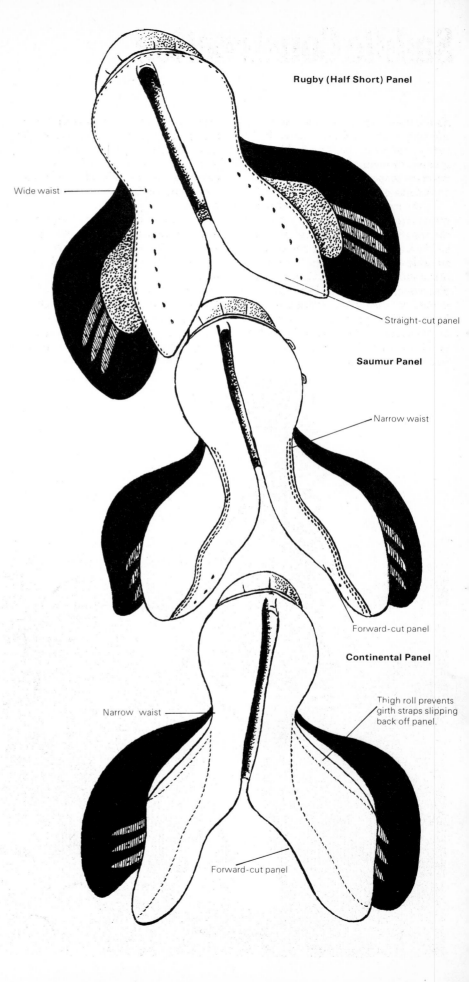

Rugby (Half Short) Panel

Wide waist

Straight-cut panel

Saumur Panel

Narrow waist

Forward-cut panel

Continental Panel

Thigh roll prevents girth straps slipping back off panel.

Narrow waist

Forward-cut panel

Saddle Construction

As the most expensive single item of saddlery the horse owner is ever likely to buy, and as the one cloaked in the greatest amount of mystery, the saddle deserves proper and careful consideration.

In the past, when saddle trees were always rigid and design was subject to the vagaries of the individual master saddler, a new saddle was considered suitable only for cavalry subalterns and other such lesser beings. A truly discerning horseman of impeccable standards insisted on having a second-hand saddle—an exquisite piece of craftsmanship, of course, and one that had been carefully broken-in until it had reached a state of complete suppleness and dark beauty that met his exacting requirements. Today, the most expensive saddles are made to precise individual measurements, ensuring that the finished article is the correct fit for the horse that is to wear it.

Over the years, many changes have taken place in the saddler's art. And although the saddler who makes his saddles by hand has changed his methods very little, the mass-manufacturer uses as much new technology as he can to make his production more efficient.

To understand the saddle as a piece of equipment, it is useful to examine its components.

The Tree

The function of the tree is to act as a skeleton around which the rest of the saddle is built. Traditionally, the tree is made of beechwood about 4 mm ($\frac{1}{6}$ in.) thick. It is formed of four shaped pieces: one each for the cantle and forearch, and two for the sides. These pieces are heated and pressed into shape individually, before being joined and covered with cloth.

Today, ever-more-successful trees are being designed in glass fibre and plastic. The world's first unconditionally guaranteed tree has been produced in a glass-fibre-based material that is claimed to be unbreakable and untwistable.

Despite such breakthroughs, the majority of saddles are still based on natural materials. Scarcity of beechwood has led to its replacement by other woods—laminated, bonded and moulded under pressure. This has brought new strength combined with lightness, and a uniformity of shape.

The head and gullet of the tree are further strengthened by steel plates, and a steel reinforcement is also laid onto the underside of the tree, from the head to the cantle. The wood is then covered in skrim, and waterproofed with a black, glue-like substance.

The major variation in trees is that between the modern spring type and the old-fashioned rigid type. The latter is still seen in hunting, polo, show and children's saddles.

The spring tree has narrower side-pieces and two pieces of light tempered steel set from the joint to the rear of the tree on the underside, 50 mm (2 in.) on the inside of the broadest part of the seat. When the wood bends, the steel brings it back into position. This offers greater resilience to the seat and allows pressure exerted through the seat to be more easily transmitted to the horse. Simultaneously, the rider is given as much security, control and comfort as possible, and his position in the saddle is maintained over the horse's point of balance.

A young competitor looking very much at home on a specially-designed children's show saddle. As with most good show saddles, it has a rigid tree and straight-cut flaps designed to show off the animal's shoulders. It also has a short seat to accommodate the small seat of the rider.

In contrast, the rigid tree is, as the name implies, without spring. It can vary in length from 360 to 450 mm (14 to 18 in.), as dictated by the size of the rider and, to a lesser extent, the horse. The dipped shape of the spring-tree saddle means that a standard 420 mm ($16\frac{1}{2}$ in.) length will accommodate all but the largest of riders. (The length of a tree is measured from head to cantle; the width is measured across the broadest part of the seat.)

One obvious outward difference in trees is a matter of round or square cantles. Which shape is chosen is of little real importance, but it so happens that many rigid-tree saddles have a square cantle and that spring-tree patterns usually take the round.

The shape of the head of the tree has more bearing on the saddle fitting, since it can be cut back to varying degrees. Cut-back heads range from one-quarter cut-back to full cut-back. The farther back they are, the better they can accommodate particularly high-withered horses.

Stirrup Bars

Stirrup bars are riveted onto the actual tree, just behind the head and at the point. Good-quality saddles always have forged bars. Only on the cheaper saddles are cast bars in evidence; these can break and are therefore less reliable. The words 'forged' or 'cast' must be stamped on the metal.

The stirrup bar is generally made in two pieces: the first is the bar itself, and the second a movable catch called a *thumbpiece* which can be closed when the stirrup leather is in position. It then operates as a safety catch which, in theory, opens to release the leather should the rider fall. Many horsemen, however, regard it as safer never to close the thumbpiece.

The practice in Australia is to have a stirrup bar made in one continuous piece of metal, curved upwards at the end. This avoids the danger of the safety thumbpiece sticking in the event of a fall.

The Seat

The seat and its *setting up*, as the process is termed, takes up much of the saddler's time and skill.

With the tree as foundation, pre-strained webs about 65 mm ($2\frac{1}{2}$ in.) wide are fastened tightly to the cantle. This process is called *webbing up*. A piece of stretched canvas is tacked down firmly on top, and small pieces of shaped felt and leather (bellies) are

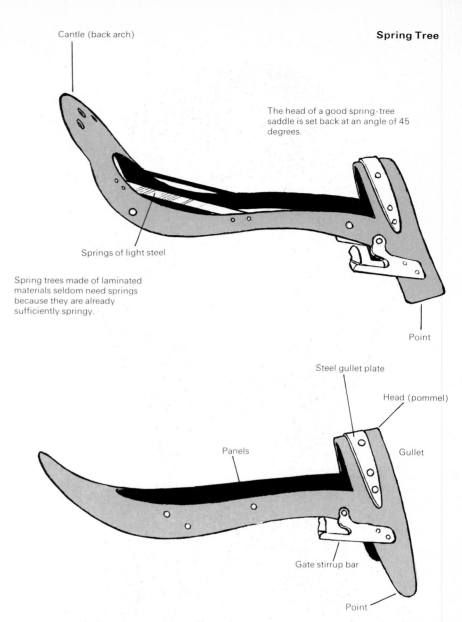

Cantle (back arch)

Spring Tree

The head of a good spring-tree saddle is set back at an angle of 45 degrees.

Springs of light steel

Spring trees made of laminated materials seldom need springs because they are already sufficiently springy.

Point

Steel gullet plate

Head (pommel)

Panels

Gullet

Gate stirrup bar

Point

Conventional Rigid Tree

The Saddle Tree

- A broken saddle tree can damage a horse's back. Regular checks, particularly if a horse falls, should be made to the saddle and any necessary repairs carried out immediately.

- A used saddle should not be bought unless it can be checked. If the tree is damaged, it is not worth having.

- To check that a tree is sound, the saddle should be placed between the legs with the seat facing the ground. The cantle is held firmly, using both hands, and moved from side to side. Any signs of looseness indicate a broken tree.

- If a saddle is to fit correctly, the tree must suit the shape of the horse's back. There are three common fittings—broad, standard and narrow.

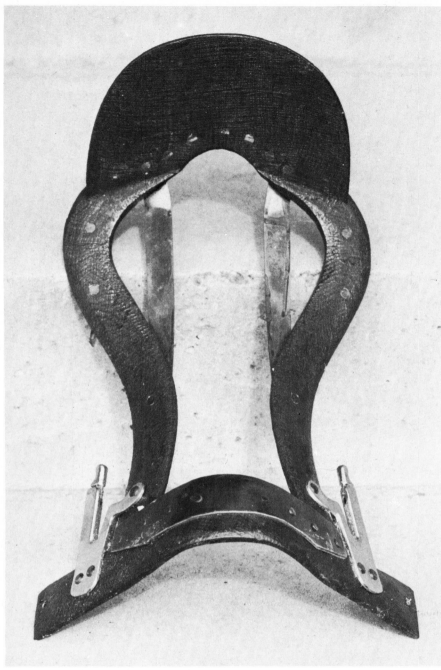

A spring tree, viewed from above. This is the type of beechwood tree around which a general purpose saddle is built by hand. The gullet, reinforced by a steel gullet plate, forms the saddle head. Behind are the wooden side panels, from which light steel strips run to join the cantle and produce the spring of the saddle.

horse, but at the expense of a certain degree of sensitivity between the horse and the rider's leg aids.

At the turn of the century, the growing demand by the competitive horsemen of the polo field for more immediate response from their mounts prompted the development of the short panel. This type of panel cut away the fullness of the early pattern. Compounded with a growing determination by the majority of horse riders to adopt the forward seat, this ultimately led to the Saumur and Continental panels. These two are now almost always the types favoured for modern dipped-tree saddles.

The Saumur, French in origin, is narrower in the waist than earlier panels, again to allow closer contact between horse and rider. It incorporated extra knee support from the outset and now often has an additional roll placed on the outside panel, under the flap.

The Continental panel has a still narrower waist and has an inconspicuous thigh roll at the rear. The main purpose of the roll is to keep the girth straps from slipping back off the panel.

Panels are made either of felt covered with leather, or of leather, serge or linen stuffed with wool. Felt ensures a close fit to the back and is very hard wearing. But it cannot be so easily altered as the wool-stuffed types that are now more popular.

Leather, provided that it is well looked after, makes the ideal covering because it is so durable and easy to clean. And it keeps its shape. It is a much better long-term proposition than, for example, serge, which is difficult to clean and which absorbs sweat that will eventually form into hard balls in the woollen stuffing and will irritate the horse's back.

Linen wears well and can, of course, be scrubbed. Used on its own, however, it will work loose and become slack and puckered; it must therefore always be put on over serge.

placed on the edges of the tree at the broadest part of the seat. The whole structure is then covered with tightly-stretched serge (serging), which is stitched down to form the shape of the seat.

At this point, a small incision is made between serge and canvas. The wool that pads the tree itself is inserted through this hole.

The final stages are the stretching on of the snug pigskin seat (blocking and setting) and the welting to this of the skirts, cut out and backed, that cover the stirrup bars. When extra padding is required, as is the case in some jumping saddles, a piece of sorbo rubber may be placed between the pigskin and the

serge of the seat.

A cheaper method is to use jute instead of canvas in the setting up of the seat. But jute is less comfortable and not so hard-wearing.

Panels
The panels are the cushion between the back of the horse and the tree. They can take four basic shapes: full, short, Saumur and Continental.

The full panel, the oldest design, was much loved by military gentlemen of the last century. When properly made, the quilted part should be thin but have a slightly thickened roll for the knee. These full panels provide a very comfortable arrangement for the

The seat is set up on the basic skeleton of the tree. First, pre-strained webs are fixed tightly from head to cantle and secured by tacks known as *tingles*. Next, strap webs are fitted across the seat, and these will form the anchor for the girth straps. Shaped pieces of leather known as *bellies* are fitted to keep the seat in shape. Then the seat is covered with wool or a synthetic material before the leather work is carried out.

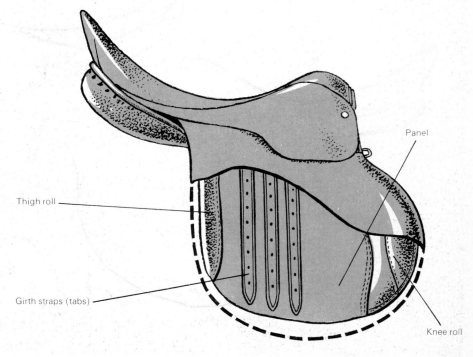

Panel

Thigh roll

Girth straps (tabs)

Knee roll

The Construction Process

On the production line, the process of constructing a spring-tree saddle begins with the saddler deciding on his tree and patterns. One man is responsible for each saddle, but such work as sewing and cutting is done by others.

Once the patterns are cut out, the saddler checks them before beginning to web up the seat. He then takes the process through from blocking the seat to setting it. Other workers hand-stitch such parts as the panels before the saddler again takes over to stuff the panels and to lace them in. He then stuffs and finishes the saddle, which is later cleaned with oxalic acid.

It takes just over two full days for an experienced saddler to make a spring-tree saddle by hand. He can therefore turn out two or three a week. On the production line, the same saddler could make at least twice this number, which is why few saddles are hand-made today.

But what still exists is variety, a vast range of saddles to suit almost every possible activity. Thus, extremely wide-fitting, deep-seated examples may be bought by the owner of an Arab horse; show pony enthusiasts have their straight-cut saddles; traditional hunting folk can order rigid-tree, square-cantled, leather-lined ones; flat-race jockeys can buy tiny, forward-cut pigskin saddles weighing less than 1 kg (about 34 oz); and the first-time pony or donkey rider may purchase a simple felt pad. It is possible to buy saddles with reversed-hide padded knees, backward-set girth straps that do not interfere with leg feel, and lined rawhide girth straps for greater strength.

The list is long, but the golden rules remain: to choose a saddle which fits both horse and rider, which suits the rider's purpose and which is of the finest quality that the purchaser can afford to buy.

Saddler's metal furniture, including headcollar shank clip-on hook; buckles for the girth, the stirrup leather and the throatlatch; a hook stud; a headcollar stop and a lunge-rope swivel. The best metal furniture is made of brass or stainless steel.

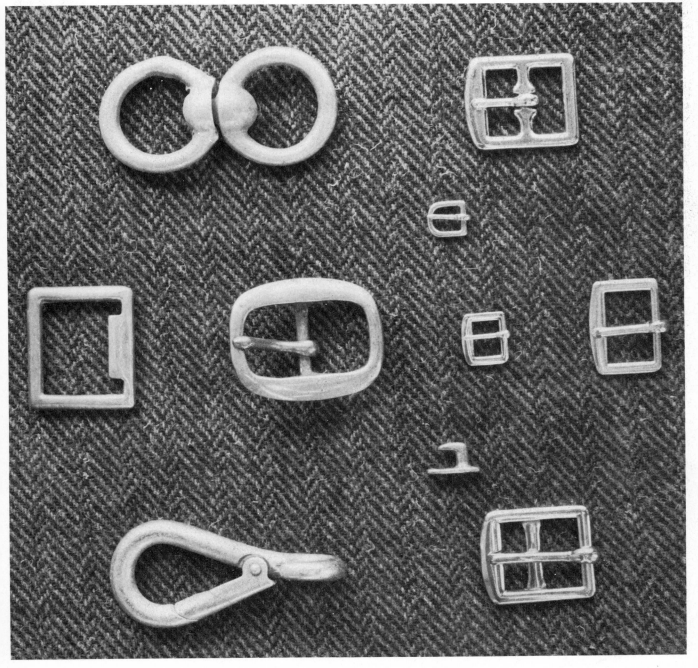

The General Purpose Saddle

The modern general purpose saddle, as used by the majority of riders today, has evolved over a period of many years. It was in the early 1950s, however, that the present-day model began to emerge as the most popular form of saddle for the everyday rider.

Anyone who has ever spent a long day on horseback and who has experience of both the modern saddle and the old-fashioned straight-cut version will vouch for the difference in comfort between them. Over the years, millions of riders have used the old-fashioned saddles and have thought them extremely comfortable: but ideas and riding styles change and the modern rider prefers the cushioned comfort of today's general purpose saddle.

When the forward seat became more fashionable both for hunting and for racing, the shape of the general purpose saddle was altered to accommodate this new position. To obtain the forward seat, it was necessary to redesign the saddle to a certain extent, with the emphasis placed upon a forward-cut saddle flap. This was in complete contrast to the old style of straight-cut flap, which allowed for the long length of stirrup leather and the straight leg position of the time.

With the leather shortened, in the new style, it became possible for the rider to shift his weight forward, thus releasing the horse's loins and quarters from additional weight and allowing the horse to use the 'power house' section of his anatomy. However, the general purpose saddle flap and panel are cut less far forward than those of the jumping saddle, and therefore allow a longer leg position than they do.

The New Structure and the Old

There are few basic differences between the general purpose 'English' saddles used in Europe and in America. There are, however, many differences between the modern and the old-fashioned patterns.

The modern general purpose saddle is made generally with a spring tree, although rigid patterns may still be bought, particularly those designed for children. The head of the tree is sloped backwards and cut away to give clearance on a horse with pronounced withers. Not all saddles are cut back to

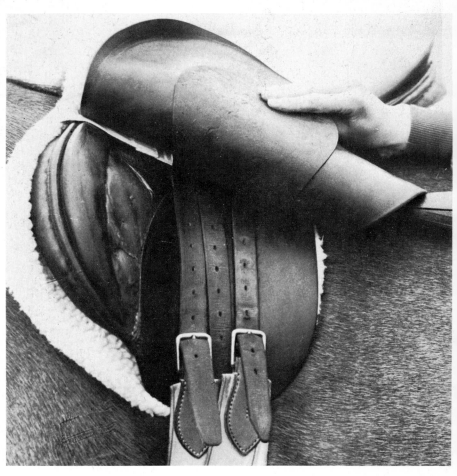

A look beneath the flap of a modern general purpose saddle. The panel has a basic type of knee roll but no thigh-roll. A fitted buckle-guard, rather than a loose one fixed to the girth straps, protects the flap from wear by the girth buckles.

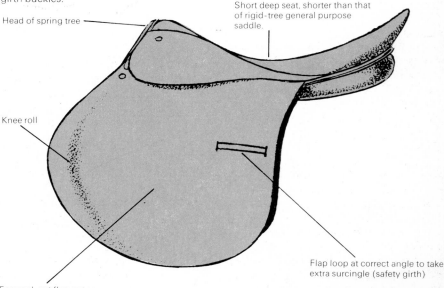

Spring-Tree General Purpose Saddle

Head of spring tree

Short deep seat, shorter than that of rigid-tree general purpose saddle.

Knee roll

Flap loop at correct angle to take extra surcingle (safety girth)

Forward-cut flap not so pronounced as with jumping saddle

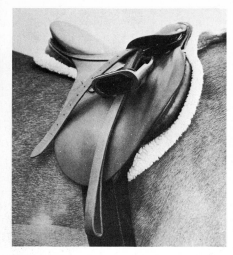

A modern spring-tree general purpose saddle and numnah, both correctly fitted. The stirrups are put up in this way for safety and convenience when they are not in use.

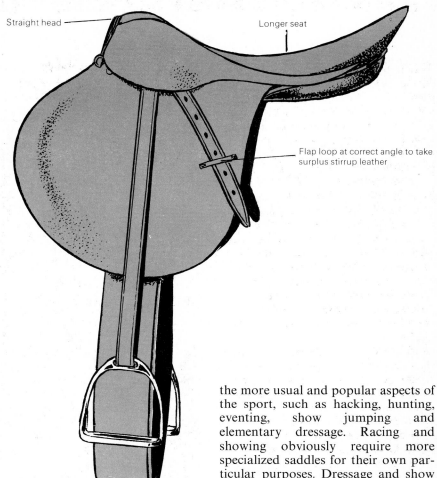

Rigid-Tree General Purpose Saddle

Straight head

Longer seat

Flap loop at correct angle to take surplus stirrup leather

such a degree, but they are markedly different from those with the old-fashioned rigid tree in that the head is set back at an angle of 45 degrees to the tree.

In older saddles, the rigid tree is broad at the waist and does not encourage a good position, since it pushes the rider's body away from close contact with the horse. In the modern saddle, the waist is much narrower and the rider has therefore more contact with the horse's back. This enables the seat bones to be used far more effectively as an aid.

There is, however, a disadvantage in this, in that the smaller bearing surface reduces the overall area for weight distribution. It is essential that these saddles are regularly serviced and restuffed to reduce any risk of sore backs if the bearing weight becomes too great on any one spot.

Seat and Rolls

The actual seat of the general purpose saddle is deeper and thus shorter in overall length than that of the older saddle. Often, it is padded with foam rubber under the pigskin seat to give the rider extra comfort and security. Flaps may be padded at the front, in the same way.

The stirrup bars are recessed into the tree in such a way as to eliminate any unnecessary bulk under the thighs. These bars are not set as far forward as those of the jumping saddle, nor as far back as those of the show or dressage saddle.

Many general purpose saddles have strong padded rolls fitted into the panel—which is generally Continental—to help to keep the rider's leg in the correct position. The rolls are placed on the front of the panel to position the knee, and behind to support the thigh when the rider is in a forward position.

Use

As its name implies, the general purpose saddle may be used for almost any equestrian activity, and certainly for the more usual and popular aspects of the sport, such as hacking, hunting, eventing, show jumping and elementary dressage. Racing and showing obviously require more specialized saddles for their own particular purposes. Dressage and show jumping, too, boast their own individual patterns, but it is perfectly possible to practise both to a reasonable standard using a good, well-made general purpose saddle.

If a general purpose saddle is readily to be used for all purposes—including, for instance, competing and a day's hunting in lashing rain—the lightweight varieties available on the market should be ignored. Many of these have either very thin panels or even half panels, often made from synthetic materials. They will not last long when used for everyday riding.

Checking a Saddle

- If a saddle receives hard daily wear, the tree may twist or even break. Before the rider realizes that something is amiss, it may have already injured the horse's back.

- Regular checks for straightness should be made while the saddle is fitted to the horse.

- Sometimes, an observant rider can tell by the feel of a saddle that the tree is defective.

The Jumping Saddle

The modern jumping saddle has been developed from the forward-seat principles of the Italian horseman Frederico Caprilli. Caprilli, a cavalry officer, revolutionized cross-country riding and jumping when he invented the forward seat at about the turn of the century. In 1890, he won his first jumping competition. Three years later, he and Lt Pompeo di Campello won the High Jump in Rome, astonishing spectators by clearing 1·4 m (4 ft 7 in.), when the average fence stood about 1·15 m (3 ft 10 in.).

At this time, the world of educated riding was dominated by an Englishman, James Fillis, who was then chief ecuyer at the Russian Imperial Cavalry School in Petrograd. Caprilli acknowledged Fillis as an authority on High School riding but disliked his principles for cross-country riding and for jumping. He considered that they imposed an artificial balance upon the horse.

Caprilli himself worked upon the basis of control without constriction of the natural movement of the horse. His style entailed sitting well forward throughout the entire parabola of the jump, instead of sitting back on the descent, as was practised until the turn of the century. Obviously, the shape of the ordinary hunting saddle or cavalry officer's saddle was found to be quite unsuitable for this new approach.

Therefore a new type of saddle had to be designed with the express purpose of keeping the weight of the rider well forward. The first jumping saddle was built by Pariani in Italy. It was then copied all over the world, with varying degrees of success. At first, many manufacturers simply cut more-forward flaps for saddles that still had the old-fashioned hunting tree. But the shape of the pommel, the flat seat and the set-back bars all helped to push the rider back behind the movement of the horse, rather than allowing him to maintain the forward seat. Gradually, the entire design of the jumping saddle was altered until it complied with the principles of Caprilli.

Jumping Saddle Stirrup Bars

Because the primary function of the saddle is to keep the weight of the rider firmly over the moving centre of gravity of the horse throughout the jump, the stirrup bars are fitted differently from those of other patterns of saddle. They are placed farther forward by sloping the points of the tree, to which the bars are attached, farther towards the front. This keeps the bars and leathers clear of the rider's thighs. Often, these bars are recessed well under the tree, so that bulk is even further eliminated between rider and horse, and the points themselves are flexible to give closer contact with the horse.

Flaps

The main outward difference between ordinary saddles and those designed purely for jumping lies in the shape of the flaps. They are cut farther forward than those of any other saddle to accommodate the knees of the rider when he is riding at the correct length, which is many holes shorter than that required for such sports as dressage. For this reason, the jumping saddle is often uncomfortable for general riding, since it was not designed to be sat down upon for long periods, but to be 'sat above'. Usually, the flaps are large to prevent the rider's legs being pinched. Often, they are padded with foam so that the rider can press into them with his knees for extra security.

Panels

Jumping saddle panels are invariably made of leather and are generally of the Saumur or Continental pattern. They echo the forward-cut shape of the flaps. Most panels have knee rolls at least. The best of these is strong and high, to keep the top of the rider's thigh in position. Some panels are fitted with thigh rolls, again to anchor the leg position, but this time from the rear of the panel. Thigh rolls are now becoming less popular. The modern trend is to do without both types of roll, to give the rider greater 'feel' of the horse. Sensitivity is becoming the watchword of the jumping saddle trade and panels are being made in fine calfskin and even in bridle leather.

Often, girth straps are set back out of the way of the rider's legs—in the

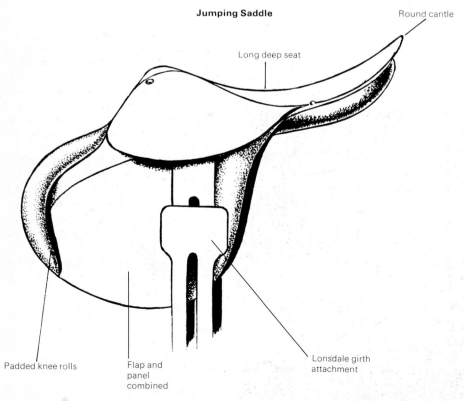

Jumping Saddle

Round cantle

Long deep seat

Padded knee rolls

Flap and panel combined

Lonsdale girth attachment

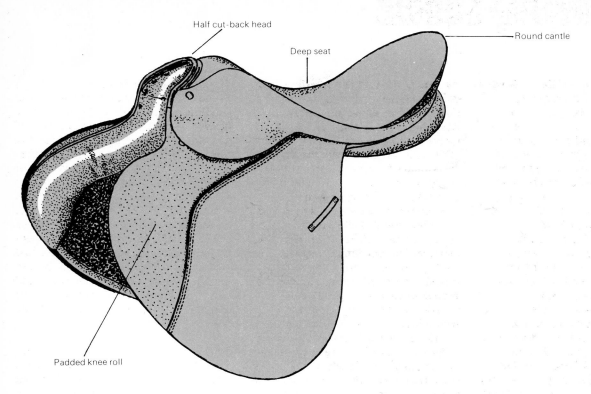

Half cut-back head

Deep seat

Round cantle

Padded knee roll

**Jumping Saddle
with Half Cut-Back
Head**

position where the thigh rolls would ordinarily be fitted. Another way of eliminating bulk is to elongate the girth straps and fit a short, Lonsdale girth. In this case, the flap and panel are often combined, again eliminating bulk between rider and horse.

Seat
The seat of the jumping saddle is slightly longer than normal, because the short leathers used force the seat back when the rider is sitting down.

In the past, most jumping saddles were built with an accentuated dip to the seat. Today, particularly in the United States, flatter seats that conform more to the shape of the back of the horse are in demand. These are called 'flat' saddles and were designed by William Steinkraus, the veteran United States Equestrian Team (USET) show jumper. Again, the object is sensitivity and feel. However, the rider is given very little assistance to remain securely in the saddle and

must therefore be a performer of high standard.

Many jumping saddle seats, particularly the deep-seated patterns, are lined with sponge rubber for the rider's comfort.

Tree
The spring tree is fitted into most, but not all, jumping saddles. Its deep seat is out of place in the flat saddles. This tree gives maximum comfort to horse and rider over fences, whilst allowing the rider close seat contact so that he can use his seat bones to drive the horse forward. This is an important aspect of a jumping saddle.

Most patterns have round cantles, but the flat saddles are fitted generally with square ones. Trees may be made from wood or from glass fibre and other man-made materials, depending upon the weight and strength of saddle required.

Most are available in sizes from 35 cm (15 in.) for junior riders, to 45·7 cm (18 in.).

Getting the best out of a modern spring-tree jumping saddle. Helped by the shape of the saddle panels, with their knee rolls, the rider maintains a position over the horse's centre of gravity.

The Dressage Saddle

Dressage is perhaps one of the oldest of today's popular equestrian activities, but the history of the dressage saddle is somewhat obscure. In the seventeenth century, the celebrated English horseman William Cavendish mentioned types of saddles suitable for schooling horses in his famous book *A General System of Horsemanship*. He favoured an elaborate version of the deep-seated medieval saddle.

During the eighteenth century, saddles changed fairly dramatically and by the nineteenth century the elegant Somerset saddle had appeared. This had knee rolls and fine quilting, and looked little different in shape from the dressage saddle of today.

Since then, only relatively minor improvements and modifications have taken place. These have been inspired by the experience of well-known horsemen.

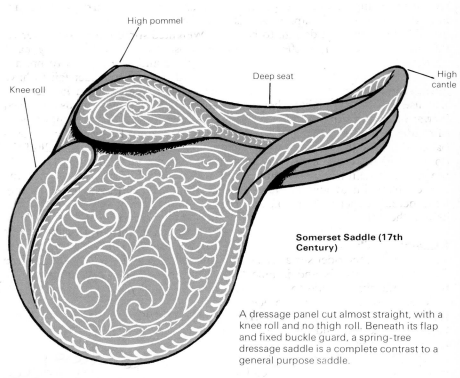

Somerset Saddle (17th Century)

A dressage panel cut almost straight, with a knee roll and no thigh roll. Beneath its flap and fixed buckle guard, a spring-tree dressage saddle is a complete contrast to a general purpose saddle.

Tree

The deep spring tree used in modern dressage saddles helps to place the rider securely in the centre of the saddle. Because of its resilience, it allows the seat to mould to the rider, who is able then to transmit seat pressure as a driving aid to the horse—something that is vital for the impulsion and collection required.

As with all saddles, the aim is to provide the rider with maximum control, comfort and security, and to keep the weight as nearly as possible in line with the centre of balance.

In dressage, this point of balance shifts slightly backwards. As higher degrees of collection are reached, the quarters carry a correspondingly greater portion of the weight.

The tree is therefore shaped to conform as closely as possible to the line of the horse's back.

Panels, Seat and Flaps

The saddle panels must bear the weight of the rider evenly over as large an area of the horse's back as possible. This is particularly important in dressage riding, as the rider remains in a very upright position for virtually all movements, and the weight rests in a smaller area than in other styles of equestrianism. The seat is short and rarely exceeds 400 mm (16 in.), even for men.

Dressage saddle panels and flaps are

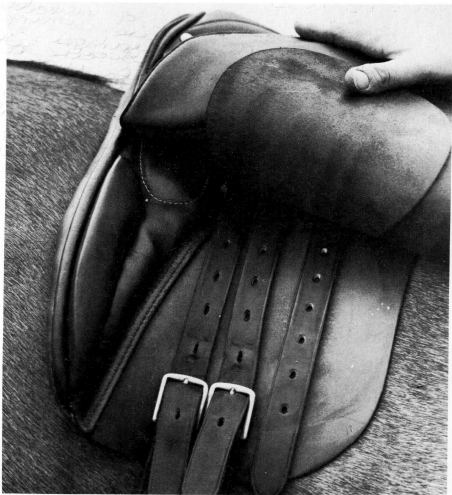

almost straight cut, allowing for the considerably longer leg position used. The saddle panels very often have a roll to support the upper leg. Lightly recessed padding may be incorporated into the front of the flap, which is usually of Continental design, to help the rider to maintain an effective leg position.

Stirrup Bars

Because the tree is straight rather than forward-sloping as in most other types of saddle, the stirrup bars are farther back, allowing the leathers to hang down the centre of the flap. This helps the rider to maintain a straighter leg and enables him to give the leg aids unhindered—either in front of, on or behind the girth.

Removal of Bulk

To ensure that the rider sits as close to the horse as possible and is able to transmit the slightest aid to the horse with ease, bulk beneath the leg is reduced to a minimum. The stirrup bars are recessed and fitted under, instead of on top of, the tree.

Many saddles also have only two girth straps, these being elongated for use with a Lonsdale girth. The Lonsdale girth is a short belly girth and is used so that no buckles remain under the saddle flap. It is important to ensure that this type of girth is of the correct length for the size of horse, so that it does not obstruct the effectiveness of lower leg aids. Care must be taken also to see that it does not chafe the horse's elbows.

Other types of leather, lampwick and tubular web girths are popular for use with dressage saddles and are preferred by many to the Lonsdale because of the ease with which they may be adjusted. An assistant is often required, or dismounting necessary, to alter the Lonsdale girth.

Narrow or fine stirrup leathers are also popular to reduce bulk between horse and rider. Some leathers are designed to be fastened at the stirrup, rather than at the stirrup bar—again to reduce bulk.

Weighted stirrup irons are preferred by most dressage riders. They hang straighter and do not tend to bounce upwards should the rider fail to have his weight evenly placed in them for any reason. Rubber treads are used universally to help to prevent the foot slipping out of the iron. In all movements of dressage, just the ball of the foot rests in the stirrup.

The use of a numnah under the dressage saddle appears to be growing fast in popularity, but is a contradiction of the basic need of the rider to be as close to the horse as possible. If it is felt necessary to use a numnah, the thinner linen varieties are probably the most appropriate, felt or sheepskin being too bulky.

Numnahs could be a fashion, but this trend may have come about through faulty design in some modern dressage saddles. The designers appear to have concentrated too much on the rider's position, and have failed to distribute the weight evenly over the weight-bearing surface of the horse's back.

When choosing a dressage saddle, care should be taken firstly to ensure that the saddle fits the horse. It should then be ridden on to ascertain whether it is still comfortable for the horse. At the same time, it should be tried for comfort and size for the rider. It must not force an unnatural position, but constructively assist the rider to sit centrally with an effective long leg.

Yearly overhauls by the saddler are particularly important for dressage saddles, to check whether the stuffing needs adjustment. Uneven pressure on the horse's back may severely hinder performance.

Dressage Saddle

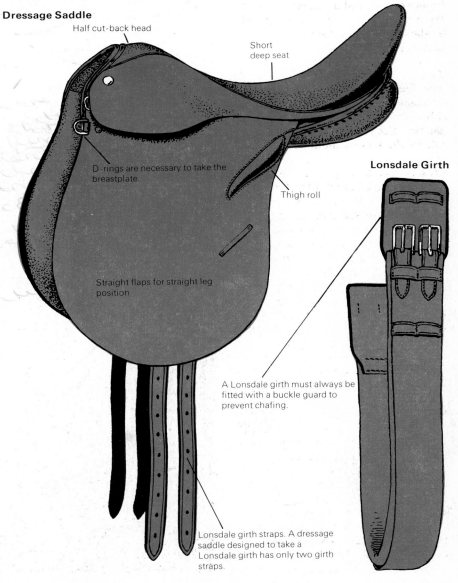

Half cut-back head

Short deep seat

D-rings are necessary to take the breastplate.

Thigh roll

Straight flaps for straight leg position

Lonsdale Girth

A Lonsdale girth must always be fitted with a buckle guard to prevent chafing.

Lonsdale girth straps. A dressage saddle designed to take a Lonsdale girth has only two girth straps.

Specialist Dressage Saddles

There are two corners of the European continent where riders still practise the classical art of equitation. To perfect their skills and complement the image of an age gone by, they favour the elegant high saddles of the seventeenth, eighteenth and nineteenth centuries. These famous classical schools are, of course, the military Cadre Noir at Saumur, in France, and the Spanish Riding School in Vienna, Austria.

Selle à Piquer

The Cadre Noir was established in the middle of the nineteenth century. Previously, it had been the royal guard. In 1972, the École Nationale d'Equitation was formed and took over the management of the school at Saumur.

The aim of the Cadre Noir (so called because the riders wear black uniforms) is to teach and to perform *haute école* riding in the old French tradition. To do so, they employ the eighteenth-century tournament saddle called the *selle à piquer*.

The saddles, which are made specially for the Cadre Noir by a private saddler in Saumur, provide padded *battes* that hold the legs in place, these having evolved from the high pommels and cantles of the medieval saddles. The saddles are covered in beige-coloured reversed hide. The suede holds the rider firmly in place when the horse performs the complicated and rigorous haute école movements. The saddles are not fitted with stirrups.

However, the horses of the Cadre Noir are fitted with these saddles only for specialized training and display or quadrille riding. At the beginning of their training and for everyday work, they wear modern 'English' saddles.

Danloux saddle

A pattern of modern French saddle used by the Cadre Noir and many other horsemen is the Danloux. This saddle originated at about the same time as the spring tree. It was designed by the great French riding master Robert Danloux, and quickly became popular. It was not, however, considered to be as good as its Italian counterparts—particularly the Toptani—since its leather was of a lesser quality and its broad seat was built around a weak tree.

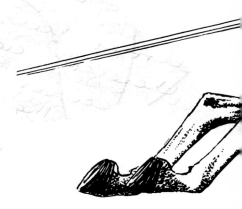

Saddle Used by the Spanish Riding School

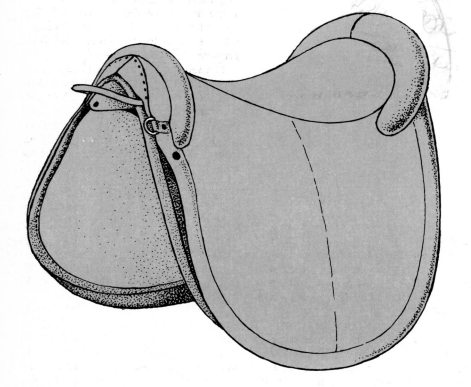

The Danloux saddle of today is a far better construction, but the forward-seat principles remain. It has a Saumur panel with short knee rolls on the top. These are set above the knees to control the leg position without pushing the legs away from the horse. Short thigh pads, set high on the panel, do the same behind the rider's legs.

The Danloux tree is shaped in such a way that its lowest point is in the front half of the saddle. This ensures that the centre of gravity of the rider matches

still longer and heavier than the 'English' saddle.

The *selle royale* is covered completely in white deer skin. The flaps, which are wide but not excessively long, are made in the same piece of leather as the seat, with a seam running vertically from the bottom of the nearside flap over the seat and down to the bottom of the offside flap. The flaps are stitched round at about 40 mm (1½ in.) from the edges. There are no skirts.

The pommel is a padded roll fitted across the front of the saddle. The cantle is formed by a second padded roll extending down to the top of the rider's thigh, after having curved round the shape of his seat. This helps to keep the rider secure when performing airs above the ground such as the levade, the courbette and the capriole.

The seat is dipped, but not excessively. The top of the panel has a knee roll.

Unlike the *selle à piquer*, the *selle royale* is fitted with stirrups and leathers. These may be removed for work in hand or between the pillars, or they may be clipped back behind the cantle. For ridden work, however, stirrups are used. The leathers, instead of passing under the rider's legs, are attached under the flaps, thus minimizing bulk between rider and horse.

The saddle is worn with a golden-inlaid crupper that was intended originally to secure the saddle during battle, and is now employed chiefly for decoration. A golden-inlaid breastplate is worn for practical schooling purposes as well as for display.

The *selle royale* is worn always with a saddle blanket. This is now purely for show, the blanket being fitted around the saddle rather than actually between skin and panel. Each blanket is designed to denote the rank of the rider: a single-embroidered band indicates that the rider is a novice, a double band indicates that he is a senior rider and a triple band denotes a rider of the advanced corps. The school commander is allowed an additional golden fringe, worn in the past only by the horse of the Master of the Emperor. The basic colours of the blankets are red with a golden hem or green with black.

As with the Cadre Noir, the Spanish Riding School horses wear 'English' saddles for everyday training. These are straight-cut saddles with narrower flaps than the *selles royales* and lower cantles. The stirrup bars are in the normal position.

that of the horse. The pommel is not cut back, yet is roomy enough to take the withers of most horses without discomfort.

The bars are positioned exactly above the girth to put the rider's legs in the correct place. They are also movable, and as a result are safer than normal patterns that have a thumbpiece.

Selle Royale

The Spanish Riding School bases its equitation upon the styles of the Italian and French riding masters of the sixteenth and seventeenth centuries. To achieve this, the famous Lippizaner stallions wear a special, custom-made saddle known as a *selle royale* or as a *school saddle*.

The saddle has evolved from the 'great saddle' of the seventeenth century—which weighed about 27 kg (60 lb) and was padded to extremes—but it is now lighter and far more practical, as well as being beautiful. It is

The Cross-Country Saddle

The need for a saddle designed specifically for cross-country riding has been apparent in the last few years because of the tremendous increase in the popularity of horse trials and the advent of cross-country races. Formerly, riders were content to compete in good hunting or jumping saddles. But as the standard of courses has become more demanding, it has become increasingly obvious that a more specialized saddle is necessary.

Today's courses require a more athletic horse and a rider well prepared for all the variations of fences, terrain and speed that are encountered. The saddle must offer added security yet allow freedom of movement to cope efficiently with the different types of fences, and at the same time maintain all the attributes necessary for the horse's comfort.

In addition, weight plays quite an important part. Depending upon the size of the rider, the use of a heavyweight or of a lightweight saddle can make quite a difference. This is particularly so in the three-day event, when distances of up to 27 km (17 miles) are covered in approximately 90 minutes, and the minimum weight is 75 kg (165 lb). Very light riders therefore need heavier saddles so that they can carry less dead weight in the form of lead. Heavier riders look for light saddles so that they do not ride over the optimum weight. But all require substantial and versatile saddles for security whilst jumping very varied obstacles at different speeds.

Characteristics

Although still in a fairly experimental stage, saddles for cross-country riding are slowly beginning to appear. What most riders feel is needed is a forward-cut saddle with a spring tree that is not too deep-seated and is without too high a cantle. It should be well balanced but allow the rider to shift his weight unhindered in order to jump the variety of fences encountered on a cross-country course. It must be possible also to shorten the leathers for some phases, such as steeplechasing.

It is important therefore that the saddle has flaps that are cut well forward and are designed to allow plenty of room for the knees. The knees play a particularly important part in cross-country riding by acting as bracers.

Flaps with suede padded knee rolls are generally preferred, because they allow the rider to press into them without forcing the legs away from the horse. A full panel of Continental design is best. An added roll placed on the outside of the panel to the rear will assist the rider to maintain a secure leg position.

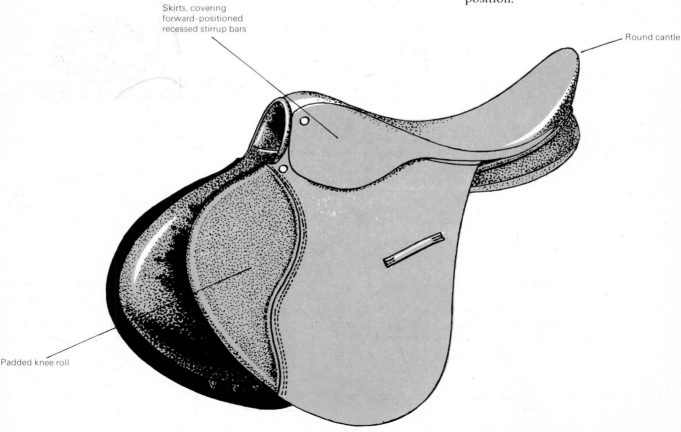

Skirts, covering forward-positioned recessed stirrup bars

Round cantle

Padded knee roll

Safety

As safety must be one of the most important considerations in any fast-moving sport, it goes without saying that one should consider only the best when choosing a saddle for cross-country riding. The girth straps must be strong, and the *D*-rings on the front of the saddle must be fixed to strong leather, otherwise they will be pulled off when a breastplate is attached. Sometimes, *D*-rings have very insecure fixings. Breastplates or breastgirths should be used for all cross-country riding to prevent the saddle slipping back. Horses fit for this sort of work will carry very little extra flesh and it is never worth taking risks.

A pair of webbing girths is best for fast work. They could have elasticated ends, but it must be doubled elastic: the single variety stretches too much.

A webbing surcingle completes the secured saddle. This should be placed over the saddle and either through the breastplate loop or the martingale loop to prevent it sliding back. If using elasticated girths, it is important to use an elasticated surcingle as well, so that it expands with the girths. It should be fastened right under the stomach on the girth so that it does not interfere with the rider's leg or chafe the horse's elbow.

If a weightcloth is being used, it is important before tightening the girths to pull the centre of the weightcloth and numnah well up into the front arch of the saddle, so that the weight does not press down on the horse's withers.

Irons and leathers play a vital role for the cross-country rider, and must be safe. Stainless steel irons and raw-hide leathers are best. Heavy irons help

The cross-country saddle must combine balance with comfort and security for the rider. It must be forward-cut yet not be too deep-seated or have too high a cantle. The aim is to assist the rider to stay in place over the variety of fences encountered, yet leave room for movement during fast changes of direction. Cross-country riding is one of the most rigorous of equestrian sports and fully deserves its new specially-designed saddles.

the lightweight rider and are also less likely to bounce around. Aluminium irons may snap and are not to be recommended for this type of sport, when safety must take priority over weight.

Because of the strain placed on the cross-country saddle, it should be checked carefully by a saddler twice a year, particular attention being paid to the stitching.

The Show Saddle

The show saddle is derived from the saddles used by British dealers from the latter part of the nineteenth century up to the outbreak of World War II.

The aim of the dealer's saddle was the purely commercial one of presenting the horse in the best possible light. To do so, it was necessary to show that the horse possessed a very adequate amount of shoulder in front of the saddle and a generous length of rein.

In order to display to advantage the extent of the horse's front and the breadth of his shoulder, the saddle was made with a straight flap or with a flap that was cut to slope slightly back towards the rear. In addition, it was made to fit very closely to the horse's back so that it did not interrupt the top lines of the animal. This was achieved by building the saddle on a skeleton short (Rugby) panel, which was made of felt and measured no more than 19 mm ($\frac{3}{4}$ in.) in depth.

The modern show saddle has the same aims as the traditional dealer's saddle. It achieves them in much the same ways.

Tree

Generally, the tree of the show saddle is rigid, since its function is to show off the conformation of the horse rather than to help the rider to use his seat more effectively. The rigid tree, being flatter than the spring tree, conforms better to the long and low requirements of the show saddle.

This is also the case with the pommel. To keep the pommel low, yet clear of the withers, the show saddle often has a cut-back head. This may range from quarter cut-back to full cow-mouth. It means that the height of the withers is not accentuated and therefore does not interrupt the top line of the horse.

For the same reason, the cantle is also low. Many show saddles have square cantles, but some are made round.

Flaps

Show saddle flaps, apart from being cut straight in the same way as those of the old dealer's saddle, are wider at the top than those of other types of saddle.

They are designed to accommodate the rider's legs in the show position. Otherwise, the legs would bear directly upon the horse.

Stirrup Bars

Ideally, the show saddle should be made with extended stirrup bars. These bars should continue well to the rear, so that when the stirrup leathers are fitted, they divide the flaps vertically down the centre.

The normal stirrup bars found on general purpose saddles place the rider's knees too far forward for the show position. On a straight-cut saddle, these bars would project the knees beyond the flaps.

Show saddle skirts are therefore cut wider than usual. They may be left plain, or covered with pigskin.

Panels

Modern show saddle panels are still made of felt in the Rugby pattern, to fit closely to the horse's body shape. Often, they are lined with leather; but some show saddle manufacturers use linen.

Point Strap

A common fitting on show saddles is a point strap. This is an additional girth strap placed under the point of the tree. It allows the saddle to be placed farther back, whilst the girth is still fitted into the horse's girth groove, thus accentuating the extent of the shoulder and the front.

Because of its position, the point strap also helps to prevent the saddle from slipping forward. This is particularly helpful with children's show ponies, which may have less shoulder than horses. Another advantage is that it tends to pull the saddle closer down onto the back, which again helps to give the uninterrupted back line.

If the saddle has been fitted with three ordinary girth straps and the saddle tends to slip backwards rather than forwards on a slab-sided animal, the use of the two rear straps may help the situation. Another solution to both problems is to fix pimpled rubber at the top of the saddle panels.

Disadvantages

While the straight-cut show saddle clearly shows the conformation of a

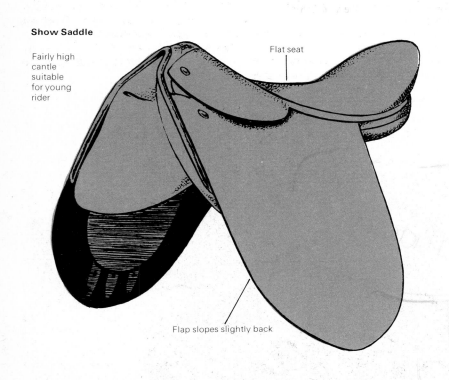

Show Saddle

Fairly high cantle suitable for young rider

Flat seat

Flap slopes slightly back

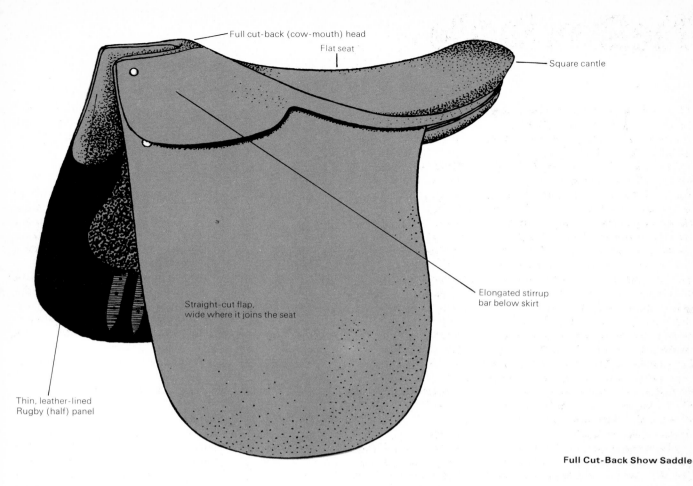

Full cut-back (cow-mouth) head

Flat seat

Square cantle

Elongated stirrup bar below skirt

Straight-cut flap, wide where it joins the seat

Thin, leather-lined Rugby (half) panel

Full Cut-Back Show Saddle

horse to its best advantage, there are certain disadvantages in its use. In the first place, the flat seat and elongated stirrup bars tend to place the rider well back towards, and often even on, the cantle and to force his legs forward in an exaggerated manner.

This not only places the rider on top of, rather than in, the saddle, but also behind the movement. This must lead to problems in bringing out the best paces and performance from the horse. When this is achieved, it is in spite of the saddle rather than because of it.

Although show judges must by now be used to these saddles, they may possibly find it difficult to appreciate the true paces of the horse if they have to perch above them. But they should be experienced enough to know whether a horse has a good length of rein and shoulder, whatever saddle he is wearing.

These disadvantages are particularly apparent in performance show classes, such as working hunter, where the horse must jump a round before being shown. Some riders change saddles during the course of the class, but there are saddles produced specifically for working hunter classes.

These have deeper seats and slightly more forward-cut flaps.

Spring-Tree Dressage and Other Saddles
Some competitors, particularly those who do not specialize in showing, now use spring-tree dressage saddles to show in. These combine the straight-cut flap with a deeper seat, which gives the seat more effect.

The supreme exaggeration of the show saddle is found in the saddles designed for the Tennessee Walking Horse and American Saddlebred. These saddles are seen with cow-mouth heads, extremely wide flaps and very flat seats.

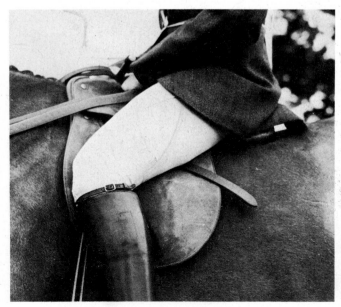

An English pattern show saddle in use. The flaps and seat are made of reversed hide and the panels are full rather than Rugby. The shape of the saddle tree throws the rider back towards the cantle, and the wide top of the flap keeps the rider's legs off the horse's sides.

The Racing Saddle

Racing saddles have a very individual design, and are usually made by saddlers who specialize in their production. A jockey riding regularly needs at least three saddles of different weights so that he can get near to whatever weight is set for each race without using excess lead. Nothing is more uncomfortable than a weightcloth bulging with lead. It makes the jockey feel insecure and unpleasantly remote from the horse.

The flat-race jockey, whose own weight and the weight set both fluctuate, may need up to eight saddles. On the other hand, the point-to-point jockey who is nearly always riding at either 168 lb (12 stone; 76 kg) or 175 lb (12 stone 7 lb; 79 kg) will be able to make do with one or, at the most, two saddles. In making a choice, he will have to balance saddle comfort against the degree of wasting he is prepared to put up with.

The most important feature of a racing saddle is its weight. This ranges from 0.2 kg ($\frac{1}{2}$ lb) for flat racing to perhaps 60 times this for point-to-pointing. But it is well to remember that extremely lightweight saddles can be frighteningly uncomfortable and skimpy.

Steeplechase Saddles

The best lightweight saddle for steeple-chasing should have a cloth lining on a panel that is lightly padded. Generally, these panels are full.

The front of the flaps does not have to be excessively long from front to back, as the jockey's knees should not extend too far forward when racing. In fact, too-long front flaps often bend back, which is a nuisance.

Steeplechase saddles usually have more dip in the seat than those used for flat racing: but the cantle of the saddle should be flat enough to allow the seat of the jockey to slip off the end of it when he is sitting back on a horse blundering over a fence.

The tree is full. Weighted saddles are made by adding lead to the tree. Obviously, because of the centre of gravity of a horse jumping and gallop-ing, this lead should be placed nearer the front of the tree than the back.

The steeplechase jockey should not choose a saddle weighing much less than 0.7 kg ($1\frac{1}{2}$ lb), which with girths,

surcingle, leathers, stirrups and pad will usually add up to 1.4 kg (3 lb). For the average jockey, the second size of saddle would be 2.3 to 3.2 kg (5 to 7 lb). The third could then perhaps be 4.6 to 6.4 kg (10 to 14 lb).

For the jockey habitually on a light saddle, it is the height of luxury to ride on a larger one. He can then actually ride the horse rather than appear to be perched on the back of a naked wild animal.

Flat Racing Saddles

In flat racing, where there are no jumps to unseat the jockey, greater liberties can be taken with weight. It is here that the proverbial 'postage stamp' saddles are seen.

The lightweight saddles are inevitably more complex than the heavier ones. Those under 2.7 kg (6 lb) often have no stirrup bars: con-sequently the leathers must be slotted through the tree itself. Panels are cut to the minimum and may be no thicker than 6 mm ($\frac{1}{4}$ in.) between tree and back. The saddles are made of light-weight pigskin throughout, apart from the panels, which may be of silk or nylon instead of leather. Lightweight trees are made from plastic or glass fibre, and are therefore fragile and not hard-wearing.

Whatever the weight, the principles of all racing saddles are the same: flat back, stiff forward flaps and as much comfort for the jockey as possible.

It is essential to use a protective pad or numnah with all racing saddles. It may be tempting to omit this when there is a weight problem, but a light-weight saddle without a pad will always give a horse sore sides.

In commonest use is the saddle-shaped numnah made of foam rubber covered in cloth. However, a simple rectangular felt pad that reaches down on both sides to below the saddle flaps is more effective in protecting the horse's sides against the girth buckles. It also gives a materially more sub-stantial feel to the saddle for the jockey. The drawback of the felt pad is that it weighs about 0.5 kg (1 lb). A plastic type of material encased in a thin cloth makes a lightweight version that can weigh less than 0.2 kg ($\frac{1}{2}$ lb).

It is advisable to use either a breast-plate or breastgirth with a light saddle. If there is any doubt about a horse's conformation, this may be advisable with all saddles.

Weight being an ever-hovering menace in many racing careers—and the equation of 0.5 kg (1 lb) equalling one hour in the Turkish baths—jockeys go to considerable lengths to

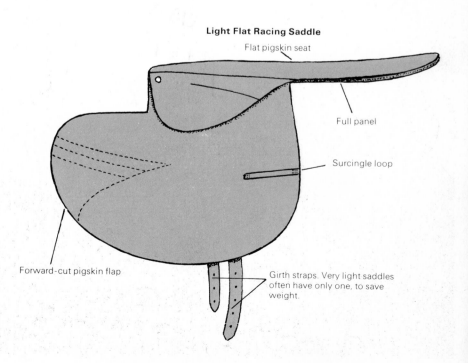

Light Flat Racing Saddle

Flat pigskin seat

Full panel

Surcingle loop

Forward-cut pigskin flap

Girth straps. Very light saddles often have only one, to save weight.

hone down the weight of their equipment, using such items as specially-made lightweight breastplates and breastgirths, aluminium irons, light-weight pads and even wafer-thin top boots for themselves.

However, since racing can be frightening, the jockey must have absolute confidence in all equipment. A balance must be struck between lightness, and safety and comfort.

Race Exercise Saddles

Race exercise saddles have a more or less standard form. They are a larger version of the racing saddle and should be a suitable shape for riding short.

The main thing to guard against is their giving horses sore backs. This is much more of a risk with the flat-backed racing type of saddle than with the conventional competition saddle with its high cantle.

The race exercise saddle usually has a full panel covered in serge or leather. It should be well padded, particularly under the seat.

The saddle tree should not be too long, so that the riders are not given the opportunity to sit too far back on the horse when riding out short. Riding in this way is the fashion in racing stables, but despite its suitability for galloping and jumping fences, it is not ideal for walking or trotting. Riders should take care to sit forward with the lower leg drawn back.

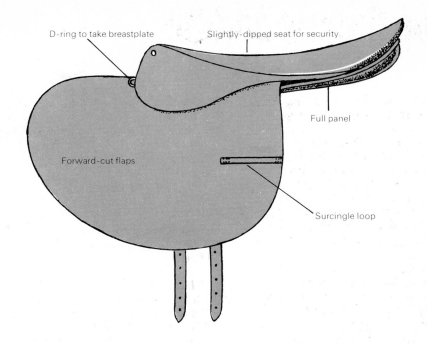

Steeplechase Saddle

D-ring to take breastplate

Slightly-dipped seat for security

Full panel

Forward-cut flaps

Surcingle loop

The race exercise saddle must stand up to a lot of work. It should certainly be no lighter than 3·2 kg (7 lb), and 4·6 kg (10 lb) is probably a better weight. In addition to not protecting the horse adequately, light saddles do not stand up to use. However, a new race exercise saddle has been designed with a half tree that is detachable for quick repair.

The weight of a racing saddle is of paramount importance, but safety is a major consideration too; one factor in safety is comfort.

The Hunting Saddle

The English hunting saddle has changed remarkably little over the past 200 years. Until about the time of World War II, it was one of the most popular riding saddles in many countries, and it is still made today.

It is interesting to look at old hunting prints and at photographs taken in the early days of this century, showing the very old-fashioned hunting saddles. The flaps on these appear to have been rather larger even than those used today. Breastplates seem to have been necessary on many of them, too.

These very old hunting saddles have been likened to frying pans because of the shape of their seats. They were very flat, sitting low down on the horse's back with the very minimum of pommel. In the days before numnahs, they must have sat down very tight upon the withers. But it should be remembered that in those days horses were seldom clipped out and, therefore, the winter coat would provide a certain amount of protection—a point borne out by the fact that when horses are given a hunter clip today, the saddle patch is left unclipped, as well as the legs.

The hunting saddle design is in extreme contrast to that of the dressage saddle. Because of the sometimes excessive scooping up of some of the seats of dressage saddles, the rider must sit at least 10 cm (4 in.) above the horse, which is somewhat surprising when the closest possible contact with the horse is recommended now for dressage riding.

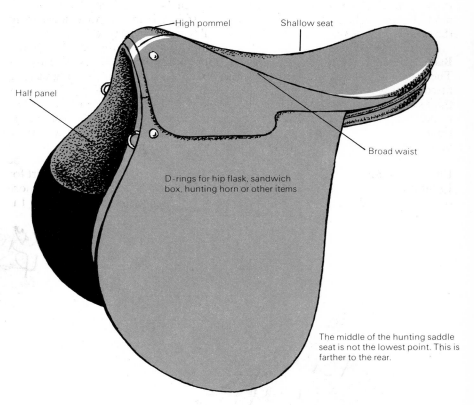

High pommel

Shallow seat

Half panel

Broad waist

D-rings for hip flask, sandwich box, hunting horn or other items

The middle of the hunting saddle seat is not the lowest point. This is farther to the rear.

English Hunting Saddle

Seat

The shape of the seat of the English hunting saddle is shallow and its cantle is low and square. The pommel is high enough to combine with these two points in shifting the weight of the rider back towards the loins of the horse. This may be seen clearly from the riding position known as the 'hunting seat', where the rider looks as if he is determined not to fall 'out of the front door' at least. Many riders still hunt in this position.

D-rings are fitted around the bottom of the seat and below the pommel. They take wallets containing hip flasks and sandwich boxes, as well as the huntsman's horn and other more essential items.

Panels

The panels of the hunting saddle are either full or, now more commonly, Rugby style. These are lined with leather, linen or serge. They may be quilted and stuffed with flock or horsehair, which makes them comfortable for the horse—particularly if the panel is full—but lessens the contact that the rider has with the horse through his thigh and seat.

Some panels have no forward rolls to anchor the rider's legs, making it extremely difficult for the rider to maintain a still leg position, particularly when he is tired. For it is when the rider tires that he begins to move about most noticeably, and this brings discomfort and possible soreness to the horse.

The chief problem about the saddle with a roll in front of the knee is that, as different riders have different lengths of leg, the roll may come at an awkward place, forcing the rider to ride either longer or shorter than he should. The less exaggerated the knee roll, the less likely it is to be a nuisance. In the same way, a too-high cantle will not be comfortable for every rider's seat.

Tree

The tree is traditionally rigid. It is also very broad at its waist, which tends to remove the rider's thigh farther from the horse. Hunting saddle trees sometimes have cut-back heads to accommodate high withers, although not to the same extent as show saddles.

Bars and Points

The bars and points of the saddle are fitted directly beneath the rider's thighs. This again pushes the seat backwards towards the cantle if the rider is to be comfortable, and minimizes contact with the horse.

Fit and Comfort

In hunting, at least as much as in any other form of riding, it is essential that a horse's saddle fits properly. Today, although the old rigid tree is still made and used, many hunting men and women are accepting the spring tree to allow for greater comfort and contact between horse and rider. The spring tree saddle is much more likely to fit well than the rigid type.

Ideally, the hunting saddle should not be too heavy, as a horse already has enough weight to carry through a long day, particularly if his rider 'rides heavy' as many hunting people do. The German types of saddle—now rightly popular for most purposes—tend to be too heavy for hunting.

The hunting saddle must be designed to provide ample comfort for horse and rider, since in hunting more than in other forms of riding the emphasis is on the length of uninterrupted and strenuous usage. The reason why hunting saddles have changed so little over 200 years is that practical experience from long days in the field, long hacks to the meet and home at the end of the day, taught our forebears the best sort of saddle for the job. Many modern riders agree with their conclusions.

The tree of an English hunting saddle is traditionally rigid, the seat shallow, the cantle square and the panels devoid of such 'new-fangled' trimmings as knee rolls and thigh rolls.

Children's Saddles

Saddles of special design are produced to help the young rider from infancy to teens. These saddles vary according to the size and age of the rider and to the type of activity for which they will be used. Babies who will merely be led around on a pony are best seated in a basket saddle; those who are older and ready to compete can have smaller versions of adult competition saddles.

Because children grow quickly and their riding ability develops quickly, their saddles must be checked and changed frequently. Only in that way can a child get the best from a pony and be able to maintain the correct seat and leg position that is vital at this early stage.

Pony Pads

From the age of two or three, a child can ride safely on a pony pad. This should be used with a crupper to prevent it slipping forward over the withers, particularly if it is used on a donkey. Donkeys have very straight shoulders, which do not hold saddles in their correct place for long without mechanical aids.

There are many patterns of pony pads on the market. They are all softer and more comfortable for the young rider than leather saddles with trees, but they vary in the degree of assistance they give the rider in maintaining a good position.

One of the most simple and old-fashioned types is made completely of felt, except for strips of leather to hold the stirrup bars (which are simple buckles) and girth straps. It is completely flat and pliable and gives very little support to the child. It has the advantage of fitting any shape of pony at any time of the year, and any size of rider.

Some pony pads have a reinforced head, which takes the pressure off the pony's withers. Other modern refine-ments are foam-padded, leather-covered seats and swing hook bars which make attaching the stirrup leathers easier for small children. Web girths are sometimes attached to the stiffened leather flaps of the saddle, as are the safety handle or straps at the saddle head. The child can hold the handle or straps for safety—without using the pony's mouth via the reins—to achieve some sort of balance.

Pads of advanced design now also have built-in knee rolls and forward-cut flaps designed to help in jumping and across country, full, leather-lined panels that assist in keeping the saddle on top of the pony rather than slipping underneath him, and a suede-covered seat, designed to keep the rider on top of the saddle.

There is also a half-way-stage saddle between the pure pad and the children's saddle proper. This has a half-tree, usually laminated. It has a deep seat, knee and thigh rolls and forward-cut flaps. In the opinion of many, this saddle helps the young rider to achieve a better riding position earlier than does the plain, old-fashioned pad.

Basket Saddles

Even infants can ride—or, rather, be carried by a quiet pony—provided a basket saddle is used. Some people mistrust basket saddles, because they have been known to slip and to decant their unwary occupants. They must therefore be carefully and correctly adjusted and secured by a pair of girths and a crupper. The child inside must also be held securely with a type of seat belt across the front of the basket or round the waist, or with a complete baby harness. The saddle may be fitted with stirrups and leathers, but these are not essential and may even be rather dangerous if there should be a fall.

The pony, which should be bomb-proof and never left unattended, is protected against being chafed by the basket weave of the saddle by thick, quilted padding.

Pony Club Approved Saddle

When the child graduates to a leather saddle with a tree, by far the best buy is a secondhand, general purpose saddle on the same lines as those produced for adults. It will be well broken-in, and

Handle

Leather trim to provide extra strength

Felt pad seat and flap

Peacock safety iron

Girth. Two girths may be fitted for safety.

Pony Pad Saddle

Basket Saddle

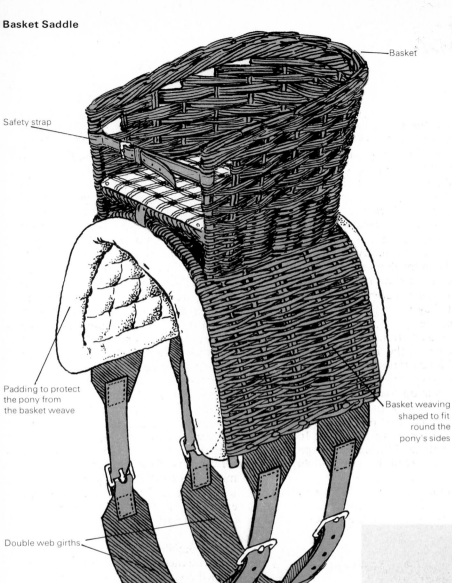

Basket

Safety strap

Padding to protect
the pony from
the basket weave

Basket weaving
shaped to fit
round the
pony's sides

Double web girths

are, however, good value for money, and for the more advanced rider there is a type of forward-cut approved saddle that has knee rolls and a fairly good depth of seat.

Whatever brand of saddle is chosen, a forward-cut type is better for children than the straight-cut showing pattern, so that jumping and really active riding are comfortable. However, a forward-cut saddle will not be so suitable for the show ring, because it will not give the illusion that the pony has a tremendous front. Nevertheless, it will be far more suitable for every other type of activity. Many straight-cut show saddles are suitable only for the most decorous riding: if the rider decides to jump a fence, he may find his knees preceding him and in fact gripping the pony's shoulder instead of the saddle flap. Anyone with a child taking up serious showing would be better to have two saddles: one for the ring and the other for riding at home.

Children being what they are, it is as well to have any of their saddles fitted with D-rings. For very young children, these are useful for fastening-on an extra rein to stop a greedy pony eating the grass as he is being ridden; and they are invaluable to secure such necessary articles as rolled-up raincoats when setting out on a day-long jaunt.

therefore comfortable. Nothing is more slippery and unyielding to a young and thin-skinned rider than a stiff, shiny new saddle.

The general purpose pattern is the best, since it will undoubtedly be called upon to serve purposes as varied as attending rallies, hunting, and taking part in shows, picnic rides and the like.

One type of saddle that is useful for all these jobs is the Pony Club approved variety, which is reasonably priced and has a fairly deep seat. Such saddles carry the sanction of people who are widely experienced in saddlery for children, and have been tried and tested in all types of activity. The fact that they have been approved by the Pony Club does not necessarily make them the best, because the cost of the finished saddles had to be considered when they were being designed. They

A fine example of a show saddle designed for a young rider on the same principles as show saddles built for adults. There is an even greater variety of saddle patterns on the market for children than for adults. Apart from basket saddles and pads, children have scaled-down versions of almost every adult saddle.

The Side-Saddle

Women in Europe rode either astride or pillion until the fourteenth century, when the side-saddle was introduced. This was a small seat with a horn at the front. It had back and side supports and a footrest called a *planchette*. The rider sat sideways, facing left, and was usually led, since such a position was impractical for controlling a horse.

Eventually, the planchette was replaced by a stirrup for the left foot, the right leg being placed over the horn. Side-saddle riding, as opposed to sitting, was born. And during the years that followed, many changes were made to bring the side-saddle to its present safe and comfortable form.

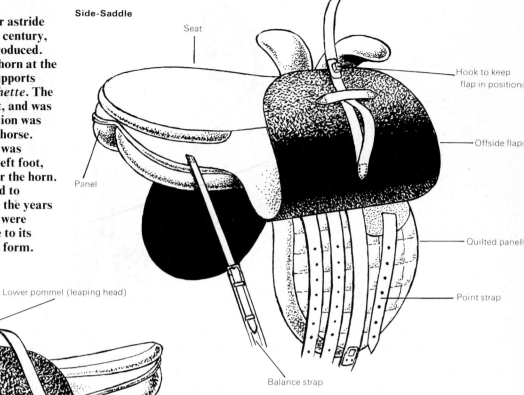

Side-Saddle

Seat

Hook to keep flap in position

Offside flap

Quilted panel

Point strap

Balance strap

Panel

Upper pommel (fixed head)

Lower pommel (leaping head)

Safe

Nearside flap

Flap strap (belly strap)

Thigh roll

Point strap angled at 15 degrees from vertical

Seat
The side-saddle seat is wide and preferably covered in doeskin. It should be absolutely level from front to back and from side to side.

Tree
The tree is fragile and can break easily. Usually, it is made from wood and cast iron. Modern trees are lighter than the older ones because they are made of laminated wood.

The tree has a cut-back head, to the left of which is a large hook about 230 mm (9 in.) across at the base, tapering and curving to 100 mm (4 in.) across the top. This is the fixed head (upper pommel), which is an integral part of the tree itself.

Leaping Head
The lower pommel is called the *leaping head*. It is screwed into the tree and can be adjusted to suit the width of the rider's thigh.

Some saddles have two sockets on the left for this pommel, a low one for ordinary riding and a higher one for jumping. The leaping head should always have a lefthand thread to tighten it. A righthand thread would be unsafe when pressure was put upon it.

Panels
The panels are of the full pattern and must be equal on both sides. But, when viewed from behind, there should be 20 to 25 mm ($\frac{3}{4}$ to 1 in.) deeper stuffing on the left than on the right to help to keep the saddle seat level during use. The saddle channel should be deep.

The covering of the panels is linen or serge, or a combination of the two. Leather is also used; it makes cleaning easier but is inclined to slip.

Flaps
The flap on the nearside is large, extending beyond the front of the saddle to accommodate the rider's right leg. This extra piece is called the *safe*. Sometimes, it has padding beneath it, but this can lessen leg contact.

At the bottom edge of the flap is a flap strap (belly strap). Under the flap are two or three girth straps and one

Above An unorthodox view of the side-saddle in use. The apron has been removed to show how the rider's legs fit over the upper pommel and below the lower.

Left A side-saddle in use, hidden by the apron of the rider's side-saddle habit. The art of side-saddle riding—and consequently the art of making saddles—virtually disappeared around the 1930s. Now, lady riders are rediscovering the techniques and demanding new saddles from the saddlers.

angled strap attached to the point of the tree to take the balance strap. This must slope back at 15 degrees from the vertical. Some Champion and Wilton saddles have a small buckle instead of a strap.

There are several types of offside flaps. The most common is plain and small, fastened down with a hook into an eye on the flap strap. The Martin and Martin saddles popular in the United States have a patent spring

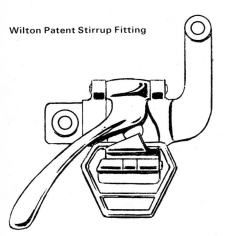

Wilton Patent Stirrup Fitting

under this flap to raise it and to keep it in place.

The fashionable show saddle has girth tabs on the outside of the flap, protruding from a small skirt. Usually, on the offside there are three girth straps, the most important of which is the point strap. The front girth buckle must be fastened to this to hold the saddle in place.

Balance Strap

The balance strap is made of leather and is 25 mm (1 in.) wide, with buckles and keepers at each end. Its purpose is to prevent the saddle back from swinging and rubbing the back of the horse. Some Champion and Wilton saddles have balance straps with holes to fit into the saddle buckles.

Stirrup Irons

A vital part of the side-saddle is its safety stirrup, without which it is a dangerous piece of equipment. Originally, the stirrup leather was threaded through a roller bar attached to the saddle. This led to much ingenuity in producing stirrups that would collapse and break open in emergencies.

Today, a safety stirrup must be used with these fittings. The three common patent fittings produced to release the leather in dangerous circumstances are the Owen, Champion and Wilton and

Mayhew—not interchangeable.

The top of the leather should have its patent fitting and the bottom should have a hook, which passes through the iron and back on itself to adjust on the holes in the leather. A leather sleeve covers this adjustment to protect the flap and the rider's boot. Side-saddle irons need extra-large eyes to admit the adjustment hook.

Girths

The Fitzwilliam girth, being double, gives extra security, but other flat girths may be used. Lampwick is often worn on greys. String is unsuitable.

The show saddle, with its outside girth straps, needs a special girth with high-quality buckles and keepers on the exposed offside. Sometimes, for extra elegance, the balance strap is shortened and stitched onto the actual girth. This is considered unsafe for hunting or strenuous exercise.

Measuring a Side-Saddle

● The length of a side-saddle is governed by the length of the rider's thigh bone.

● The saddle is measured from the centre of the cantle to the centre of the cut-back head or to the front edge of the fixed head.

● To wear a side-saddle, a horse must have good withers. On a rounded pony or a horse with over-muscled shoulders, the saddle slips.

Military Saddles

Throughout much of history, soldiers relied upon horses, ponies and mules for transport. Military saddles were constantly being changed and developed to increase their efficiency. Not only did they have to provide the fighting man with a comfortable seat upon which to travel, but they had to be secure and unimpeding in battle.

The problems to be overcome in the design of military saddles were very basic. The saddles had to be tough enough to stand up to constant, gruelling use, often in bad conditions. They had to be comfortable not only for the rider but also for the horse: a horse suffering from saddle sores or girth galls was a liability to an army, and might continue to be for weeks. In addition, military saddles had to be fitted with the means of carrying many items of soldierly equipment.

Cape Fan Military Saddle

The name *Cape fan* is derived from the trade name of the saddle tree used in this saddle. Other names for the saddle include *colonial, staff officer's, semi-military* (to distinguish it from the Universal saddle) and *yeomanry*.

The saddle was first seen in the Cape of Good Hope as a modification of the English hunting saddle. By 1877, it was in use by the military all over South Africa, and it was adopted officially by the British Army in 1879. It is in use today in many parts of the world, particularly by mounted police forces.

The tree of the Cape fan saddle is similar to that of the hunting saddle, but it has sidebars that extend to produce pronounced fans at the rear and burs at the front. Both are designed to give the saddle tree greater bearing surface on the back of the horse. Fans have the additional advantages of preventing the cantle from pressing down onto the spine, and they take such loads as rolled blankets.

Traditionally, the tree is made of beech, and has points and hinged spring bars for the leathers. The forearch is raised quite high to prevent it sitting down on the horse's withers.

The head is generally full for police work, but officers' patterns may be cut back.

To accommodate a wide variety of riders, the saddle seat is large. Seat and skirts are cut in one piece. Two *D*-rings are attached to the fans to take the rifle bucket, baton case and spare shoe case, or other items of equipment.

At first, the Cape fan saddle had no panels; a numnah and military blanket were used instead. (A military blanket measured about 1·7 by 1·4 m [5 ft 5 in. by 4 ft 8 in.] and was folded so that there were no uneven folds or wrinkles in it. A numnah was usually felt, about 10 mm [$\frac{3}{8}$ in.] thick.)

Padded full panels have replaced the blanket and numnah. Some of them are detachable. They are strapped or screwed to the tree and may be removed for re-stuffing or replacing.

The saddle weighs approximately 8 kg (18 lb) complete. It was designed to carry the rider's personal luggage, but it is not suitable for taking heavy packs.

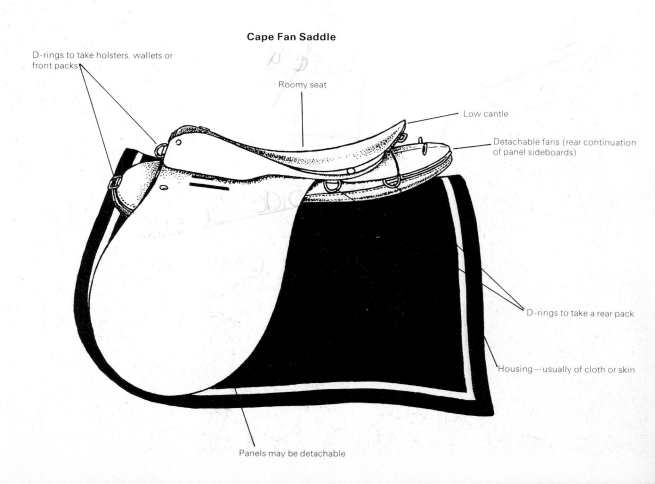

Cape Fan Saddle

D-rings to take holsters, wallets or front packs

Roomy seat

Low cantle

Detachable fans (rear continuation of panel sideboards)

D-rings to take a rear pack

Housing—usually of cloth or skin

Panels may be detachable

McClellan Cavalry Saddle

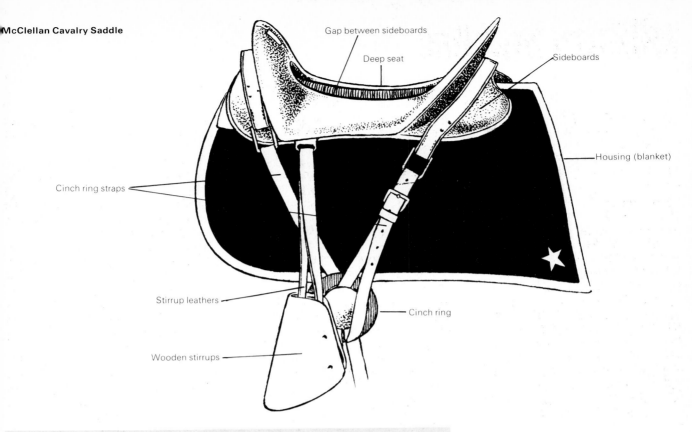

Gap between sideboards

Deep seat

Sideboards

Housing (blanket)

Cinch ring straps

Stirrup leathers

Cinch ring

Wooden stirrups

McClellan Cavalry Saddle

McClellan Saddle

The basic saddle of the United States military until World War II was the McClellan saddle. It was adapted from the Hussar saddle by the American general George Brinton McClellan.

The saddle has a narrow beech or poplar tree without points. It is covered tightly in leather and stitched round the edges. The tree extends into short burs and fans and has a slightly dipped seat and high arches. The rigging is centre fire, and is held at the cantle and pommel by brass screws. At first, a braided horsehair cinch was used that had a ring at each end to secure it to the cinch rings on the saddle. Later, flap straps and a leather girth were adopted.

The stirrup irons may be either English or wooden and hooded in the Western tradition. The saddle has no pads and is worn above a thickly-folded blanket.

The McClellan saddle weighs about 7·5 kg (17 lb) and forces the rider to sit very upright and therefore to ride light. It does not give as much security as its British counterpart.

The Cape Fan Military saddle in use by mounted police. The saddle burs and fans—the extensions of the tree at the front and rear of the saddle—give a far wider bearing surface over the back of the horse than do most saddles. This leads to fewer sore backs, making the saddle a popular choice among the military of many nations since the late 1800s.

Hussar Saddle

The Hussar (light cavalry) saddle is a Hungarian pattern that has been used by the military throughout Europe since the eighteenth century. It is still in use, particularly by the Household Cavalry and by the King's Troop, Royal Horse Artillery in Britain.

It is an extremely strong and simple saddle based on the design of the old Mongol saddle. At first, the tree was of beech and had no points. Its frame was glued and pegged and fastened with rawhide. Later, steel trees that had points of thick felt were fitted. The tree has burs and long fans that allow the saddle to bear quite a lot of weight. The tree sidebars are laced together with tight rawhide so that the channel is wide and high to keep any weight from the horse's spine. The high channel also allows for a good flow of air, which helps to prevent saddle sores on long journeys. The stirrup leathers slot through holes in the tree.

The saddle seat is short—approximately 420 mm (16½ in.)—and deeply dipped. It lies between a high pommel and even higher narrow cantle (spoon) of approximately 280 mm (11 in.). This allows the rider to maintain a firm and deep seat with either a short or long leg position.

In the Austrian cavalry, the seat and flaps of the saddle were made in one piece and were quilted and removable. Now they are usually of ordinary stretched leather and are often covered with a shabraque (shabrack). This also covers the horse behind the saddle, and the holsters. It is usually of leather and may itself be covered with sheepskin and secured by a surcingle.

In the British cavalry, a blanket was folded up to 15 times and used instead of panels. Since 1860, however, panels stuffed with horsehair and lined with serge have been in use.

Web girths are worn with the saddle, fixed permanently to the offside to prevent their loss.

Two major advantages of the Hussar saddle for military purposes are that it can be completely taken apart, and that it is designed to carry a great deal of extra equipment.

Phillips Saddle

The Phillips saddle is in use by the United States military today. It is a modern, forward-seat saddle that combines the characteristics of the English hunting saddle with those of the French officer's saddle. There are also two styles of Phillips military pack saddles.

North American Indian Saddle

The North American Indians had their own battle saddle. It had a light wooden frame shaped to the horse's back, and a straight seat of hide forming almost a right-angle with the pommel and cantle, which were 200 mm (8 in.) above the seat.

The cantle was wide and cut away in the centre; the rider could catch his heel in it and throw himself out of sight on one side of the horse to escape detection.

The shape of the seat, coupled with the very short length of stirrup leather used, did not allow the rider to sit up straight. He was forced into an unnatural position, lying almost on his back.

Universal Steel Arch Saddle

The Universal Steel Arch saddle was a revolutionary design in the field of military saddles. It was produced in the 1890s and has since undergone many modifications.

The steel tree is made up of sidebars extending into fans and joined by two high and rounded arches. It is extremely strong and is able to bear heavy weights. The front arch is held in place by clips and the rear arch by sockets. Struts at the rear arch prevent it from being wrenched from its

Universal Steel Arch Military Saddle

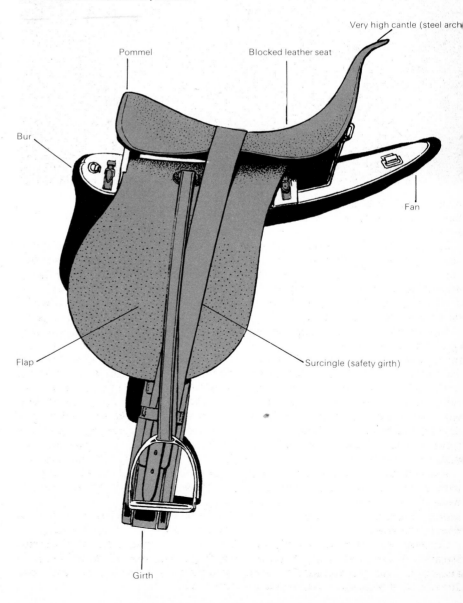

The Universal Steel Arch military saddle being used by troopers of the British Household Cavalry. The shaped and blocked saddle seat, and the panels, require the rider to use a straight-legged and very upright position. The saddle is fitted with burs and fans.

Pack Saddles

Pack saddles have played a major role in war and peace for centuries. Although pack animals cannot carry loads anything like as heavy as those that may be moved by driven animals, the pack animal has the advantage of being able to travel on almost any terrain.

On a riding saddle, the 'weight' moves about and gets on and off again at intervals. But the pack is a dead weight that stays on the saddle all day. To prevent the animal being injured by this constant, unyielding weight, a pack saddle must be designed and fitted even more carefully than a riding saddle; and the pack must not be allowed to move about on the animal's back.

There are many patterns of pack saddles, some civilian, others military or civilian patterns adapted by the military. They can all be divided into two categories: those with trees and those without.

ockets. Both arches are jointed so that they are able to fit any horse without adjustment.

The saddle seat is supported by double webbing stretched from the rear arch to the front. It is long and blocked (made from wet leather that is dried in place to form a tight skin over the framework of the tree).

The stirrups are fitted onto the tree by a buckle attachment, rather than through it, which can cause sore backs. They are set slightly farther back than those of the hunting saddle. At first, the saddle tree was built with points. These were later removed, when a new form of girth attachment was designed to prevent the saddle from shifting without using points.

These girth straps are a V-shaped arrangement of two straps, the wide arms of the V being attached to the saddle sidebars. The longest arm is fitted at the rear.

Separate felt numnah panels are issued with the saddles. The flaps are straight cut and are buttoned to steel studs in the sidebars for easy removal.

Aparego Pack Saddle

The aparego (albarda or asparego) tree-less pack saddle is Spanish and is still used widely today. It is made of long stems of straw sewn up into two linen cases so that they measure about 100 mm (4 in.) across and are long enough to reach from hip to withers.

Both ends of these cases are joined by padded straps that pass over the animal's back. Straw stuffed into a sack to form a thick pillow is placed on top of the bundles. A linen saddlecloth is used, and the whole thing is secured by a surcingle.

The actual load is fitted in the form of two large bundles and numerous small ones. They are all roped in place so that they leave the animal's spine completely free of weight.

Otago Pack Saddle

The Otago pack saddle was first seen in the mines of New Zealand's South Island. It later became known as the *British universal pack saddle*.

It consists of a large cushioning pad secured onto the back by a breastplate and breeching. It has long sidebars to spread the weight of the load, two girths to secure it and hooks on the pommel and cantle to take the ropes.

This saddle was said to be extremely comfortable for long journeys, but often it weighed as much as 18 kg (40 lb).

Mark V Adjustable Tree Pack Saddle

The Mark V adjustable tree pack saddle is still in use by military today. The tree arches are jointed onto the sidebars so that they can adjust to any size of back. The sidebars themselves are wooden and shaped to fit the back.

Panels stuffed with horsehair slot inside leather pockets on the sidebars, and there are various hooks and loops to take carriers for the loads. A double girth, breeching, crupper and breastplate are all used to keep the saddle secure.

Most modern military pack saddles are, however, jointed adaptations of the steel-tree cavalry saddle.

The Australian Stock and Other Saddles

The stockmen of Australia and New Zealand have always preferred to ride on the Australian stock (buckjumping) saddle than on any other pattern. One reason for this is the fact that it is almost impossible to fall off a horse that is wearing one. Another is the great comfort of the saddle for both the rider and the horse, which is a vital requirement of any saddle used for hours at a time.

The tree of the stock saddle is very deep and curving (the dip of a saddle is measured by dropping a perpendicular from a line between the cantle and the pommel). The seat is rather short and has a very high cantle. On the other hand, the pommel is often set particularly low. The reason is that the Australian and New Zealand stockmen do not use the lasso as much as the cowboys of America and therefore have no need for the horn that is part of the Western stock saddle.

Large thigh pads are set outside the flaps—which are short—between the thigh and seat of the rider. The tops of the flaps are also fitted with knee pads, so that the rider's legs are secured at back and front.

Usually, the stock saddle is secured with a surcingle rather than with a normal girth or cinch. It is threaded through eyes in the saddle flaps and is passed right across the seat for additional safety. When the saddle was first used, it was fastened over the pommel and behind the knee pads.

Cruppers are used on young horses or those with too little shoulder. They pass under the seat and fasten at the front to a stick that juts out on both sides.

Stirrup irons are usually of the Simplex safety pattern or the stock saddle pattern. The stock saddle iron has four bars making up its tread. This provides a wider, and therefore more comfortable, bearing surface for the foot than do most irons.

Because of the shape of the stock saddle, many Australians believe that Count Toptani used it as a model for his deep-seated jumping saddle. One saddle that is similar in design to the stock saddle is the park saddle. This has less dip to the seat and smaller knee and thigh pads.

Mongol Saddle

The Mongolians have used the same type of saddle for centuries. It is said that not only did they invent the saddle tree, but the saddle as well.

Mongolians ride in a totally different style from Europeans. They crouch forward, drawing back their feet in stirrups with very short leathers. They are extremely comfortable in the saddle; their forebears virtually lived on horseback.

The saddles have very short and deep seats with little room for movement. To compensate for this, they also have short burs and fans—extensions of the tree side-bars at the front and rear. These spread the weight of their load over a wider area of the horse's back. The cantle is of medium height but the pommel is extended quite high to help protect the top of the rider's leg from attack in battle.

The tree of the Mongol saddle has straight side-bars and rounded ends. It has no points. Sometimes the saddle is fitted with permanent blanket padding to act as a cushion on the horse's back. Often, however, the cushioning is simply a thick, folded blanket. Slipper stirrups are worn to lessen the chance of the rider losing his stirrups.

Argentine Recardo Saddle

Pad saddles were the only types of saddles known until about AD 400. Finding any still in use today seemed to be a remote possibility: but in fact at least two of these pads are in daily use in certain parts of the world, and have been so for hundreds of years.

Of these two, the Argentine recardo (riding) saddle is probably the better known. It is made of blankets folded and placed on the horse's back. These are followed by two pieces of flat

Australian Stock Saddle

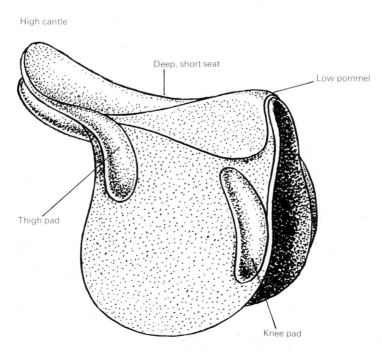

High cantle

Deep, short seat

Low pommel

Thigh pad

Knee pad

leather with rounded ends. Two pillows made of straw—each about 45 cm (18 in.) long—are added, one on each side of the spine. They are joined by leather thongs. A girth made of wide rawhide is placed right round the pad, and rings are attached to be used as stirrups. A sheepskin is placed over the whole thing to form the seat. This is secured by a surcingle.

Near East Donkey Pad Saddle

The second pad saddle in extensive use today is the Near East donkey saddle. Unlike other riding saddles, it is fashioned specifically for use on the hindquarters of the animal, rather than on the back behind the withers. The rider sits well back. In northern Africa and parts of Asia, this is considered to be the correct way to ride a donkey.

The pad has a flat cantle fitted slightly in front of the top of the donkey's dock. It has a high pommel to stop the rider slipping forward, and the seat is a piece of leather stretched from front to back. Stirrups are not used, but a girth fastens around the saddle and is adjusted well back towards the donkey's hind legs.

Dutch Dressage Saddle

A rather more modern saddle, yet again designed for a particular type of animal, is the Dutch dressage saddle made by Jonas-Bouman. Many Dutch horses have long backs, which upsets the balance of most saddles and causes the rider to sit too far back. This saddle is built to accommodate this on a maximum 45 cm ($17\frac{1}{2}$ in.) tree. It is made from imported English-treated hides that are a maximum of 2·5 mm ($\frac{1}{10}$ in.) thick. It has a deep seat, very long flaps and thickened panels with leather inserts. The stirrup bars are placed quite far back to maintain the correct leg position.

These saddles, although not available new today, are still popular with a number of people including Dutch dressage riders.

The Sikh (Khatee) Saddle

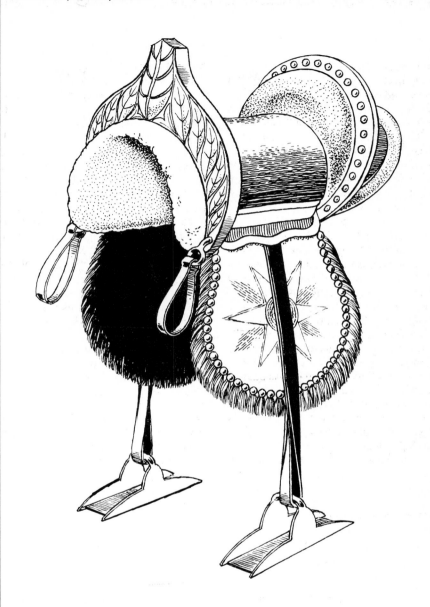

In the eighteenth and nineteenth centuries, some Indian cavalry regiments used the Sikh (Khatee) saddle in preference to those used by British regiments in India. It was considered to be particularly comfortable for the horse. One officer of Probyn's Horse wrote that it would not gall the horse, even under hard conditions. However, he warned against fitting any padding between the saddle and the horse as this would result in sore withers.

Panel and Seat

The panel and seat were combined. They were formed from a padded semi-circle called the *koorjeen*, which was shaped to fit the back of the horse rather than the seat of the rider. The panel and seat extended only a short way down the sides of the horse. However, they were elongated behind the cantle to give a greater bearing surface—in the same way as the Cape fan saddle, only as a single piece.

Pommel and Cantle

The pommel was a high, firm projection at a right-angle to the seat. It protected the top of the rider's legs during battle and helped to give him a secure seat. The cantle was similar, but was rounded to fit the back of the rider's seat.

Skirt and Stirrups

The rider's knees and thighs rested on rounded, and often decorated, skirts, from which the stirrup leathers were suspended. The stirrups themselves were narrow horizontal platforms that gave the rider an extremely secure base in fighting.

Girths

Girths pass underneath the belly, usually in the girth groove behind the elbows, and are buckled to the girth straps on each side of the saddle. They are therefore extremely important pieces of equipment and should never be worn if they are in any danger of breaking.

For the comfort of the horse, girths must be fitted properly. Otherwise they can cause girth galls (sores). Obviously, a girth should not be so loose that it allows the saddle to slip, but for ordinary riding it should not be put on as tight as it will go. The only circumstance in which it should be pulled up as tightly as possible is for racing, racing girths being made of webbing with elastic inserts. In this case, after tightening the girths, each foreleg in turn should be lifted up and pulled forward to minimize the risk of pinching.

A horse should be girthed up gradually. If the girth is pulled up sharply in one haul, it is likely to pinch and wrinkle the skin, causing the horse pain: he might be tempted to retaliate. The girth should be fitted well back from the elbows and should be drawn up gently to a loose fitting, before being tightened. A hand should then be run down between girth and skin to smooth out any wrinkles. Once the rider is mounted, the girth should be tightened again and, after walking a short way, it should be checked once more.

Balding Girths

The Balding is one of the most popular leather girths. It is designed to prevent galling and was perfected by a William Balding, of Rugby in England.

The leather is split into three behind the horse's elbows and plaited to give the elbows and forearms maximum room and prevent chafing. The only problem here is that the pressure is not evenly spread behind the elbows.

Atherstone Girths

Again, the Atherstone girth is shaped to avoid chafing at the elbows. It is sometimes made with an elastic insert, but it has the same pressure problem as the Balding.

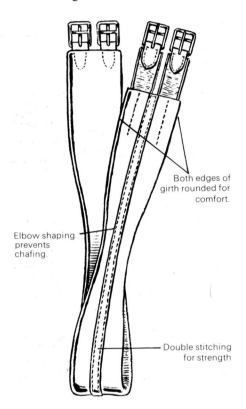

Elbow shaping prevents chafing.

Both edges of girth rounded for comfort.

Double stitching for strength

Three-Fold Girths

The three-fold leather girth is made usually of baghide and may have a serge or flannel inlay. It should be fitted with the rolled edge to the front for comfort; but once the edges begin to wear, they can cause chafing. The girth is rather warm because it does not allow air to circulate.

Lampwick Girths

Lampwick girths are now deservedly popular, particularly as summer girths.

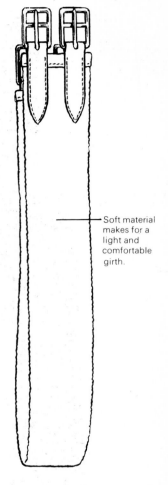

Lampwick Girth

Soft material makes for a light and comfortable girth.

They are made of tubular wick, are soft and pliable and are ideal for thin-skinned horses. Again, although lampwick girths are among the least liable to cause galling when new, they will fray eventually, usually in the area of the elbows.

German Cordstring Girths

The German cordstring girths are made of thick, round cotton strings held in place by strong cross-weaves. These girths are generally better than nylon, since they are stronger, cooler

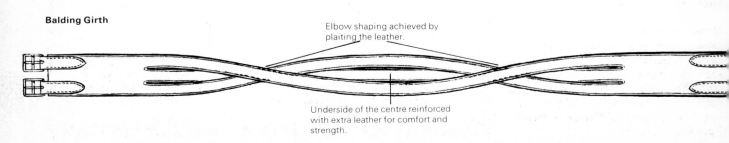

Balding Girth

Elbow shaping achieved by plaiting the leather.

Underside of the centre reinforced with extra leather for comfort and strength.

and wider. They are usually about 125 mm (5 in.) wide. When made from Terylene, these girths are even softer and easier to maintain.

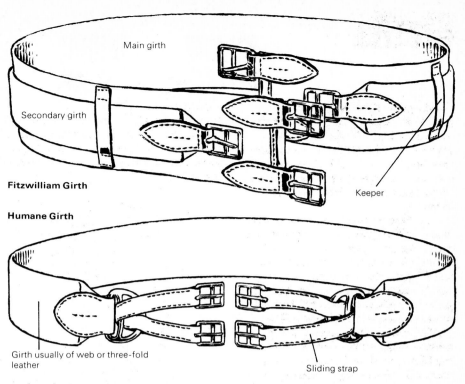

Main girth

Secondary girth

Fitzwilliam Girth

Keeper

Humane Girth

Girth usually of web or three-fold leather

Sliding strap

Tongue should fit into a groove on the top bar. Rolled metal on the top bar eventually cuts into the girth strap.

Strands keeping cord in place must be checked for fraying.

Fitzwilliam Girths

The Fitzwilliam girth has always also been known as the side-saddle girth. It is seldom seen today.

It is a double girth made of web underneath with web or leather on top, held together by a leather band. The bottom girth is 125 mm (5 in.) wide and the top 75 mm (3 in.).

Humane Girths

Humane girths are made either of web or of three-fold leather. The buckles are set on a sliding strap passed through a ring, allowing a little movement in time with the horse's action. These girths are now quite rare. They can generally be made to order.

Web and Elastic Girths

Web and elastic girths are made mainly of web, but have elastic inserts fitted on one side to give when the horse is at full stretch. For this reason, they are used mostly in racing, but they do have a place in any show jumping or cross-country competition.

They are usually 65 mm ($2\frac{1}{2}$ in.) wide for steeplechasing or hurdling, where they are often used singly and are fitted with light roller buckles. When used with a surcingle, the surcingle should also have elastic inserts.

Web Girths

Web girths are made in three materials: wool, wool and cotton mixtures and pure cotton. The best of these is wool, which wears fairly well. Cotton and wool mixtures are also quite hard wearing, but the pure cotton varieties are useless because the horse's sweat

rots them so quickly.

All web girths harden with sweat if they are not washed frequently. They are sold in pairs with single buckles at each end and are usually 85 mm ($3\frac{1}{4}$ in.) wide for hunting or training and 70 mm ($2\frac{3}{4}$ in.) wide for racing.

Tubular Web Girths

Tubular web crossover girths are made of two narrow web straps, usually white, joined at the centre with rubber pimple grips to keep them in place. These smart, neat girths are ideal for use on show ponies.

Elastic Girths

Elastic girths are another type popular in the racing world because of their tremendous give and grip. Sweat does tend to rot them, however, so they are best kept solely for the racecourse and not used for training.

Care of Girths

● Leather girths tend to dry out with the action of the horse's sweat. They should be well greased with a leather dressing.

● The three-fold type of girth should be unfolded for cleaning. It will stay more supple if a piece of cloth soaked in a leather preparation is placed between the folds.

● Nylon cord girths are washable and strong, and when new are among the least likely to cause galls. But the bands holding the nylon strands together must be checked for fraying. If the strands work loose they can cause sores.

Girth Accessories

Girth Extensions

Horses coming up from grass are often so much fatter than normal that their girths will not fit. Instead of going to the expense of buying a new girth that will probably only be needed for a short period, it is possible to buy a girth extension strap. This provides an effective and inexpensive answer to the problem.

Girth Sleeves

The girth sleeve acts as an additional protection against galling, particularly on a young horse or one that has just come up from grass and is in soft condition. Usually, it is made either of sheepskin or of rubber: a tyre inner tube is a good homemade substitute.

The girth is threaded through the sleeve, which should reach to just above the level of the horse's elbows. The girth is then buckled as normal. In stables where a number of horses are in work and are using the same girths, disposable rubber girth sleeves may be used to prevent the spread of skin disorders.

Girth Safes

The girth buckles on the saddle not only cause an uncomfortable lump under the rider's legs but can in time damage the saddle flaps. Therefore, it is necessary to fit girth safes on each side for protection.

These are inexpensive, flat pieces of leather through which the girth straps are slotted. They form a protective cover between the buckles and the saddle flaps and rider.

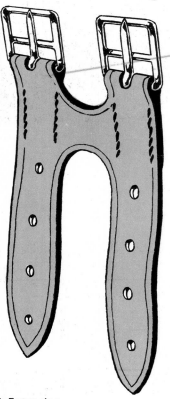

Girth Extension

Girth extensions are ideal for the ever-changing girths of small ponies. They should not be fitted permanently.

Sheepskin Girth Sleeve

To avoid girth galls, it may be advisable to use a girth sleeve on any horse in soft condition. Bathing the skin under girth and saddle with a saline solution also helps by toughening the skin.

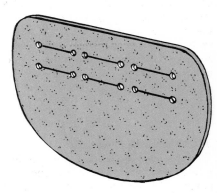

Girth Safe

Surcingles and Security

- A surcingle is not used merely to hold a rug in position. It can be used over the saddle for security in case the girth breaks or becomes unfastened. This is necessary in training, jumping and fast sports.

- The surcingle is fitted either through the two loops on the saddle flaps or under the ends of the stirrup leathers. It is buckled under the belly, and should always remain on the girth.

Stirrup Leathers

The narrow straps called stirrup leathers thread through the eyes of the stirrup irons and attach to the saddle bars. They are adjustable for length—to suit the rider—by means of buckles. Generally, the buckles are concealed under the saddle skirt, but some riders prefer to position them close to the irons, where they are less bulky under the rider's thigh. This is a particularly sensible arrangement for dressage riding.

Stirrup leathers may be made from cowhide, rawhide, buffalo hide or oak bark tanned hide. They have to be very strong, and are cut from the centre of the hide and specially dressed. In flat racing, web is used instead of leather because it is lighter. But whatever type of material is chosen for leathers, it is always wise to buy the highest quality possible in order to reduce the risk of breakage.

Buffalo Hide Leathers
The red leather of the buffalo hide is virtually unbreakable and is therefore particularly suitable for the stresses of racing or cross-country riding. It is soft, supple and oily-dressed, but after long use it has usually stretched to such a degree that the buckle end has become quite narrow. A good idea is to change the leathers round frequently so that the one on the mounting side does not become longer than that on the offside.

Rawhide Leathers
A rawhide leather is harder and therefore less likely to stretch than one of buffalo hide. It is also exceptionally strong. Show pony leathers are usually made of top quality fine rawhide or of oak bark tanned hide.

Extending Leathers (Hook-up or Let-Down Leathers)
Extending leathers are manufactured to assist elderly or short-legged riders who have difficulty in mounting from the ground. The nearside leather has a webbing extension that can be hooked up or let down. When unhooked and let down, it gives the extra length needed for easy mounting. But once the rider is in the saddle, he has only to hook-up the extension again to restore the leather to its correct riding length.

The saddle bar as it appears outside the saddle flap. For safety, saddle bars should be made of forged steel rather than cast steel because the latter may break. The movable thumbpiece (safety catch) of the bar should be left open to allow the stirrup leather to slip out of the bar in the event of a fall.

Stirrup Leathers
The stitching at the buckle end of stirrup leathers often wears thin. At the first sign of fraying, the stitching should be renewed.

Flat Race Webs
Flat race webs are made of lightweight tubular webbing with reinforced points. Usually they are much narrower than normal.

Extending Stirrup Leather

Quality Leathers
- Top-quality leathers are finished off smartly with a bevelled edge and three rows of stitching.
- The best and strongest buckles are made of stainless steel.
- The holes for adjustment are sometimes numbered so that the rider can easily check that the leathers are the same length on each side.

Stirrup Irons

Novice riders, as well as the more experienced, often ride without stirrups to improve their seat and balance. But in all the usual spheres of riding, stirrups are considered essential.

Although stirrup irons give the rider support and security in the saddle, they should not be relied on to keep him there. If a rider loses the stirrups— because the horse has shied or bucked or has made a bad mistake, such as landing awkwardly after a jump—he should still be sufficiently well balanced to remain in the saddle. Skilled jockeys and cross-country riders can lose their irons when racing at high speeds and yet continue comfortably without them.

It is usual to have the ball of the foot resting on the tread of the stirrup iron, but some show jumpers rest only the toes. When racing, however, it is advisable to push the iron right home to the heel to give that little bit of extra security.

The size of the stirrup iron is very important. Ideally, the rider's foot should rest close to the inside of the stirrup, leaving a space of 25 mm (1 in.) at the outside. An iron should never be so big that the foot can pass right through. Nor should it be so small that there is a danger of it gripping the foot in the event of a fall. With a badly-fitting iron, a rider could be dragged along helplessly behind a frightened horse.

English Hunting Iron
The English hunting iron is one of the most basic patterns of stirrup. The iron is made in many different styles, but it always has a perpendicular eye for the leather, rounded sides and a horizontal tread fitted with small metal grips. It is available in all the usual metals except aluminium, but is seen mainly in stainless steel and nickel alloys.

Heavy Dressage Iron
An extra-heavy type of stainless steel iron is the German Stübben pattern. It is one of the more expensive irons, and has a characteristic thick tread and tall, streamlined sides. Its weight makes it particularly suited to dressage riding, where the stirrups should be as still as possible.

Cock-Eyed Iron (Kournakoff Iron)
The cock-eyed iron has an eye set to the inside, out of the perpendicular. Its sides slope forward and the foot tread slopes upward. Its purpose is to keep the rider's foot and leg in the correct position, with the toe up and heel down, and the sole lower on the inside than on the outside. These irons must be marked 'right' and 'left' because, obviously, they are not interchangeable. They are not always recommended for modern dressage riding. The irons were made popular by a Russian cavalry officer named Kournakoff.

Bent-Top Iron
The bent-top iron has a top that is curved away from the rider's instep. This helps to keep the heel down and is suitable for those riders who like to push their foot fully home in the iron.

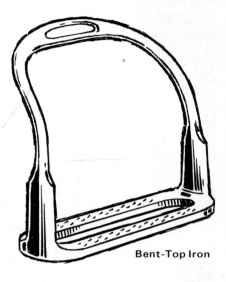

Bent-Top Iron

Australian Simplex Saftey Iron
The Australian simplex iron is one of the safest patterns. A balloon-loop forwards on the outer side of the iron ensures that the foot cannot become trapped. The simplex is as strong as a plain iron.

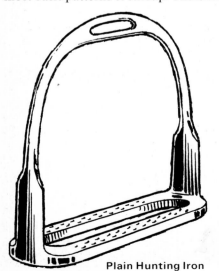

Plain Hunting Iron

Stirrup-leather eye set 31 mm (1¼ in.) away from the perpendicular towards the inside

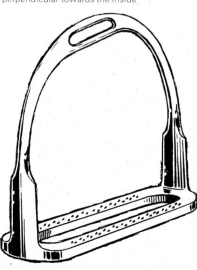

Cock-Eyed (Kournakoff) Iron

Half-moon shaping allows the foot to be released easily during a fall.

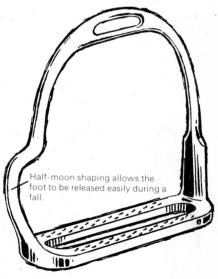

Simplex Safety Iron

Peacock Safety Iron
The Peacock safety iron is used mainly by children. It is neither as safe, as easy to maintain or strong as the Australian

Devonshire Slipper Iron
Few Devonshire slipper irons remain. They are shaped like a heel-less slipper and hang on a revolving bar from the stirrup leather. The 'slipper' itself is leather and takes the complete front of the rider's foot, making it warm, if unusual, in use.

Cradle Race Iron
A popular iron in racing is the cradle pattern. It can be made of stainless steel or, for lightness, aluminium. The tread is rounded upwards, instead of being straight. Therefore less metal is used and the iron is more comfortable for a jockey wearing a thin boot.

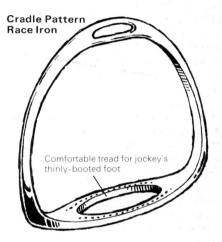

Cradle Pattern Race Iron

Comfortable tread for jockey's thinly-booted foot

simplex pattern. The idea is that the outer metal side is replaced by a thick rubber band hooked up near the eye. When the child falls, the band, in theory, comes away and frees the foot.

The disadvantages are that the rubber band does not necessarily become undone in a fall, and it can sometimes open when it should not. Because of the rubber band, the iron is also rather too narrow; and the weight placed on the iron during mounting tends to bend the tread down on the

A plain English hunting iron without a rubber tread—put up for safety. The eye of the iron should be run up the far side of the stirrup leather before the spare leather is tucked in behind.

outside, forcing the child to hold an incorrect leg position. If Peacocks are used, the left and right irons should be interchanged frequently.

Prussia Side Iron
The Prussia side iron has sides that narrow gradually from the tread to the eye, unlike the standard iron that keeps the same width all the way up. It is smart but not particularly safe.

Stirrup Wedges
These attachments are intended to have the same effect as the off-set cock-eyed iron. They are cut in such a way that the lowest part is diagonally opposite the highest.

Rubber Treads
Most riders today use rubber treads. They are fixed on top of the metal treads to give extra grip, especially for slippery-soled boots. The rubber helps slightly in keeping the feet warm. Rubber treads can be bought in different sizes to fit the various irons, and are usually black or white.

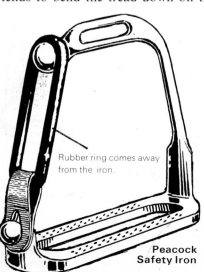

Rubber ring comes away from the iron.

Peacock Safety Iron

Selecting Irons
- Heavy irons are preferable to light ones. They free the feet more easily after a fall and are harder to lose accidentally.
- Stainless steel irons are better than those made of nickel or plated iron. They look well and are almost unbreakable.
- Nickel irons should not be used. They can bend and break.
- Aluminium irons are preferred on the racecourse because of their lightness. But they can break, and are only safe for flat racing.

Numnahs

The Indian word 'numnah' means simply 'saddle pad'. The numnah is placed on the back of the horse beneath the saddle and is designed to provide extra comfort and cushioning.

Strictly speaking, a numnah should be unnecessary if a saddle is properly fitted and stuffed. It often causes overheating and consequent soreness to the back. Again, if it is not kept clean, it can cause soreness or skin disease. And any additional bulk beneath the rider moves the seat and legs farther away from the horse and is against the design principles of most modern saddles.

A numnah can do more harm than good if it is used over a continuous and prolonged period—for instance, in hunting. The horse generally sweats, cools and sweats again during the day, the back over-heats and the skin can be easily chafed. Rubber is a particular culprit here; modern synthetic materials usually offer better circulation of air to the back.

A numnah is useful, however, if several horses have to share one saddle. A numnah can then prevent the soreness that would otherwise be caused by the saddle failing to fit any of the horses perfectly, especially across the withers.

When a horse comes up from grass and is in soft condition, it is all too easy to end up with saddle sores on the pressure points along the back, especially under the cantle and along the horse's sides. A numnah helps in such a case, but another way to avoid this soreness is to bathe the back with a saline solution to harden the skin.

Numnahs are always needed under lightweight race saddles. These numnahs are made usually from thin, cloth-covered foam or felt. They protect the horse's back and prevent the jockey's boots chafing the horse's sides.

In general use, numnahs have the advantage of making saddle panels easier to clean. But this does not mean that panels should not still be cleaned regularly.

Fitting

Numnahs are cut to the shape of the saddle they will be placed under. The shapes range from dressage through hunting and general-purpose to race and race-exercise. In every case, the numnah is cut just a bit bigger than the saddle. Its size must also be related to that of the horse. Generally, three size fittings are available for ready-made numnahs: horse, cob and pony.

The methods of attaching a numnah fall into three general types: strap and buckle, loop, and pocket.

The strap and buckle fits onto the girth straps at each side, above the buckle guards. It is fastened in front of the panels. Consequently, it can be fitted without removing the buckle guards, but the buckles are rather cumbersome. With this type of fastening, and with the loop type, the numnah sometimes has a tendency to slip back from the withers.

The loop variety is probably the most popular. The two straps have a loop at each end which slips onto a girth strap at each side. As a result, the buckle guard has to be removed and replaced every time the numnah is fitted. The straps are made either of leather or of strong elastic.

The third method is the pocket numnah. This has fabric pockets that fit snugly over the saddle panels at each side, under the girth straps. They are very secure, but give twice as much bulk beneath the rider's leg as the other two methods.

Numnahs are made in a variety of materials and in a variety of colours, sometimes rather gaudy.

Sheepskin Numnahs

The sheepskin numnah was once the most common form available. Now, largely because sheepskin is expensive, it is being replaced by other types.

Real sheepskin numnahs can be made to the customer's own pattern. They are usually cut from two skins and are joined along the back. They are either left unlined, or are lined with linen or thin panel hide.

These numnahs are not easy to clean. They must be washed by hand in warm, soapy water, well rinsed and re-shaped before drying. While still not completely dry, the knots should be combed out. If they are unlined, the inside should be rubbed with warm glycerine oil to keep it supple.

If properly cared for, a sheepskin numnah should last a lifetime.

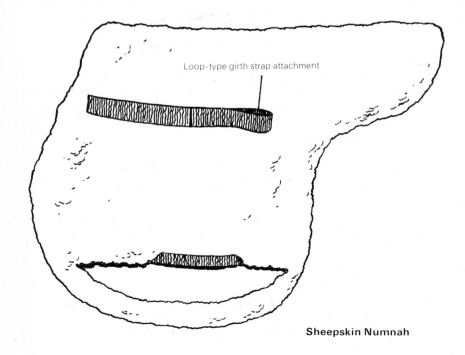

Loop-type girth strap attachment

Sheepskin Numnah

Synthetic Numnahs

There are many varieties of synthetic numnah available. One of the cheapest and best is the linen-covered plastic foam numnah, which neither heats nor draws the back, as the now outdated sorbo rubber variety did. Nylon-covered foam is not good either, since this also draws the back.

Mock sheepskin is now a popular alternative to the real thing. Many numnahs of synthetic sheepskin stretch and are non-slip, and some claim such attributes as sweat-resistant girth panels to prevent chafing. Yielding, textured fleece helps to give a good moulding even when a horse has a prominent spine or withers.

Synthetic numnahs are generally made in a quilted pattern. They are not thick, but are good for soaking up the sweat. Some simulated sheepskin numnahs are made of cotton rather than of synthetic materials.

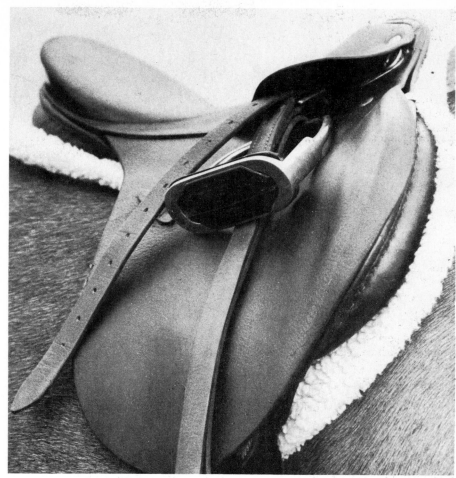

A synthetic fleece numnah. It is important to fit a numnah so that it does not press down on the spine of the horse causing soreness. The front of the numnah should be pushed up into the saddle gullet to prevent this.

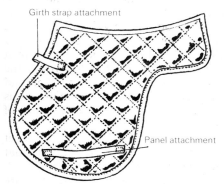

Girth strap attachment

Panel attachment

Quilted Cotton Numnah

Woollen Weave Numnahs

Wool woven onto a fabric backing makes a numnah of natural resilience and durability. When the wool is actually woven into the fabric, the numnah takes up moisture well and does not chafe.

Leather Numnahs

Filled leather numnahs are not as soft on the horse's back as are most other varieties, but are, however, very easy to clean. How long any numnah will last depends largely upon wear and tear and how well it is looked after, as well as upon the type of material chosen. Any numnah with leather fittings must always be washed by hand to stop the leather cracking.

Felt Numnahs

The felt numnah is one of the best for a horse with a bad back. If the horse is suffering from a skin trouble such as warbles, a hole can be cut in the felt to take the pressure off the sore spot and allow the rider to keep the horse in work.

Although felt is generally thin, it does not become uncomfortably flat. Thick felt numnahs can be made to order, but they may be expensive. All felt numnahs are easy to wash.

Self-fastening straps envelop the saddle panel.

Felt Numnah

The Use of Numnahs

- Using a numnah is not a remedy for a badly-fitting saddle. Nor will it compensate for faulty stuffing, except as a temporary expedient.

- One argument against using numnahs is that they tend to cause the horse's back to overheat. An overheated back is more likely to become sore.

- A numnah must be kept scrupulously clean and soft, otherwise it will irritate the horse's back.

- For the sake of appearance, a numnah should project an equal distance all round the edge of the saddle. A more important requirement is that it should conform with the shape of the horse's back.

Saddle Accessories

Wither Pads

The wither pad is a pad just large enough to cover the withers and prevent a saddle from clamping down too tightly on them. With a well-fitting saddle, this should not be necessary. But as a temporary measure, if there is any likelihood of a saddle touching the withers when the rider is mounted, a wither pad is essential to avoid soreness. In racing, a wither pad is valuable in helping to make a very lightweight saddle fit the horse comfortably.

Most wither pads are oval, though some are kidney shaped. The best are double-knitted, making stuffing unnecessary. Sheepskin is also good, and foam plastic wither pads are available. Most of the stuffed varieties are useless, since pressure forces the stuffing away from the point it is supposed to be protecting.

Weightcloths

Weightcloths are used only for racing or in competitions where a specific minimum weight has to be carried, such as in top-flight show jumping, horse trials or team cross-country chasing. But lightweight riders occasionally use weightcloths on exercise to get their horses used to carrying more weight.

There are two types of cloths available generally: one is an extension of the saddle cloth, the other is an extension of the breastplate. They are not necessarily interchangeable because they have different qualities.

The saddle cloth variety is the most common. It lies over the horse's back under the saddle and has pockets to hold the lead weights. This type of weightcloth is made usually of linen lined with rugging and has leather pockets. The cloth used for flat racing is often lined with silk and has pigskin pockets. But many lightweight event riders prefer the weightcloth itself to be heavy so as to reduce the amount of lead that must be carried.

The breastplate pattern is used most frequently by women riders, because usually they must carry more weight than men. The breastplate places the weights in front of the saddle and therefore closer to the horse's centre of gravity. A built-in steel frame stops the weight from pressing down onto the withers.

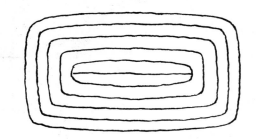

Cloth-covered wither pad. The stitching keeps the stuffing in place when under pressure from the saddle.

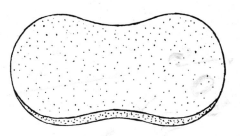

Kidney-shaped foam rubber wither pad fits the withers and the saddle pommel.

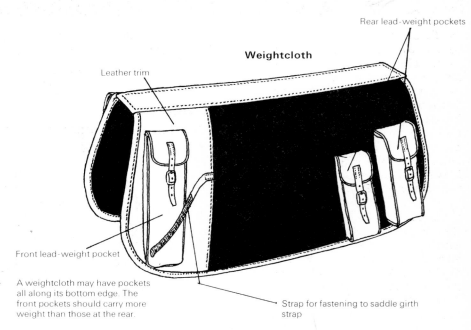

Weightcloth

Rear lead-weight pockets

Leather trim

Front lead-weight pocket

A weightcloth may have pockets all along its bottom edge. The front pockets should carry more weight than those at the rear.

Strap for fastening to saddle girth strap

Saddle Cloths

A saddle cloth is worn on the horse's back under the saddle in the same way as a numnah. But it is not padded and is not shaped to fit the saddle, being usually a simple square or rectangle of fabric. Primarily, it is worn only for appearance, although it does keep the saddle panels clean.

The saddle cloth is usually made of cotton or linen, either in white, plain colours or checks. Some cloths have a special design or bear the monograms of clubs, regiments, commercial firms or equestrian teams. Riders who are chosen to represent their country in equestrian events are entitled to bear an emblem showing the country's flag on their saddle cloths.

Young horses or those that are cold-backed appreciate a folded woollen blanket placed as a saddle cloth under the saddle. Because the blanket is warm, the horse relaxes.

A white linen saddle cloth and number cloth fitted under a very light racing saddle. Although saddle cloths are often worn simply for appearance, it is necessary to use one with a light racing saddle to prevent the horse's back becoming sore. Riders who represent their countries in equestrian sports usually use a saddle cloth with the national flag motif in one corner.

Saddle Covers

Saddle covers, as their name implies, fit over saddles to protect them when they are not in use. Some are made-to-measure and have handles and zip fastenings so that they can be carried. Strong varieties, in heavy corded canvas with brass zips and nylon handles, are ideal when travelling abroad. And waterproof covers can be invaluable at shows and other events if the weather is wet.

Cruppers

A crupper is used to prevent a saddle slipping forward onto the withers, and is worn both by riding horses and driving horses. It is a padded leather loop that passes under the tail at the dock and is then attached to the centre of the back of the saddle. The attachment is an adjustable strap and buckle. The loop of the crupper should be filled with linseed, which gives out a certain amount of grease and therefore keeps the leather supple and prevents chafing.

Cruppers are worn mainly by small, fat ponies with not much shoulder or withers. On such animals, the saddle tends to slip out of position. They are also used during breaking. In this case, they should be fitted with additional buckles at each side of the dock piece so that they can be adjusted easily without upsetting the young horse.

Saddle Cover

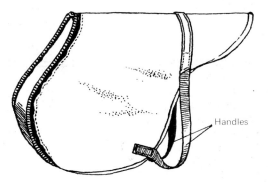

Handles

Weightcloths

● When choosing a cross-country saddle, allowance must be made for the fact that a weightcloth may have to be carried.

● With a saddle-cloth type of weightcloth, a numnah should be worn to prevent the horse's back becoming sore.

● If saddle cloths are allowed to wrinkle they will irritate the horse's back. Irritation can also be caused by a saddle cloth that has become coated with stale sweat and hairs.

Breastplates and Breastgirths

Breastplates and breastgirths have the same function—that of holding the saddle in place at all times. They are particularly necessary on 'herring gutted' horses and on horses that are fit but under extra strain—for example, horses in a race or a cross-country competition. In such circumstances, a saddle can slip back and cause an accident unless it is firmly anchored. Horses with a conformation that tends to make a saddle slip back should always be fitted with a breastplate or breastgirth.

Although these two pieces of equipment have the same purpose, they look different and fit differently.

Breastgirth

The more simple is the breastgirth, often called the *Aintree breastgirth*. Its main component is a girth of webbing, elastic or leather fitted round the front of the horse's chest, just above the points of the shoulders. Generally, this girth is lined with either sheepskin or soft leather to prevent chafing of the horse's chest. It is held in place by an adjustable leather strap resting in front of the horse's withers and by a leather loop and buckle sewn onto each end of the girth and fitting onto the saddle girth. The polo pattern breastgirth has a centre slot or loop on the inside to take a standing martingale.

The elastic breastgirth allows for some give when a horse is at full stretch. Like the webbing varieties, it is generally available in various colours.

Breastplate

A breastplate is made completely of leather, the weight and width of which depend on the use to which the breastplate will be put. Breastplates made for hunting are the stoutest. Those for flat racing are narrow and light.

Breastplates do not fit round the chest. They are attached to the saddle girth at one end by being passed between the horse's front legs. They then branch upwards into a V-shape round the horse's neck and are attached by straps and buckles from this to the D-rings on either side of the front of the saddle. The ring at the breast should always be fitted with a leather safe to ensure that it does not dig into the horse.

In jumping, a breastplate can become rather tight round the forelegs, restricting movement. But it has the advantage of being able to be fitted with a running or standing martingale attachment to the breast ring, obviating the fuss of having a full martingale and breastgirth. These types of martingale attachment are not, however, recommended for steeplechasing, because the pressure on the reins could interfere with a horse's freedom and cause a fall.

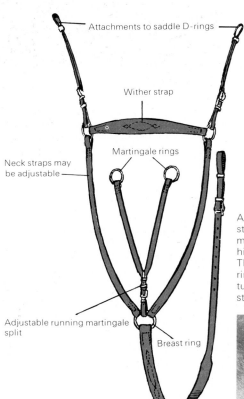

Attachments to saddle D-rings

Wither strap

Neck straps may be adjustable

Martingale rings

Adjustable running martingale split

Breast ring

Breastplate

A hunting pattern leather breastplate. The strap and buckle attachments to the saddle may be moved from the D-rings to those higher up the saddle, underneath the skirts. These are often found to be safer. The breast ring is used to take the martingale splits that turn the breastplate into a running or standing martingale.

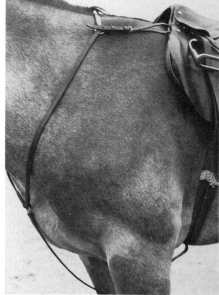

Adjustable wither strap

The breast strap may be sheepskin-covered, or may be plain leather, web or elastic.

Adjustable girth strap attachments, fitting under saddle flaps

Breastgirth

Spurs

Spurs are an artificial aid used to clarify the normal leg aid. They are fixed to the rider's heels, parallel to the ground, and are attached either by straps or by special holders at the back of the boots known as *spur boxes*.

Spurs are brought into play when the rider uses the legs, pricking the horse's sides. They should be used only by riders who have complete control of their lower legs.

Modern spurs have two main functions. Either they are used for decoration or ceremony, or they act as a functional aid. The latter type is generally the less severe. Spurs with long, straight necks are the best for ordinary schooling.

There are many patterns of spurs, and many schools of thought about which are the most effective. But the two commonest patterns of spur shanks (sides) are the Prince of Wales and the hunting.

A rowelled spur is a more effective aid than a blunt spur, since the rider will almost certainly use it with more care and thought. The points should be fine but not too sharp. If applied properly, a rowelled spur causes less pain—and certainly is less injurious— to a horse than a blunt spur that is strongly applied and that probably results in bruising.

Prince of Wales Spur

The shanks of the Prince of Wales spur are offset, the longer side being worn on the outside of the foot. The spur has either a dummy neck (of varying lengths) or is fitted with fine points or sharp rowels. The neck droops slightly. Generally, the spur is secured to the boot by a single strap of leather or plaited nylon which passes through its loop ends and is buckled. The spur is used for hunting, eventing and show jumping.

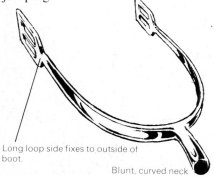

Long loop side fixes to outside of boot.

Blunt, curved neck

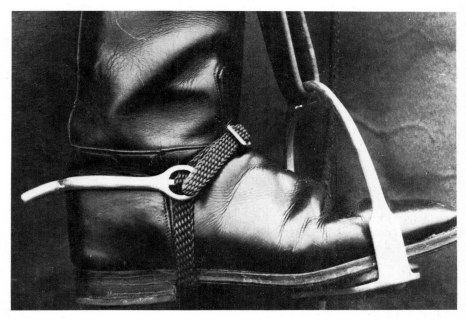

A modern plaited nylon spur strap used to secure a Prince of Wales pattern stainless steel spur. The slightly-drooping spur neck is of a good moderate length to give accurate aids, and it is not set with rowels. The shanks are offset, with the longer side on the outside of the rider's foot.

Hunting Spur

The hunting pattern spur has sides of equal length and, again, can have a dummy or a rowelled neck. The spur straps are attached to studs on the spur and are buckled. This type of spur usually has a straight neck.

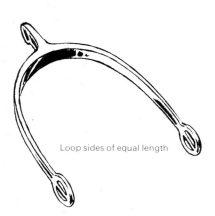

Loop sides of equal length

Race Spurs

Race spurs are usually of the Prince of Wales pattern, but are made of light-weight materials. Most often they are made of aluminium.

Competition Spurs

Blunt spurs are compulsory for the Fédération Equestre Internationale (FEI) standard dressage tests and for advanced horse trials. But no particular pattern of spur is specified. Spurs are allowed at intermediate and novice horse trials, for Pony Club activities and in polo games.

German Spurs

Spurs in Germany are usually of a single-strap pattern; they are similar to the Prince of Wales but have very long shanks.

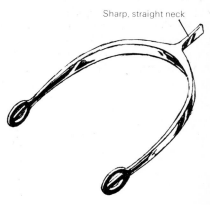

Sharp, straight neck

No-Strap Spur

The no-strap spur is, as its name implies, strapless. It is clamped tightly to the heel of the boot by tapering shanks. The neck is usually rowelled.

Box Spur

This spur is worn with riding trousers and is often ceremonial. It is kept in place without straps and is set into a spur box at the heel of the boot.

WESTERN RIDING

Western Bridles and Bits

Western bridles, bits and other head-gear run the gamut from inexpensive bridles with simple snaffle or curb bits to handsome silver show bridles with silver-engraved bits. Between these extremes is a vast range of equipment, some of it specifically for curing the various training problems that arise.

The bits and headgear used also vary from one part of America to another, and with the particular event in which horses are shown or otherwise used. 'Western' horses are used for such wide-ranging events as cutting (cattle), rodeo, showing, gymkhana, cowboy polo, pleasure and competitive trail riding, and everyday ranch work.

The following are the most popular bits and bridles used:

Ring snaffle
The ring snaffle, such as the *D*-ring, or eggbutt, is the standard snaffle bit in America. It is used also on racehorses, so much so that it is known as the *D-ring* or *D-cheek race snaffle*.

Shank Snaffle
The shank snaffle is a bit that has a snaffle mouthpiece combined with long shanks (cheeks) that give the rider leverage. It is used with a curb strap (curb chain).

Two of the most popular shank snaffles are the *Argentine* and the *Tom Thumb*. The Argentine has flat cheeks, which are long and have rings for the reins on a level with the mouthpiece. It works on the same leverage principle as the curb, but because the mouthpiece is jointed (broken) it combines this with the snaffle's nutcracker effect.

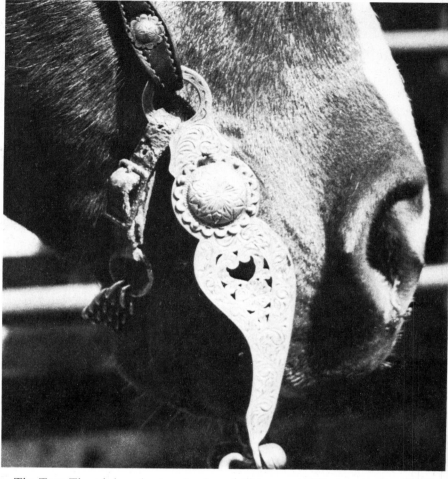

The Tom Thumb has shorter shanks than the Argentine shank snaffle. They are rounded, rather than flat. The Tom Thumb works on the same principles as the Argentine, but its shorter shanks give the rider less leverage, and the bit is consequently milder.

Some authorities say that because the shank snaffle is not a true snaffle,

A silver-mounted Western shank snaffle. The bit has a snaffle mouth married to curb cheeks. The attachments of the reins to the bit cheeks are of a typical Western design.

it should not be referred to as such. The prefix 'shank', however, is used to differentiate it from a true snaffle. The action of the shank snaffle is the same as that of a curb, yet it always has a snaffle mouthpiece.

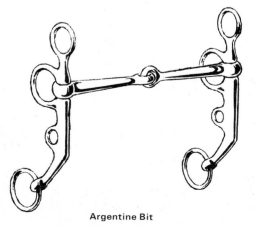

Argentine Bit

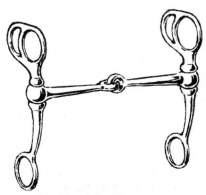

Tom Thumb Snaffle (Colt) Bit

Hackamore

The hackamore, which has already been discussed in detail, is a headstall with a thick nosepiece called a *bosal*, which is made of braided rawhide. The bosal should be kept soft and pliable so as to stop the nose or jaws becoming sore. Some hackamores, especially in Texas and the east, are made with a simple rope nosepiece.

Curb

A curb bit is a leverage bit that has shanks and a solid-bar mouthpiece rather than a jointed one. The shanks vary in length and in design. Many are plain, but some are silver-mounted.

The length of the shanks obviously determines the amount of leverage the bit exerts upon the mouth and poll. Mouthpieces range from straight-bar varieties to those with a high port that offers more room for the tongue.

Spade

The spade bit derives its name from the spade (spoon or port) that rises from the mouthpiece. A true spade has braces (sidebars) extending from the cheekpieces to the bottom of the spoon at each side, to prevent the horse putting his tongue over the bit. Some braces begin halfway along the mouthpiece.

Spade mouthpieces are always straight-bar. Their spoons, which may be rounded or flat at the top, often have a central roller (cricket) to act as a pacifier. Copper rollers on the mouthpiece increase moisture in the mouth even more. The bit cheeks are usually silver-mounted in beautiful designs.

Spades are seldom used today because of the great length of time needed to train a horse to work well in them. The spade has a particularly undeserved reputation for being cruel. The real severity of the spade, as with any bit, depends upon the hands of the rider using it.

Half-Breed Bits

True half-breed bits are those that are like spade bits but have the side braces and the spoon removed, and this is the reason for their name. The true half-breed always has a straight-bar mouthpiece and a narrow port of about 38 to 45 mm (1½ to 1¾ in.) wide and about 38 mm high, often with a roller.

As with the spade, the cheeks are usually silver-mounted in intricate designs. They are also loose-jawed (slide-cheek or loose-cheek), fastening

Fiador

Headpiece (crownpiece)

Browband

Cheekpiece

Bosal of plaited rawhide

Mecate (hair rope reins)

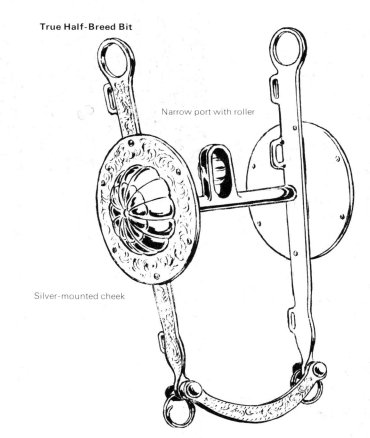

True Half-Breed Bit

Narrow port with roller

Silver-mounted cheek

loosely to the mouthpiece rather than being fixed.

Training Bits and Headgear

In the south west and along the west coast, the majority of trainers break colts using a ring snaffle. They prefer this bit because it affords easier control of the colt and because they feel they can teach lateral flexion better with it, the colt learning quickly to 'follow his head'.

The colt is then generally put into a hackamore, especially if he is to be trained for reining and cow-horse work. In fact, in classes for this work, young horses are often shown in the hackamore through their five-year-old year. The theory is that the colt may be taught to perform such Western movements as to figure-eight, slide and spin and handle cattle, without his mouth being damaged.

Even though a young horse may be shown in a hackamore, many trainers school in the snaffle bit. It is felt that there is still no substitute for the snaffle for schooling and training, regardless of the age of the horse.

From the hackamore, the horse is put 'into the bridle' or 'straight up in the bridle', as it is often referred to. This means using a bridle fitted with a curb or a half-breed, which are the most common bits used in this part of the country. Once again, the trainer often schools the horse in the snaffle and running martingale, even though he may be already used to the curb or half-breed.

In some parts of the country, trainers often use a hackamore to break a colt initially, then put him into the snaffle or shank snaffle for all schooling. The Tom Thumb and Argentine shank snaffles are particularly popular for this.

Bits for Showing and Competing

Many major shows in the United States are governed by the rules of the American Horse Shows Association (AHSA) or the American Quarter Horse Association (AQHA). AHSA rules allow young horses to be shown in some events in the hackamore until they are six years old, and the AQHA permits it until they are five. After this, horses in judged events, including reining and pleasure, must be shown in standard bits, such as curbs, half-breeds or spades.

In recent years, specialized events called *Snaffle Bit Futurities* have been growing tremendously in popularity. These futurities operate under their own rules and are limited to three-year olds of any breed that are shown in snaffle bits. Each horse is shown in a reining pattern and must also work cattle.

Pleasure futurities for horses of either two or three years old are also very popular. In these, horses may be shown in curbs, snaffles or hacka-mores, depending upon the rules of each futurity.

In timed events such as barrel racing, pole bending and calf roping, held as part of horse shows, rodeos and gymkhanas, almost any type of head-gear is permissible. Hackamores are very popular for these events, partly because they afford excellent control and partly because the rider, being preoccupied with making the best possible time, does not then have to worry about hurting the horse's mouth.

Generally, hackamores are used with a tie-down to keep the horse's head in position. This is a strap, rope or wire used in the same way as a standing martingale, but attached either to a breastgirth or to the cinch (girth). Again, if the rider is concentrating on time, he will do better if the head is anchored into position. This can be difficult for some horsemen to appreciate, but there are often thousands of dollars at stake as prize money in timed events.

Bridles

Silver-mounted or silver-trimmed bridles (headstalls) are extremely popular in the American show ring for judged events, such as pleasure, trail horse, equitation and reining. The

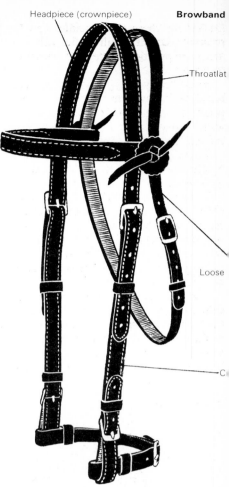

Headpiece (crownpiece)   **Browband**

Throatlat

Loose

C

A silver-mounted browband bridle—one of the two major styles of Western bridle. A separate throatlatch runs through an elongated browband and over the poll of the horse.

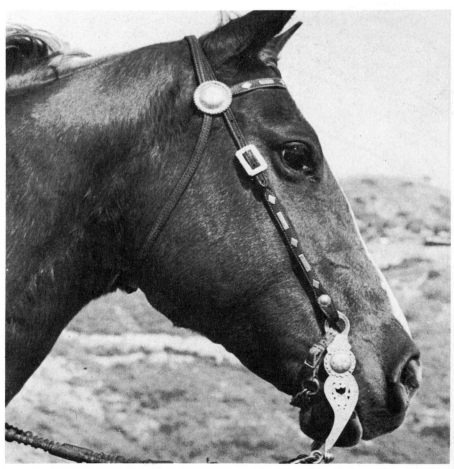

114

leather for these show bridles can be round or flat, although the flat varieties are more practical since they are easier to repair.

Some heavy-duty bridles have been lined with rawhide, but this is not practical. The rawhide becomes soft with sweat, then dries hard and inflexible.

There are two styles of Western bridle; the browband and the one-ear (split-ear).

The browband bridle, which is fitted with headpiece, cheekpieces, browband and throatlatch, is the most popular variety. It is double-sewn, and the headpiece and the throatlatch are made separately, being joined by three double loops.

The one-ear has a headpiece with a split in it on one side, through which the horse's ear passes. This anchors the bridle and there is therefore no need for a browband or throatlatch. This pattern is used often on working stock horses.

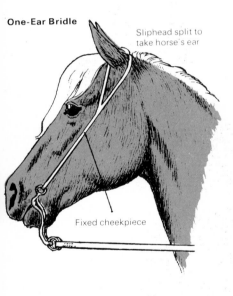

One-Ear Bridle

Sliphead split to take horse's ear

Fixed cheekpiece

Nosebands are hardly ever used, except for decoration or by the Argentine gauchos. But a halter is often fitted either over or under the bridle so that the horse can be easily tethered. In judged events, nosebands, including cavessons (cavasons) are not permitted. Curb chains are permissible.

On the west coast, most riders use reins and a *romal*. The reins are closed and on the end is attached the *romal*— a long strap of leather. Often the rider holds the *romal* when he is working cattle and needs to ride single-handed. The horse is turned by neck-reining.

In other parts of the country, split reins are more popular. They are simply reins that are separate, not joined together along their length. When dropped, they hang down in front of the horse, who is trained to halt when they are in this position, and therefore does not need to be tied up.

Other American Bridles and Bits

American Saddlebred, Arab and Morgan Bridles and Bits

American Saddlebreds, Arabs and Morgans all have rather more ornate bridles than the ordinary patterns of English bridle. Browbands and nosebands are made of leather, but are coated in plastic in eye-catching colours. These colours are chosen not only to co-ordinate with the clothes of the rider but with the colour of the horse, too.

Saddlebreds are invariably schooled in some type of snaffle with a running martingale. Even a prospective five-gaited horse receives all his training in a snaffle, and not until he is proficient in all five gaits is he put into a full double bridle. (The five gaits are the walk, trot, slow gait, rack and canter).

Both three-gaited and five-gaited Saddlebreds are shown in double bridles with curbs that have exceptionally long cheeks of between 178

and 203 mm (7 and 8 in.). The mouthpieces may have low or high ports, some of which are square and some of which have rollers set inside to help to make the horse mouth.

American Race Bridles

Race bridles are often known as the 'English' pattern, although they have the American style of separate throatlatch passing over the poll. Usually, race bridles are of excellent quality leather that is no more than 16 mm ($\frac{5}{8}$ in.) thick. Most are brown but a few are made in white leather.

Californian Elevator Bit

The elevator bit is a new pattern of bit, invented by Jimmy A. Williams, of California. It is a smooth, broken snaffle with a long shank. It is used with a snaffle rein and a curb rein in the same way as a Pelham, but with far greater leverage. The bit is designed to elevate the head by the use of the snaffle rein and achieve flexion with the curb rein.

Tennessee Walking Horse Bit and Bridle

Tennessee walking horses have a bit designed specially for them. This is known simply as the *walking horse bit*. It is a curb with extremely long cheeks of between 203 and 254 mm (8 and 10 in.). This length gives the rider enough leverage to control the horse for the showy running walk and rocking-horse canter. Mouthpieces of walking horse bits are fitted with ports of medium height.

Bridles for Tennessee walking horses always have a cavesson noseband and curb chain to act with the bit. Tiedowns and martingales are never used.

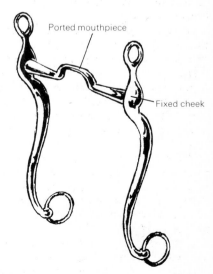

Ported mouthpiece

Fixed cheek

Walking Horse Bit

Bridle Facts

- The most usual materials for Western bridles are rawhide and latigo (soft, oil-tanned leather). Nylon bridles are popular for timed events because they are durable and require little upkeep.

- Expensive silver-trimmed bridles are not suitable for everyday use, and are reserved solely for the show ring.

- The use of snaps (spring hooks) instead of buckles at the bit end of a bridle facilitates changing bits over or using the same bridle on different horses.

Western Saddles

The Western saddle now used in America is descended from the saddle on which the knights of the Middle Ages went into battle. Early in the sixteenth century, the Spanish Conquistadores brought the heavy, deep-seated saddles to the Americas, and from these the true Western stock saddles have been developed over the years.

Modern Western saddles retain the traditional high cantle, deep seat and set-back stirrups to give the characteristic straight-legged seat. But the pommel has become a tall and flat-topped horn to take the stock lasso.

These saddles are extremely strong, but they are also heavy, their weight depending largely on the amount of metal used to decorate them. This weight is distributed over a wide area of the horse's back, however, and the Western horse appears to bear the weight easily, even during days of continuous work.

Western saddles vary according to the type of riding for which they are designed. There are, for example, saddles specifically for cutting and roping cattle, trail riding, barrel racing and general use, and even for riding broncs in rodeos.

The basic parts of all Western saddles are similar.

An ornately-tooled Western saddle with a wide fork designed to help the rider maintain a secure seat. The saddle is fitted with double rigging shown by the extra cinch at the rear. This rear cinch may be fastened fairly loosely since it is secondary to the front cinch. The front cinch is set back from under the saddle point. Full rigging means that the cinch is fastened directly below the point.

Western Virtues

● A well-made Western saddle will fit almost any horse. It is constructed to give a good universal fit over a folded blanket.

● The Western is designed to provide comfort and security rather than to aid fine horsemanship. And, although heavy, it is kind to the horse because it holds the rider firmly in position.

● Perhaps the greatest merit of the Western saddle is that the weight of saddle and rider is distributed over a large area of the horse's back.

Tree

The tree, the skeleton of the saddle, is today made either of hardwood or of a synthetic material such as glass fibre. Usually, it is covered with rawhide or with bullhide, sometimes of double thickness. Bullhide is the tougher of the two.

There are four basic types of trees, designed to fit the four main types of withers and backs common in Western horses. The *regular tree* is designed to fit a horse with prominent withers and a back with a pronounced slope, such as the Thoroughbred. The *semi-Quarter horse tree* is built for the horse with an average back and withers. The *full-Quarter horse tree* is wider and is for the animal with flatter, 'mutton' withers and a broad back. Finally, the *Arabian tree* is built to cope with the short, level back and unpronounced withers of the typical Arab horse.

For the average, all-round Western horse of today, the semi-Quarter horse tree is usually best. It will fit horses of all breeds that have good withers and backs.

Fork

The forks of Western saddles range from the narrow *A*-fork to the extra-wide fork with undercut or rounded *swells*—the leather surrounding the pommel just below the horn. The type of fork and swells affects the amount of leg room available between cantle and swells. A slick (very narrow) fork allows a lot of room. But a wide fork with rounded swells reduces it. A wide fork with undercut swells can help to brace the rider's legs and give him a far more secure seat.

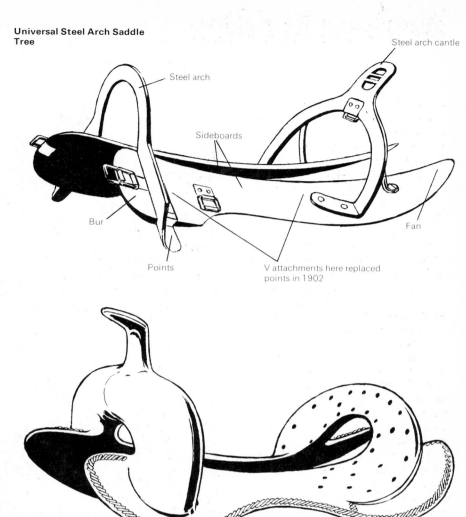

Universal Steel Arch Saddle Tree

Steel arch

Steel arch cantle

Sideboards

Bur

Points

Fan

V attachments here replaced points in 1902

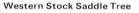

Western Stock Saddle Tree

Western Saddle Swells

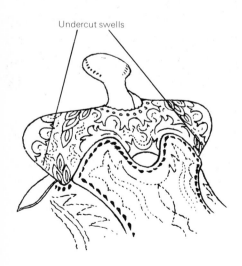

Undercut swells

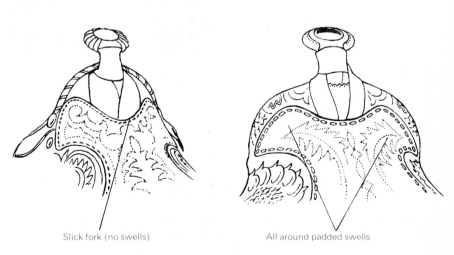

Slick fork (no swells)

All around padded swells

Horn

The horn is fixed firmly to the pommel of the saddle. It is made of steel covered with leather; the lasso (lariat or reata) is dallied (tied) over it when the rider is holding a roped animal. The horn and pommel may extend as high as 33 cm (13 in.) from the saddle. The cantle reaches only 10 cm (4 in.).

Unless a rider plans to rope cattle, any type of horn is suitable for most riding. The calf roper, however, likes a tall horn. This is sometimes called a *two-rope horn*, since it allows room for tying two or more ropes.

A dally roper, such as a team roper, likes a tall, straight horn that allows plenty of room for taking his dallies. Usually, a dally horn is covered in rubber to prevent the dallies slipping.

Seat

Seats vary in type according to the use to which they are put. A cutting horse saddle, for example, has a much flatter seat than any other Western saddle.

Most seats have quilting or other padding for comfort. This is then covered with suede or roughout leather to help keep the rider in the saddle. Often, highly complex patterns are stitched into the saddle seat.

Seats also vary in size, the correct length depending not on the horse but on the rider. Most women take a 380 or 390 mm (15 or 15½ in.) seat. Men usually take a longer seat.

Skirts

Skirts help to make the saddle fit down on the horse and stay in position. On some saddles, they also anchor the rigging.

Skirts may be round or square. The choice is often a matter of personal preference, but there are a few factors to keep in mind:

Square skirts on a short-backed horse might dig into the flank area in front of the hip bones. On a big horse, however, a saddle with square skirts looks better because it is more in proportion to his size. Some ropers feel that square skirts, or large round skirts, tend to distribute pressure more evenly and across a wider area of the horse's back than do small round skirts.

Rigging

Basically, saddles are rigged either *on-*

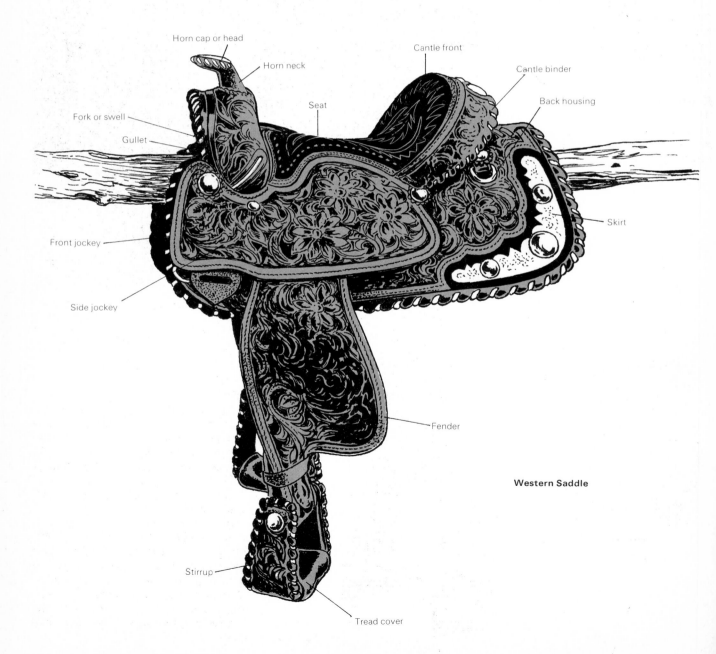

Western Saddle

the-tree or *in-skirt*. These terms indicate where the front rigging holding the cinch is attached: either to the tree or to the skirt.

Rigging is described as *full double, seven-eighths double, three-quarters double* or *single*. *Double* rigging indicates that the saddle has both front and back cinches. *Single* indicates just one cinch. With a full-double rigging, the front cinch is positioned right under the fork. The other positions move progressively closer to the centre of the saddle.

Ropers invariably use a saddle that has a back cinch to stabilize its rear. Many reining-horse riders do the same. These back cinches do not have to be pulled up as tightly as those at the front.

The nearside cinch ring has the *latigo* fixed to it. The latigo is a soft leather strap of about 1·8 m (6 ft) in length, which is passed through the ring on the cinch and gradually pulled tight.

Stirrup Leathers

The stirrup leathers are combined with sweat flaps (*fender sudadero*) and are attached to the saddle tree. They are often highly decorated.

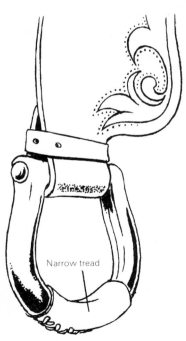

Oxbow Stirrup

Narrow tread

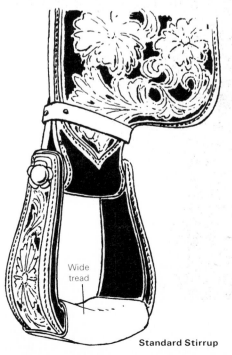

Standard Stirrup

Wide tread

A heavily-tooled Western sweat flap (fender sudadero). This forms the stirrup leather and flap combined. In front of the sweat flap is the ring cinch fastening, and below is the heavy Western stirrup.

Stirrups

Western stirrups are heavy. Generally, they are made from curved oak in the pattern known as *oxbow*. The footplates (treads) are covered in leather. The standard width of footplate is 50–75 mm (2–3 in.), but a narrow tread of about 20 mm ($\frac{7}{8}$ in.) is available.

In South America, the box pattern of stirrup known as *tapadero* is in general use. It is covered by a leather hood designed to give the rider's foot even greater protection from injury than normal patterns. All Western stirrups are intended, however, to protect the foot and to give quick release in case of a fall.

A Western saddle in use. The swells in front of the rider's upper thigh keep her almost locked into the typical Western straight-leg position. This type of saddle is extremely comfortable for the rider during long hours on horseback.

Types of Western Saddles

The following are among the most popular types of Western saddles in the United States. All are made by leading saddle manufacturers such as Tex Tan, Potts Longhorn and Circle Y, as well as by custom saddlemakers.

All-Around Saddle
As its name implies, the all-around saddle can be used satisfactorily for almost every type of activity. It is the general purpose saddle of the Western scene.

Generally, the seat is moderate in depth to allow the rider to stand easily in the stirrups for roping, or to stay in the saddle for equitation or pleasure riding. The cantle varies from about 60 to 70 mm ($2\frac{1}{2}$ to 3 in.) in height, and always has a roll at the top, called a *Cheyenne roll* (cantle binding).

Generally, this saddle is made with a full-double or seven-eighths double rigging. It can be ordered with any type of finish, from plain to basket weave or hand-tooled floral designs, with or without silver. Its weight ranges from 16 to 18 kg (35 to 40 lb), but it can be made even heavier.

Equitation Saddle
The seat of a good equitation saddle is moderate in depth. If it is too flat, the rider has trouble in sitting correctly. If it is too deep, it sandwiches the rider so that he can hardly move at all. Stirrups should be hung in such a way that the rider is able to keep a straight leg position.

Equitation saddles often have the back cinch removed so that they do not interfere with the leg cues (aids). Since these saddles are almost always used in the show ring, they generally have hand tooling of some kind and silver trim. Their weight is between 13·5 and 18 kg (30 and 40 lb).

Barrel Racing Saddle
Barrel racing saddles are used for a variety of timed events. They are therefore stripped down to make them as light as possible. Some weigh as little as 10·5 kg (23 lb), which for a Western saddle is very light indeed!

Many barrel racing saddles have undercut swells to provide more security for the rider, in-skirt rigging and just one cinch. Small skirts help to minimize weight.

Roping Saddle
Roping saddles are built for rugged use and generally have double rawhide-covered or bullhide-covered trees. They have double rigging, usually either full-double or seven-eighths double. Generally, the cinches are extra-wide, having as many as 27 strands. This spreads the sudden jerks the cinch receives—when the rider ropes a steer—over a wider area of the

horse's girth, so that he is not injured.

Roping stirrups are deeper than average to allow the feet to slip out quickly, so that the rider is not caught up after a fall.

These saddles can weigh up to 20·5 kg (45 lb), and may be ordered with any type of tooling, with or without silver.

Cutting Horse Saddle

The cutting horse saddle has changed considerably during the last 10 to 15 years. Formerly, it had an extremely deep seat, but now it is very flat. Cutting horse trainers and riders prefer the flat seat because they can stay in better balance with the horse. They say, too, that a rider who is jerked out of position during a sharp turn can get back into the saddle more easily with a flat seat than with the old deep seat.

Oxbow stirrups are standard on cutting horse saddles because it is almost impossible for the rider to lose them during the swift turns of the cutting horse—provided of course that they have been adjusted to the correct length.

Accessories

Many Western riders use breastcollars (breastgirths), some for a specific function, others merely for decoration. Ropers use them to help keep the saddle in place during hard jerks or pulls. Breastcollars must be adjusted so that there is no pressure on the horse's windpipe, or interference with the shoulder action.

Some breastcollars have a loop on the outside and are used with a tie-down to keep the head in position. The tie-down must not be adjusted too short or it will interfere with the horse's forward movement.

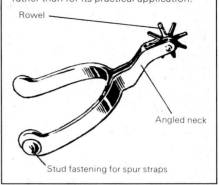

The Western Spur
The rowell spur has a 'sun' wheel of radiating points which turns freely. It is said to have originated in Spain and, certainly, it was introduced into the Americas by the Spanish. Often, the spur is highly decorated, sometimes in silver, and today it is usually worn for effect rather than for its practical application.

Rowel

Angled neck

Stud fastening for spur straps

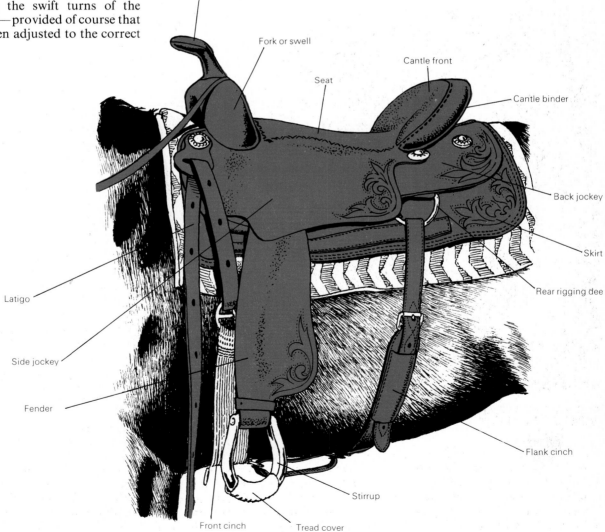

Cutting Horse Saddle

DRIVING

Driving

Harness for driving was the first equipment invented for the horse. It is appropriate therefore that driving and harness-making are at the centre of a great modern revival.

The story of harness for horses began about 2000 BC, when yokes were first used. These were mechanically inefficient not only because of their too-high point of traction but because the neck strap pressed against the horse's windpipe and jugular vein.

One form of yoke harness employed by the Romans is still in use today in India. This is the chariot rig, which is a lighter modification of the oxen yoke. It has no traces, and the traction upon the vehicle pole must come straight from the yoke.

Modern forms of harness were perfected in Asia and introduced to Europe in about AD 800. Neck and breast collars were in use by that time. Three centuries later, the whiffletree—invented to equalize the pull of the traces by joining two sets of harness—had become common.

Although driving was brought about by necessity, it soon became a means of sport and entertainment. Just as chariot races captivated Roman audiences, so, in more recent times, private drivers took to wagering upon their own skills and the speed of their animals in front of admiring crowds. These and other less-spirited types also took pains to cut a fashionable figure in society. Their horses were subjected to such cruel pieces of harness as tight bearing reins to obtain high, flexed headcarriages, and fancy, long-cheeked and high-ported bits. Generally, these fashions are now dead, though Hackneys are still shown in bearing reins.

By the early 1900s, the popularity of driving—and therefore of the harness-maker's trade—had reached a peak in Europe and elsewhere. From then, it gradually declined, until World War 1 gave rise to a need for military and farm harness.

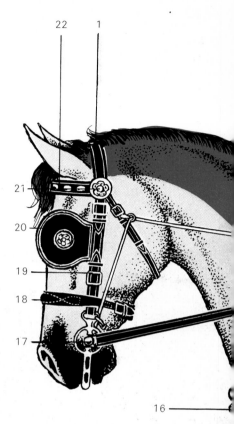

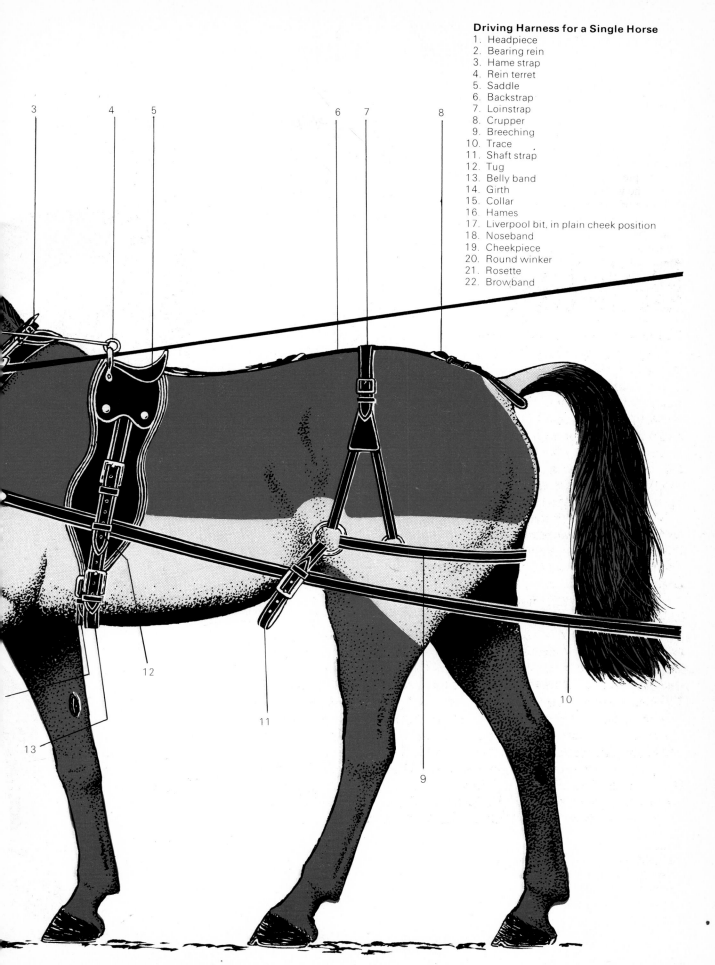

Driving Harness for a Single Horse
1. Headpiece
2. Bearing rein
3. Hame strap
4. Rein terret
5. Saddle
6. Backstrap
7. Loinstrap
8. Crupper
9. Breeching
10. Trace
11. Shaft strap
12. Tug
13. Belly band
14. Girth
15. Collar
16. Hames
17. Liverpool bit, in plain cheek position
18. Noseband
19. Cheekpiece
20. Round winker
21. Rosette
22. Browband

Driving Bridles and Bits

Bridles

The driving bridle consists of a head-piece placed over the horse's ears, to which cheekpieces are attached in the same way as in a riding bridle. The cheekpieces carry not only the bit but also the winkers and the noseband.

The browband, which passes across the forehead and is attached to the headpiece by loops, is often decorated with a design in either brass or white metal. A plain or ornamental rosette in matching metal covers the browband loops.

The throatlatch passes under the throat. It is buckled just tight enough to stop the bridle from being pulled off.

Bridles are sometimes further embellished by the addition of a purely ornamental facedrop, made of leather and decorated with a metal crest or monogram. This is buckled from the poll to hang in the centre of the forehead.

Most private driving bridles are similar to those used for riding, apart from the noseband and winker attachments. However, some are quite different, having cheekpieces with decorative swells and (in place of browbands) earbands curving from the headpiece round the front of the ears to the temples.

For heavy horses, large buckled bridles are normal. These should weigh no more than 2 kg (4½ lb), however large the horse may be.

Another pattern of bridle is called full-faced. It has a broad piece of leather joining the top of the headpiece to the browband and continuing down the nose to the noseband.

Full-face bridles are warm for the horse; but they are heavy and may also sweat up the horse's face.

Winkers (Blinkers or Blinders)

When winkers are worn, the bridle is known as 'closed'. Bridles without winkers are termed 'open'.

Winkers are available in many different designs: round, square, shell-shaped, D-shaped or hatchet-shaped. Usually, they carry the owner's crest or monogram as decoration in the centre. They are supported by two winker stays buckled to the top of the headpiece.

The purpose of using winkers is often questioned. The usual explana-

Winkers

D

Round

Hatchet

Square

tion for them is that they prevent the horse seeing the vehicle behind him and taking fright. This argument does not entirely hold water, since all military and many commercial horses have been trained to work without winkers with no ill effect.

Bits

The only direct contact between horse and driver is on the mouth, via the reins and bit. The movements made by the driver's hands are transmitted to the bars, lips, tongue, roof of the mouth, poll, curb groove and nose in the same way as in ordinary riding.

Notwithstanding the extremely delicate nature of these seven points of control, drivers of the past invented bits that were not only instruments of torture but also quickly destroyed their horses' mouths. However, the

Care and Positioning of the Bridle

- It is important to hang bridles, and all pieces of harness equipment, in a dry room. A special rack can be used which gives separate support to the winkers and ensures that the bridle is hung correctly.

- Care should be taken that the winkers are correctly positioned when the bridle is put on the horse. The horse's eye should be central to the winker, and the stay strap must not be too tight.

Wearing Winkers

- In driving, the whip may be used to encourage the horse or to distract him in an emergency. Without winkers, he may see the whip coming and anticipate the correction.

- If winkers are not worn in pair or team harness, the horse that does not need correction may see the whip and take fright.

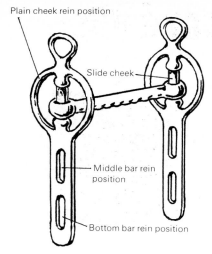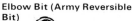

standard driving bits in use today are unlikely to damage the mouth if used correctly.

There are several varieties, the most common being the Wilson snaffle, and the Liverpool, Buxton and Elbow curbs.

Wilson Snaffle
The Wilson snaffle is a plain, jointed snaffle with four ring cheeks, two attached to the mouthpiece and two hanging loose. Usually, the reins are buckled to both rings. But if they are fastened to the fixed rings only, the mouthpiece presses on the tongue and roof of the mouth whilst the loose rings squeeze the lips. A control as severe as this should be used only in extreme cases.

Liverpool Curb
The Liverpool curb is the most common driving bit. It is similar to the riding Pelham.

A closed bridle designed for use on a heavy horse. The browband and facedrop are decorated in silver, and the headpiece rosette bears the monogram of the owner. The winkers are square. The most common driving bit—the Liverpool curb—is coupled to the reins in the least severe plain-cheek position. The bit is buckled to the noseband and cheekpiece combined, to cut down on unnecessary clutter.

Liverpool Bit

Plain cheek rein position
Slide cheek
Middle bar rein position
Bottom bar rein position

The bit has a straight-bar mouthpiece, one side of which is smooth, the other corrugated. The rough side should never be used against the sensitive bars.

The mouthpiece varies in width and may be covered in leather for softness. Ports of varying sizes may be incorporated, either to make room for the tongue or to stop the horse getting his tongue over the bit.

The bit cheeks are circular, with hooks for the curb chain, extending to straight bars. Each of the bars has two slots to which the rein billets may be buckled. The slots are called 'middle bar' and 'bottom bar'.

The reins may be attached to the bit in four different positions, with increasing degrees of severity.

When buckled to the cheek rings, the position is known as 'plain cheek', and is the least severe. When the billets are placed round the arms of the bit below the mouthpiece, a slight bearing is given on the curb and this is known as 'rough cheek'. When they are slotted into either of the two lower positions, middle bar or bottom bar, the curb action is more pronounced. Both of these fittings should be used with caution. Bottom bar should be used only for hard-pulling horses.

Liverpool bits are made in various patterns, having fixed, sliding or swivel cheeks, and a variety of lower arms. Some have room for three bar adjustments. For coaching or pairs, the ends of the bit arms are joined together to prevent the bits becoming entangled.

Buxton Curb
The Buxton is a variation of the Liverpool. It has the same action, but is much larger and more ornate, with curved arms. It is suitable for smart pairs and teams and ceremonial occasions.

Elbow Curb (Army Reversible Bit)
The elbow bit, too, has an action similar to that of the Liverpool. Its cheeks are right-angled back from the mouthpiece, away from the lips. The purpose of this design is to prevent a horse taking the cheek arms in his mouth and being able to bolt.

Although used much by professional coachmen in the past, the elbow is not often seen in private driving today. It has a variation called the *Wimbush bit*.

Elbow Bit (Army Reversible Bit)

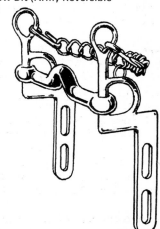

Collars and Driving Saddles

Neck Collar

A horse's neck collar—oval in shape, padded and covered with leather—should fit well enough to lie flat on the horse's shoulder. Two metal hames fit into a groove around it, and to these are attached the traces. It is by means of the collar that the motive power from the horse's shoulder is transmitted to the load. The collar therefore constitutes by far the most important piece of equipment. Careful manufacture and fitting are vital to the horse's well-being.

Usually, collars are covered in either brown or black leather—patent leather for smart turnouts—lined with soft leather, wool or serge. They are stuffed with horsehair, rye straw or flock.

Collars vary not only in size, according to the type and size of animals that wear them, but also in design. One distinctive design is the piped collar (windpipe collar) used to keep pressure off the windpipe. A tubular metal pipe fitted to the inside of the collar prevents it pressing in on the windpipe. Other familiar collars are described as plain, straight, bent and peaked at the withers.

Most collars are completely closed and are put on upside down so that the widest part of the collar passes over the broadest part of the head. They are then turned round so that the pointed ends are uppermost, and are put into position flat on the shoulders. To facilitate the putting on of a collar, it can be stretched temporarily by inserting the knee against the inside and pulling hard on it.

If a collar is too tight for a horse it will impede his breathing. If it is too loose, it will rub his neck raw in places. There should be just enough room to place the hand between the bottom of the collar and the horse's windpipe.

Open-Top Collars

Open-top (split) neck collars are made for animals that have exceptionally large heads, such as heavy horses and donkeys, and for those that do not take kindly to collars being put over their heads. These collars are open at the top so that their sides can be forced far enough apart to slip round the neck. They are then buckled securely, usually with two straps.

Breast Collar

Instead of having a neck collar, a horse is sometimes fitted with a breast collar. This type of collar consists of a padded breastpiece, to which the tug buckles are attached, supported by a neckstrap with rein terrets. The breast collar predated the neck collar. Its disadvantage is that it fits too low on the horse for comfortable pulling of heavy loads.

A heavy type of breast collar is used on such army harness horses as are still in service. One pattern has two supporting straps and a zinc collar pad to protect the horse's withers.

Although not as smart or as suitable for heavy loads as neck collars, breast collars have the advantage of being easier to fit, since with only minor adjustments they can be used on any horse. But in order to reduce the risk of chafing the horse's chest, it is advisable to use a swingletree (bar) with them.

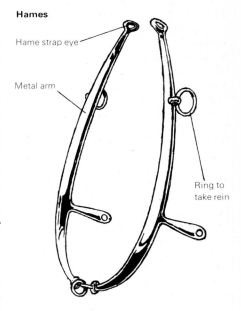

Hames

Hame strap eye

Metal arm

Ring to take rein

Hames

The hames are two tubular metal arms that fit snugly into grooves on either side of the neck collar. The traces are attached to them. Formerly, hames were made of wood. Today, they are fashioned out of high-quality steel, plated with brass or white metal.

The top ends of the hames have eyes through which a small strap, the 'hame strap', is slotted to fasten them together. At the bottom, there are similar eyes for a strap, or hame hooks for a chain or a kidney link.

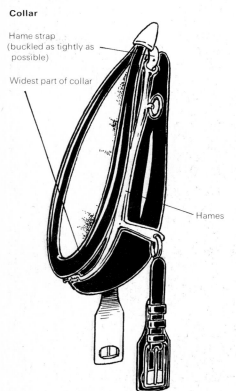

Collar

Hame strap (buckled as tightly as possible)

Widest part of collar

Hames

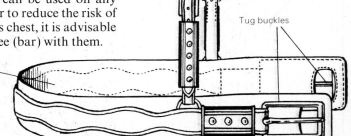

Breast Collar

Tug buckles

Padded breastpiece

Near the top of each hame is a ring, which may be either swivelled or fixed. The reins pass through it. Towards the bottom are generally two rings to which the traces are attached. But in some cases, the traces are riveted to a short projection from the hames.

Saddles

A saddle is used in single harness to take a small part of the weight of the load and to provide balance. It is heavier and more substantial than the pad, which is its equivalent in pair turnouts when there is no weight to be supported on the horse's neck.

Usually, saddles are made of leather with well-stuffed panels on either side. They are lined with soft leather or cloth. As with riding saddles, care must be taken to ensure that they do not bear down upon the spine, but on the back and ribs.

On the top of the saddle are two terrets, with rings through which the reins are threaded. In front of these is a hook for attaching a bearing rein or an overcheck, and at the back there is a D-ring for the crupper strap.

A channel provides room for the girth—which passes under the horse's belly and straps on either side —and the backband. The backband carries the tugs through which the shafts of the vehicle pass. It then runs through a loop in the girth beneath the horse's belly and is buckled, either on one side only or on both sides. Its aim is to prevent the shafts rising.

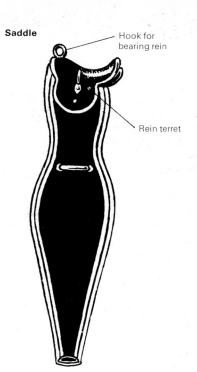

Saddle

Hook for bearing rein

Rein terret

Pads

Pads have much the same function as saddles but are very much lighter in construction, since they do not have either a backband or tugs attached. They must be well padded and their pattern should match that of the winkers and padcloth. Often, they are made of patent leather.

Pads are used in pair harness. Their purpose is to carry the tug buckle to which the traces are attached.

A well-fitting full neck collar for a heavy horse, with hames, reins and shepherd's lock attached. The hame strap joins the steel hames at the top. Lower down, a rein terret takes the rein from the bit. At the bottom, the shepherd's lock holds the chain traces.

Pad

Bearing rein hook

Rein terret

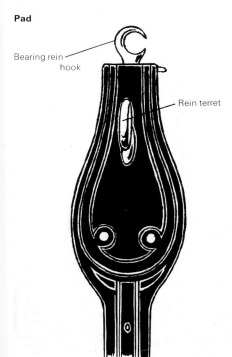

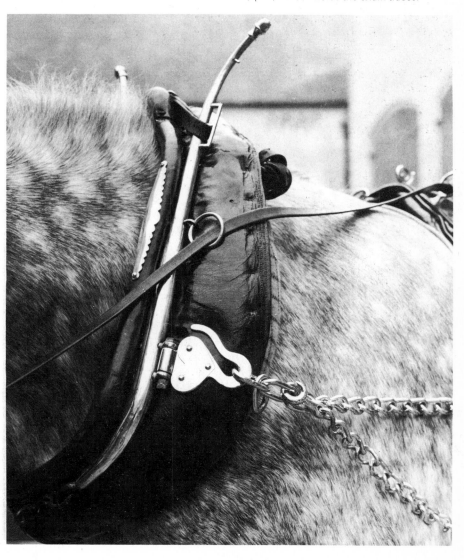

Reins and Other Driving Leathers

A pair-horse pad, fitted at the top with rein terrets to feed the reins from the neck collar terrets to the hands of the driver. The reins are looped over the terrets to stop them being broken by the horse's feet trampling on them.

Adjustable crupper backstrap

Reins

Leather driving reins are always brown, whether the rest of the harness is brown or black. Sometimes, they are stitched.

Reins should not be too wide. Approximately 25 mm (1 in.) is a good width to handle.

Each rein has a billet at one end to attach it to the bit, and the other ends are joined with a buckle and keeper. Some people prefer to dispense with the buckle and to rely on a firm keeper only. Then, should an accident occur, the driver cannot become caught up in the ends of the reins.

Reins used in heavy horse harness for farm work are usually made of rope, and are called *lines*.

Bearing Reins and Overchecks

Bearing reins and overchecks are both designed to keep the horse's head up. Bearing reins are not often used today, except in show Hackney classes and in heavy horse work on a farm. Overchecks are used mainly in the United States for harness racing.

Bearing reins may be of two different patterns: pulley or plain. Both are made of rolled leather, one end being attached to a special hook on the saddle or pad, and both require bridoon snaffle bits in addition to the driving bit.

The pulley bearing rein is attached to the headpiece by buckles on either side of the horse's face. It passes through specially-constructed rollers on the snaffle bit cheeks, then through rings fixed by small straps to the headpiece, and then to the saddle or pad.

The plain bearing rein is far less complicated. It passes from the hook on the saddle or pad, through the rings at the sides of the headpiece and is then clipped onto the bit cheeks.

Overcheck reins are similar, but pass through a ring over the horse's poll, between the ears.

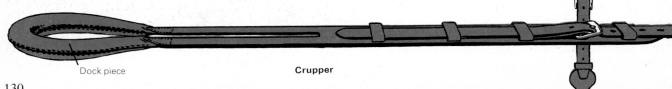

Dock piece

Crupper

Traces

Traces are usually composed of layers of leather joined together by as many as four rows of stitching. Adjustment is made either to the hame buckle or, in some cases, to a buckle on a separate short length of trace at the trace-hook end.

Traces should be of a length that positions the horse as close as possible to the vehicle trace-hooks, while keeping the quarters well clear of the foot-board. In commercial and heavy horse harness, the traces are frequently made of chain.

Martingales

Generally, the purpose of a martingale used in driving is to stop the collar riding up.

The basic martingale is a leather strap that runs from the girth up to the bottom of the collar. It is not attached to the noseband, bit or reins.

As a safety precaution, it is advisable to fasten the martingale round both collar and hames, in order to hold them together. In heavy harness, this type of martingale is often adorned with horse brasses.

Another type of martingale, called the *ring martingale*, is similar to the running pattern used in riding. Its two rings are passed over the reins to correct a too-high head carriage.

Cruppers

The dockpiece of the crupper is attached to the saddle or pad by means of the crupper backstrap. The purpose of the crupper is to keep the saddle or pad in place.

Crupper dockpieces may be fitted to the backstraps by means of one or two buckles on the dockpiece straps. But sometimes, the dockpiece and back-strap are made in one piece, and are then known as a *martingale crupper*. The martingale crupper has the advantages of looking neater and reducing the risk of reins or whip becoming entangled in the buckles. But it is more difficult to put on because the horse's tail must be folded and slotted through the dockpiece, which may prove difficult with a young or nervous horse which does not like its tail being touched.

With both designs, great care should be taken to ensure that the dockpiece is kept soft, pliable and clean. Some dockpieces are stuffed with linseed to keep them supple. Should they become hard, they will irritate the horse and cause sores that may take a long time to heal.

Breeching

The purpose of breeching is to enable the horse to take the weight of the vehicle on his quarters when descending a hill or backing. There are two main types: full breeching and false breeching. Both should be fitted in such a way that they do not interfere with the horse's quarters.

Full breeching consists of a wide strip of leather passing round the horse's quarters midway between the dock and the hocks—often 30–35 cm (12–14 in.) above the hocks. It is held in position by vertical loin straps passing up through the crupper backstrap, and is attached to dees on the shafts by means of rings and short breeching straps.

False breeching is simpler. It consists of a leather strap stretched straight across the quarters and attached to dees on the shafts. It is very practical for a two-wheeler.

With false breeching, a kicking strap is sometimes used. This strap passes over the top of the quarters and through the crupper backstrap, and is attached to dees on the shafts placed farther forward than those used for the breeching. As its name suggests, a kicking strap is designed to prevent a horse from raising his quarters in order to kick.

Long (Bristol) breeching is a third type of breeching. Here, the breeching strap is buckled not to the shaft but to the tug buckle. It is supported by a kicking strap.

Tugs

Tugs are strong leather loops connecting the shafts to the backband. They prevent the shafts moving up and down. Tugs may be either of the 'open' varieties, which do not open, or of the Tilbury or French patterns, which do.

Tilbury tugs are used principally with four-wheeled vehicles, where the shafts are usually independently hinged. This type of tug has a metal-reinforced leather-covered lower part for the shaft. The end loops back through the end of the buckle to secure the shaft.

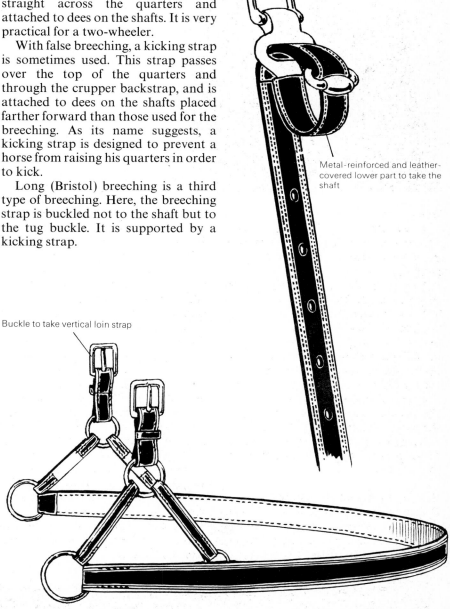

Tilbury Tug

Metal-reinforced and leather-covered lower part to take the shaft

Buckle to take vertical loin strap

Full Breeching

Single Harness

All harness, whether for heavy horses, Hackney ponies or donkeys, is basically similar. The size and design of the harness varies with the type and number of horses to be used, and with the vehicles.

Harness for the single horse comprises the following items: a *bridle*, with bit, and either with or without winkers; a *collar* which, when full, is used with hames and traces, though breast collars are worn only with traces; a *saddle*, with backband and tugs that are usually of the open variety but may be Tilbury tugs; a *crupper* and dockpiece, with breeching that is either full, long or false, and that may be used with a kicking strap; and *reins*.

Harnessing the Horse

By tradition, the first item of harness to be fitted is the collar. Next, the hames should be fitted into the grooves of the collar and buckled together at the top with the hame strap. The hame strap is a most important piece of the harness and should be checked regularly for soundness. If it were to break, the harness would drop off and the horse would be freed from the traces.

The saddle is then placed on the horse's back. The crupper is fitted, care being taken to see that there are no loose hairs in the way to cause irritation. Next, the breeching is fitted. If full breeching is to be used, this should be placed on the horse in position, ready for attachment to the vehicle.

The girth is threaded through the loop of the martingale, if this is being used, and buckled. It is correctly fitted if there is room for a hand to be run between it and the horse's body. Finally, the bellyband is made ready for the final adjustment.

The reins are then slotted through the terrets on the saddle and the rings on each side of the collar to await the bridle. This is fitted in the same way as a riding bridle, by holding the headpiece or cheekpieces in the right hand, easing the bit into the mouth with the left hand, and then drawing the bridle up over the horse's ears.

Care should be taken to check that the winkers are in the correct position and that the winker stays are not too tight. Otherwise, they will press painfully on the horse's eyes. The throatlatch is buckled, the noseband fastened and the curb chain fitted as for a riding bridle.

The rein billets are then threaded through the chosen slots on the bit rings or cheeks. The most usual position is rough cheek, the reins being fastened through the lower portions within the circle of the mouthpiece.

Once the vehicle has been drawn up, and the shafts slotted through the tugs, the traces are threaded between the girth and the bellyband, and hooked on to the appropriate fittings on the vehicle. When not in use, the traces are left to hang, looped up, from the hames so that the horse cannot become entangled in them. The breeching strap is then buckled on to the dees of the shaft and the horse is ready to be driven.

A smart pony fitted with full single neck-collar harness to a Dennett gig. Because it is a single harness, the pony is wearing a saddle rather than a pad. He is also wearing full breeching suspended from loin straps. The general impression is one of smartness, and the vehicle suits the pony's size and type.

Single Hackney Pony Harness

Harness for the single Hackney pony varies in that it is lighter than normal single harness. A breast collar is always used.

When showing a Hackney pony, a bearing rein is fitted. Therefore, the bridle has the addition of a bridoon bit and bearing rein headpiece to which this (or an overcheck) may be fastened.

Usually, breeching is not used with this type of turnout. Tilbury tugs are fitted and the horse can therefore control the vehicle, provided that the ground is fairly level and the vehicle very light. A small Hackney wagon is the type used most commonly.

The traces are attached to the trace hooks on the vehicle, or to a swingletree, by means of a crew hole, which is simply a hole at the end of the trace. Some traces have a swivel cock-eye made of metal, serving the same purpose. Others are attached to the swingletree without hooks, but their chamfered ends pass through the crew holes and are secured with leather laces.

Cock-Eye

A single Hackney pony harness. A breast collar is always used in Hackney pony turnouts. A bearing rein is another essential item, running from an overcheck bit through a special strap on the bridle headpiece.

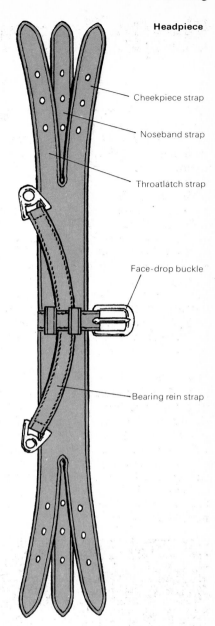

Headpiece

— Cheekpiece strap

— Noseband strap

— Throatlatch strap

— Face-drop buckle

— Bearing rein strap

Boat Horse Harness

Although in very limited use today, one form of unusual single harness still seen is the boat horse tackle. It was once commonly used on horses that walked along canal towpaths towing barges.

The harness generally includes a full neck collar with very low hames to allow the horse to walk under bridges, though a breast collar is sometimes used. A martingale, backband, crupper and hip strap are also worn.

Rope traces are attached to a swingletree, which has a swivel hook fitted to take the long towing line from the boat. The bridle is usually closed. One essential piece of equipment for the boat horse was a nosebag, from which he ate as he moved along the towpath.

Pair Harness

Pair Harness (Double Harness)

The main differences between single and pair harness relate to the vehicles used. With just two exceptions, horses in pairs are used with four-wheeled vehicles. Such vehicles have a central pole instead of shafts. And in consequence, the lighter type of saddles known as pads are used, and pole straps (pole chains or pole pieces) are fitted to join the pole head to the kidney links at the bottom of the hames.

Usually, pole straps are attached with buckles or spring hooks. They prevent the horses swinging out and away from each other. In addition, the crupper has a hip strap with two trace carriers, whilst the pad carries tug buckles to take the traces. A short martingale is used. This should pass round the base of the collar and hames for safety.

Traces

The traces may be of either the French loop or the quick-release design.

The French loop is a simple, leather-sewn loop (running loop) formed where the end of the trace is passed through a metal ring. A short piece of leather attached to the ring facilitates its opening.

The quick-release trace is another popular variety. The traces have fixed and loose moveable shackles. A loop is formed when these are joined together, and they are secured by a tongue of leather sewn to the trace and passing through both shackles. When this tongue is pulled out, the loop falls apart and the trace is freed. The quick-release type of trace is very useful in case of accident. Care should be taken, however, to ensure that the tongue is on the outside of both traces, so that it is easily released from the side of the vehicle.

Since most horses pull slightly towards the pole rather than away from it and since most coachmen prefer to have the horses' heads leaning slightly inwards, it is necessary for the outside traces to be slightly longer than those on the inside. A difference of one hole, usually about 32 mm ($1\frac{1}{4}$ in.), is too much. A useful compromise is to wrap a 12 mm ($\frac{1}{2}$ in.) piece of leather round the two central roller bolts, thus shortening the inside traces slightly. If

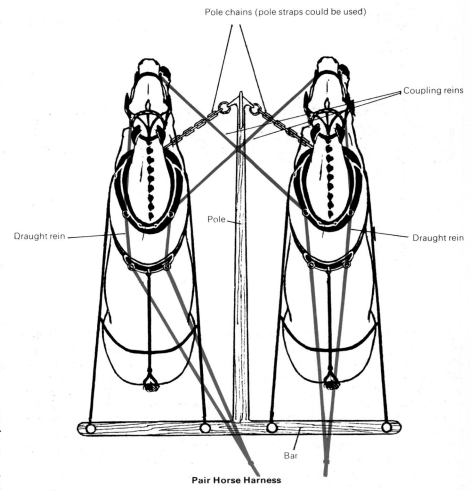

Pole chains (pole straps could be used)

Coupling reins

Pole

Draught rein

Draught rein

Bar

Pair Horse Harness

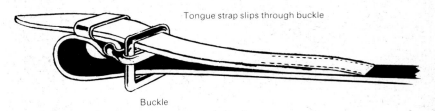

Quick Release Trace

Tongue strap slips through buckle

Buckle

swingletrees are used, the problem obviously does not arise.

Reins

In pair horse harness each rein is divided at the end into two. The outside reins (draught reins) go direct from the hand to the outside of each horse's bit. In some farm hitches, the insides of the bits are joined together by a short strap or piece of cord, but in all private driving or commercial vehicles, coupling reins are used. These enable both horses of a pair to be turned by the action of a single rein.

The coupling reins are buckled to the draught reins at a point about 0·6 m (2 ft) from the hand, and are about 13 cm (5 in.) longer than the draught reins if buckled in the centre of 15 holes. The coupling reins are attached to the inside of the bits: the near-side coupling rein to the inside of the off-side horse, and vice versa.

Pair Horse Tug Buckle

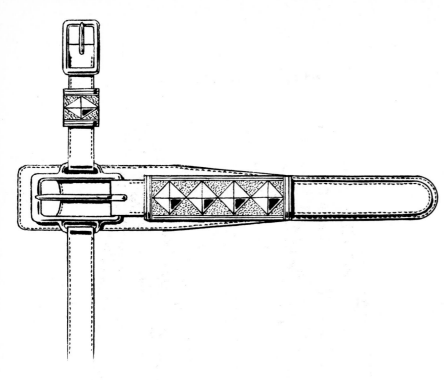

When fitting pair or any other harness, it is wise to ensure that there are extra holes in every strap or trace. Nothing is more irritating than harness that cannot be lengthened or shortened at will.

Curricle and Cape Cart Harness

Pair horse harness for a two-wheeled vehicle is completely different from the harness for a four-wheeled vehicle. It is also rare. The only two-wheeled vehicle to be built in Britain for a pair, for instance, was the early nineteenth century curricle.

In four-wheeled vehicles, the pole more or less supports itself because it is slotted into the futchells on the undercarriage. But in a two-wheeled vehicle, the weight of the pole is carried by the horses.

Saddles for curricle harness are more heavily constructed than normal. In addition to their rein terrets, they have two central terrets with rollers, through which a steel bar is fitted to hang poised above and across the backs of the horses. This bar supports the weight of the pole by means of a stout leather strap slotted through the centre. The strap is looped through a strong, leather-covered spring ring encircling the pole. A special bellyband—passing over the pole and under the bellies of the horses to be strapped to their girths—prevents the pole rising too high.

Harness for a Cape cart, a two-wheeled vehicle built and used in South Africa, differs from that used for curricles in that the pole is supported by a bar about 1·5 m (5 ft) long and made of wood. This is suspended on a level with the horses' chests by four rings at the ends of strong leather straps attached to the breast collars.

If both horses hold their heads in the same way and move identically, the coupling reins, both buckled in the centre of 15 holes, should keep their heads about 25 cm (10 in.) apart, which is the correct distance.

If one horse is more keen than the other, holds his head differently or is longer in the neck, it may be necessary to lengthen or to shorten his coupling rein. When this is done, the coupling rein of the other horse in the pair must be moved the same number of holes in the opposite direction. This will then maintain the distance between their heads. For instance, if there are 15 holes in each draught rein, and the coupling reins are both in the centre, there will be a total of 14 spare holes on each side of the buckle. If one is moved forward, the other is moved back, so that the spare holes on each side of the buckle still add up to 14.

Draught reins and coupling reins both pass through the ring terrets on the pads before attachment to the bits.

A pair of ponies harnessed to a phaeton. Light matching pads are used, rather than the more substantial saddles. Full neck collars and closed bridles have been fitted.

Tandem, Randem and Unicorn

In a tandem turnout, two horses are driven one in front of the other. The horse nearest the vehicle is the wheeler or shaft horse, and the front horse is the leader.

The Wheeler

The harness for a tandem wheeler is similar to that used for a single horse, but there are minor differences.

The rings on the terrets of the saddle or the pad are divided by rollers. These rollers allow the leader's reins to pass through the top half of the ring, while the wheeler's reins pass through underneath. As a result, the reins can be handled more independently.

Wheeler harness also has a ring, known as a roger ring, fitted to the rosettes on each side of the bridle in order to carry the reins of the leader. There is also an eye on the lower front corner of the tug buckle, to which the leader's traces can be attached with cock-eye spring hooks.

The Leader

The leader can wear either a breast collar or a full neck collar in contrast to, or matching, that worn by the wheeler. The leader carries a lighter saddle or pad than the wheeler. This is fitted, not with tugs, but with two leather slots sewn on each side, through which the tandem traces are threaded. They should be just long enough to keep the traces level.

In addition, the leader wears a bearing strap (trace carrier) which passes through the crupper back strap to hang over the horse's loins and support the traces.

Conversely, a belly strap, which passes from the girth to dees fixed on the traces at about the level of the horse's hips, prevents the traces slipping over his back if he turns round.

Attachment

There are two methods of attaching the leader: by long traces or by swingle-trees. The long traces have cock-eye spring hooks which clip directly into the eyes of the wheeler's tug buckles.

Swingletrees consist of two bars only. The rear bar has a large, central hook in front and a short chain at the back. This chain is attached to a ring at the bottom of the hames of the wheeler. The two ends of the bar are fitted with short traces with spring hooks to fix to the eyes of the wheeler's tug buckles.

The front, and longer, bar of the swingletrees has a metal eye that clips onto the hook on the rear bar, and two coiled hooks at either end, to which the eyes of the leader's traces may be fixed. Care should be taken to close the hook on the rear bar: otherwise the bit of the wheeler may become entangled in it or the lead bar may slip out. A small leather strap is ideal for this purpose.

The long-trace method of attachment has the advantage of simplicity, but there is a risk of the wheeler getting his front legs over the traces. When

Harness for a Tandem

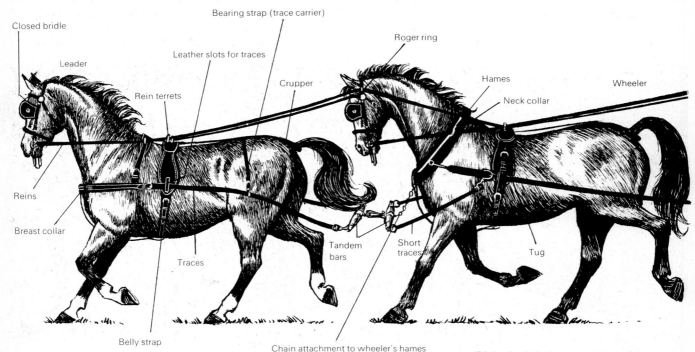

Closed bridle · Leader · Bearing strap (trace carrier) · Leather slots for traces · Crupper · Roger ring · Hames · Wheeler · Rein terrets · Neck collar · Reins · Breast collar · Traces · Tandem bars · Short traces · Tug · Belly strap · Chain attachment to wheeler's hames

Right A relatively uncommon unicorn (spike) coupling on a trio of bay Gelderlander horses from the Netherlands. The harness is similar to that used by four-in-hand teams, but the roger rings taking the reins are on the inside of the wheelers' bridles because there is only one leader.

Tandem Bars

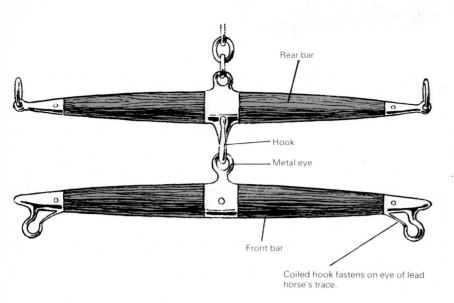

Rear bar

Hook

Metal eye

Front bar

Coiled hook fastens on eye of lead horse's trace.

The harness for a unicorn is similar to that of a four-in-hand, except that the roger rings for the reins are on the inside of the wheelers' bridles, not on the outside. This enables the reins to pass more directly to the single leader.

There is an additional ring on the wheelers' terrets for carrying the lead reins, the leader being attached to the pole head by a special lead bar. The bar has a sufficiently wide eye to pass over the crab hook at the pole head.

The unicorn team was used to enable a four-horse coach to continue its journey if one of the team went lame or met with an accident. For this reason, coaches carried an S-hook in addition to spare main bars and lead bars. The S-hook enabled the spare lead bar to be fitted to the pole head so that it hung horizontally. Without it, the lead bar, which is made with an eye for attachment to the main bar, would hang vertically when hooked to the pole head. Although the main bar is constructed to hang horizontally, it is of course too wide for use with a single horse.

Unicorn teams have been used extensively in agriculture and commerce. Also, if a particularly hard day's work was envisaged for a privately-driven pair of horses—due either to heavy going or to hilly country—it was an easy matter to use one extra horse as unicorn leader. It was also cheaper than using a team of four. Such companies as furniture removers and breweries used this hitch frequently.

bars are used, this is less likely to happen. But if it does, it is more difficult to extricate the wheeler's legs. Also, a high-stepping wheeler could damage his knees by knocking into the bars.

Randem

Three horses driven one in front of the other, are known as a *randem* turnout. Randem harnessing has never served a useful purpose other than to demonstrate the skill of the coachman.

Confusingly, the word trandem (troika) refers to three horses driven abreast, often harnessed to a curricle. For this turnout, it is necessary to fit an extra swingletree and pole socket, as well as an extra pole on the vehicle.

Unicorn (Spike)

The name *unicorn* is given to a team that consists of one leader in front of two wheelers. It is also called a *spike* team and sometimes a *pickaxe* team, although most authorities apply the term *pickaxe* to a team with two wheelers and three leaders.

Four-in-Hand

Teams of four horses are used principally for coaches. But they have been used also for brakes, wagonettes, four-wheeled dog carts and mail phaetons, and either for pleasure driving or, in modern times, for competition work.

Coaches

In addition to state coaches used on ceremonial occasions, there are (or were) three other types of coaches: mail coaches, road coaches (stage-coaches) and private coaches (drags).

The harness for state coaches and chariots is extremely ornate. It is heavily emblazoned with crests and other ornaments and is the only exception to an otherwise inflexible rule that harness should be either black or brown. State harness can be found in dark blue, maroon and even yellow, but is used only for ceremonial and state occasions.

The harnesses used for the three other types of coaches do not differ greatly from each other. Mail and road coach harness is slightly heavier and therefore stronger than the harness used for private drags.

Mail and road coach harnesses may have brown collars, in spite of the rest of the harness being black, but private drags use matching black harness with winkers, collars and pads covered frequently in black patent leather.

Embellishments on the harness of privately-driven vehicles may show the owner's monogram or crest, made in either silver or brass to match the fittings on the coach and the groom's livery buttons.

Road coaches once carried either the insignia or initial letters of their make.

Harness for road coaches has steel pole chains, painted black. They fasten with an open hook secured with a rubber band or a leather strap. The pole chains on private coaches are burnished and have spring hooks.

Other Vehicles

Four-in-hand harness for vehicles other than coaches is similar to the harness used for private coaches, except that pole straps may be used instead of chains. Also, Buxton bits may be used on the horses in a drag, whereas Liverpool bits or elbow bits are for road coach horses.

Breeching may be used on road coaches being driven in hilly districts, but would not be thought correct for drags. And while road coaches have chain-end traces or French-loop traces, drags usually use the running-loop or quick-release patterns.

Wheelers and Leaders

Coach wheelers' harness is very similar to pair-horse harness except that there are additional rings to carry the leaders' reins in the centre of their pads. There are also roger rings on the outsides of their bridles for the same purpose.

The leaders' harness is lighter than that of the two wheelers'. In a road coach, pads can be dispensed with and the traces held down with a light bellyband. Therefore, cruppers are unnecessary.

Team of Four Horses

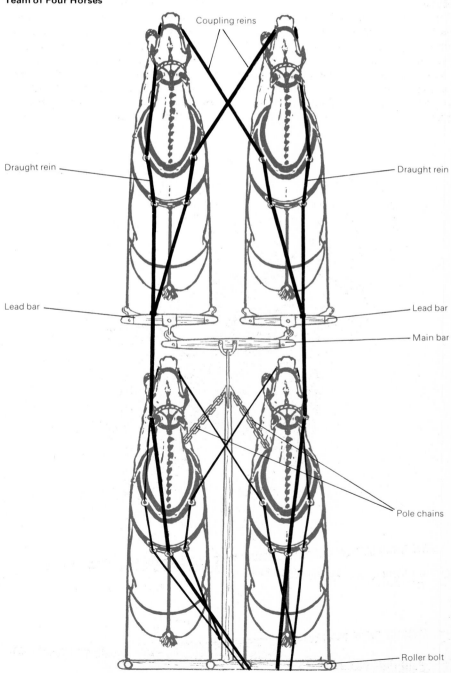

Coupling reins

Draught rein

Draught rein

Lead bar

Lead bar

Main bar

Pole chains

Roller bolt

The coach and four was once a common sight. Now it is seen mainly in the show ring or in the new driving equivalent of the ridden horse trials. Coach wheelers generally wear harness that is similar to ordinary pair horse equipment. The leaders' harness may be lighter, and pads can be removed so that the traces are held down simply by a bellyband.

Reins

The reins are coupled in the same way as for pairs: the leaders' draught reins pass through the roger rings on the wheelers' bridles; the coupling reins pass through the terrets on the pads and rings on the hames, to be buckled to their bits in the same way as for a pair.

All the reins are held in the driver's left hand, with the near lead rein over the first finger, the off lead rein under the first finger, the near wheel rein over the second finger and the off wheel rein between the second and third fingers. The whip is held in the right hand, but both hands are used to lengthen or shorten the reins or to execute turns.

This method is used in many countries. But in Hungary, the home of coaching, quite another method of handling the reins is used.

The Hungarian method involves a different arrangement of the reins. They are all coupled together to two draught reins, which are themselves joined together with a short strap known as the *frog*. This is held in the driver's left hand with the knuckles uppermost. Turns and changes of direction are made by drawing back the coupling reins with the right hand or by moving the position of the left hand on the frog.

It has been widely considered that this method, although ideal for the open country of its origin, is less suitable for city streets than the more common style. However, the Hungarian coachmen are exceptionally successful in international competitions which involve negotiating difficult driving obstacles.

Cock Horse

The only remaining items of harness peculiar to four-in-hand driving are those of the cock horse. A cock horse was used to assist coaches up steep hills. It was ridden and attached in front of the leaders by means of a rope running between them and hooked to the pole head.

The cock horse's harness consists of a collar, bridle with winkers, riding saddle, crupper, traces and a bar supported by two straps from the backstrap. The traces are attached to this bar, which pulls the rope and thus assists the team with its load.

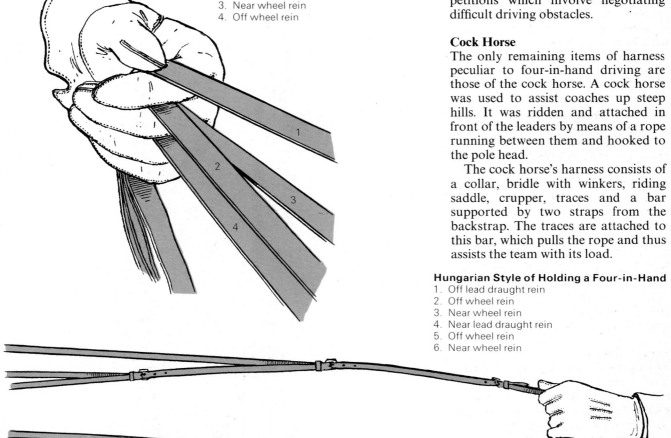

English Style of Holding a Four-in-Hand
1. Near lead rein
2. Off lead rein
3. Near wheel rein
4. Off wheel rein

Hungarian Style of Holding a Four-in-Hand
1. Off lead draught rein
2. Off wheel rein
3. Near wheel rein
4. Near lead draught rein
5. Off wheel rein
6. Near wheel rein

Heavy Harness

Single Heavy Harness (Thill or Ridger Harness)

Single heavy harness consists of a heavy, square-shaped saddle, heavy collar with hames, crupper, breeching, open or closed bridle and reins. Forward and backward draught is transmitted from the horse to the vehicle through the shafts.

The saddle is often made of wood. It has a channel for the *ridger chain*, which is hooked to the shafts and supports them. The heavy collar has hames made of wood or metal; a short length of chain joins the hames to hooks on the shafts of the vehicle.

Crupper and breeching are attached to the rear of the saddle, and the breeching chains are fastened to hooks on the shafts. A pair of hip straps keep the trace chains up out of the way of the horse's legs.

The bridle, with or without winkers—which are usually square—is fitted with a ring snaffle bit or a Liverpool bit. The reins are sometimes made of cord. A plough horse also has bearing reins attached to the bit rings, usually looped over the top of the hames.

The mouthpiece of the bit may be hooked to the ring cheeks with an open hook or a strap. It can then be easily removed from the horse's mouth to allow him to eat and drink.

Heavy Pair Harness

Heavy and commercial pair harness varies considerably—from the minimal harness used in former days by omnibus companies to the extensive regalia used by brewers and millers and in heavy farm wagons.

For buses and trams, the harness consists simply of bridle, collar and hames and traces with two short pole chains running from the kidney link at the bottom of the collar to the pole head. When such harness was in daily use, pads were thought unnecessary and, as the vehicles had good brakes, no breeching was required. Carriers and tradesmen used medium-sized horses known as 'vanners' or 'parcel carters'. The harness of such horses is slightly fuller and includes a pad.

Sometimes, the harness has long breeching extending to the trace tug buckles on either side. Its effect is to transfer some of the weight of the vehicle to the pole head and to the base of the collar. Without it, all the weight of the load will bear down from the top of the collar onto the neck of the horse when descending a hill.

Pole chains are frequently attached

Heavy Horse Wearing Thill Harness

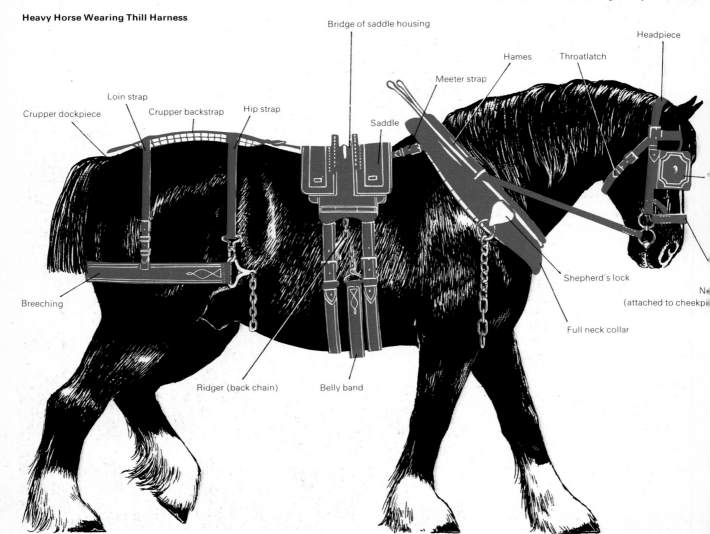

Crupper dockpiece · Loin strap · Crupper backstrap · Hip strap · Bridge of saddle housing · Saddle · Meeter strap · Hames · Throatlatch · Headpiece · Breeching · Ridger (back chain) · Belly band · Shepherd's lock · Full neck collar · N (attached to cheekpi...)

to the rings in the kidney links by means of a patent quick-release knot known as a 'shepherd's lock'. The shepherd's lock allows the pole chains to be detached quickly in the event of an accident.

Housens

The heaviest types of harness have massive hames that extend 20 to 30 cm (8 to 12 in.) above the top of the collar. They are backed by leather shields known as *housens*. These are often richly decorated, but they have a practical use. When folded down, the housens prevent rain running down the horse's withers.

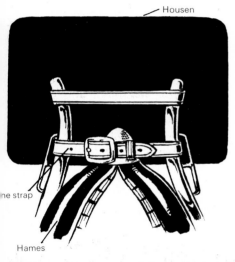

Housen

ne strap

Hames

Brasses and Other Ornaments

All heavy horse harness is embellished with brasses of varying design. These were intended originally to ward off evil spirits. Latterly, they have been used purely for decoration and to depict the trade of the owner.

The first brasses were made by hand from hammered brass sheets known as *latten*. Cast brasses appeared in the 1820s.

Other ornaments include fly terrets (swingers, danglers or hodders) and bells. Fly terrets were made from the middle of the nineteenth century. They were fitted on top of the headpiece and on the browband and collar, and helped to ward off the flies in summer.

Bells were often attached to pads. Their purpose was to warn other road-users of the horses' approach, particularly in the dark, because lights were rarely used.

A pair of Shires wearing full heavy horse neck collar harness with closed bridles and chain traces. The vehicle pole separates the two horses; the pole chains keep them at equal distances from the pole. Heavy horses in full dress harness are an increasingly familiar sight in the show ring and on short-haul delivery services in some cities.

Trace Horses

Heavy horses were once driven one in front of the other, but this type of turnout was not given the status of 'tandem'. The leader was referred to simply as the *trace horse*.

In the past, spare horses were often available at the foot of a hill, ready to be hooked on in front of a single horse to help with a particularly heavy load. Some firms sent their single-horse turnouts out in pairs, so that each could help the other. The trace-horse chain traces were then hooked either to the shaft of the vehicle or to the traces of the horse in the shafts.

Bodkin Hitch

The bodkin hitch is primarily a farm hitch, used in ploughing heavy land. Two horses are hitched as a pair, but a third horse is then yoked in front of them. The leading horse helps by walking in the plough in front of his comrade, while the other horse walks on the land.

To compensate for the fact that two horses are pulling on the same bar, the two-horse swingletree is fitted with an iron crab, along which a crab hook may be run so that it is resting just to the inside of the two furrow horses.

Multiple Hitches

Most of the multiple hitches seen today are in the show ring. Beautifully turned-out multiple teams are shown wearing immaculate chain harness. But for serious work such as farming, single and pair harnesses are the most popular.

In the 1920s and 1930s, however, the multiple farm hitch was the driving horseman's answer to the appearance of the tractor. Even now, some farmers prefer to use a lot of horses rather than a lot of horsepower in the form of machinery.

The multiple hitches are extremely complex, but have many advantages. They equalize the pull on the horses, keeping each individual horse cooler and more comfortable because he does not have to take all the strain of the job. They also eliminate side-draught.

The biggest multiple hitch recorded is the 40-horse hitch driven by Dick Sparrow of Iowa. The head of the front horse in this turnout was about 30 m (100 ft) from the driver.

141

Light Trade Harness and Accoutrements

Light Trade Harness

Basically, light trade harness is the same as harness used in private driving. But for the single horses, the saddle is heavier and the traces have chain ends.

Furniture and fittings may be made either of brass or of white metal—usually white metal because its upkeep is easier. The browband has a clenched metal front.

Full breeching is always used. The bit is always of the Wilson snaffle variety.

Accoutrements

Whips

The whip is an extremely important piece of equipment in driving. It should not be used to punish the horse, but to divert him and at times correct him. It should always be carried in the right hand, so that it is readily available for use.

Generally, whips are made of holly, but they may also be made of black-thorn, yew or hickory. A driving whip consists of a long stick to which a quill is attached, forming a bow at the top. The whole is covered with strong black thread. A thong of plaited hide is attached, culminating in a lash.

Although driving whips have been made with coloured lashes, it is more correct for them to be plain. They should never be whitened.

Obviously, whips vary in size. They range from that used for a four-in-hand team, which has a stick 1·5 m (5 ft) long, to a lady's whip for a pony single turnout, measuring half that length. The thongs for singles and pairs are usually about the same length as the stick. For tandems or teams they are double the length of the stick.

At the base of the whip is a leather-covered handle, finished with a metal cap or ferrule. The cap or ferrule is made of either brass or silver to match the fittings on harness and vehicle, and is often engraved with the crest or monogram of the owner.

Although most whips have straight sticks, variations have been produced.

Light Trade Harness

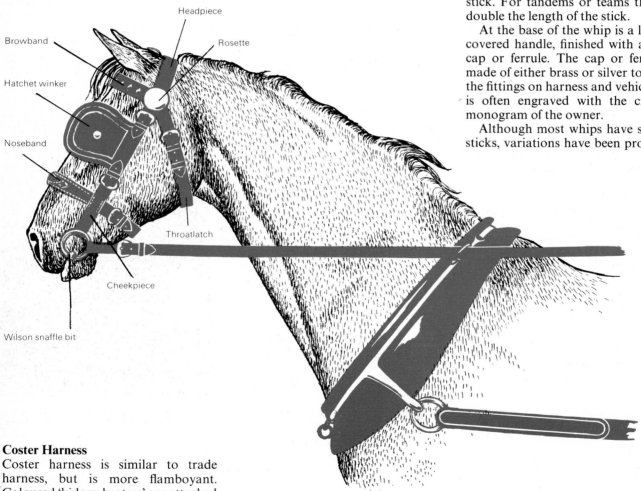

Headpiece
Browband
Rosette
Hatchet winker
Noseband
Throatlatch
Cheekpiece
Wilson snaffle bit

Coster Harness

Coster harness is similar to trade harness, but is more flamboyant. Coloured 'kidney beaters' are attached to the crupper back strap (scarlet or bright yellow are the favourites) and these match the leather on the face drop and under the saddle.

At shows, coster horses and ponies are hitched to gaily-painted vehicles. Their manes and tails are plaited with wool and pompoms.

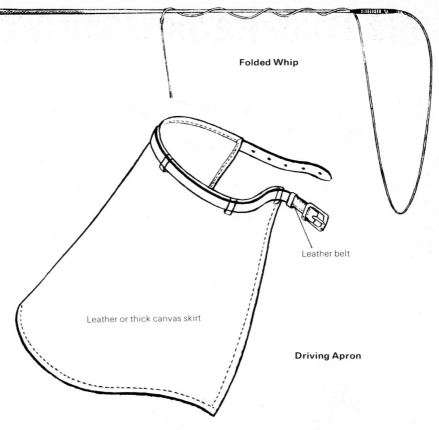

Folded Whip

Leather belt

Leather or thick canvas skirt

Driving Apron

Some sticks have an angular bend and are called 'dog-leg' whips. Others are scarred and are known as 'rabbit-bitten' whips. For travelling convenience, particularly when carried as spares on coaches, jointed whips have been made, and whips with parasols on the end were introduced for ladies to take on summer drives.

Gloves

Gloves are essential for driving—as anyone who has tried to hold a hard-pulling horse will confirm. They should be made of leather, preferably dog skin, and thick enough to stop the reins cutting into the hands. It is advisable also to buy gloves at least half a size too large, or 25 mm (1 in.) too long in the fingers. If they are tight, they numb the fingers.

It is also wise to carry a spare pair of gloves made of crocheted string for use in wet weather. Leather gloves become slippery when wet.

Quarter Sheets

In addition to rugs and aprons for the driver, some protective clothing is needed for the horses.

Although some people use full-size rugs, these are both bulky to store and difficult to put on and take off in a hurry. Quarter sheets, which fit over the horses' loins, are good protection against the elements when horses are standing still. They are secured either under the back strap or with a loop hooked onto the pad or saddle.

Spares Kit

Driving equipment is incomplete without a spares kit for use in emergency. Such spares as hame straps, traces and reins should be regarded as essential. A good knife, pieces of leather and matches are other useful items in case of trouble.

Rugs and Aprons

Knee rugs and aprons, although not strictly necessary, are usually worn for driving. They not only give a tidy appearance, but also protect the driver's clothes from dust and flying hairs from the horses, and resin and dirt from the reins.

Aprons fitted with a leather strap are the most convenient. They should be made wide enough to wrap right round the body.

For summer use, there are aprons made of linen, often with a Tattersall

check design. For more protection and warmth, aprons tailored from Bedford cord in a shade of beige known as 'drab' are considered correct.

Large rugs, made of boxcloth and lined with either checked tweed or fur, were produced for use with coachmen-driven carriages and coaches. Rugs made of waterproof materials, were manufactured for the same purpose.

Rugs and aprons can be embellished with the owner's crest or monogram. But such markings should be small and unobtrusive.

A Hackney pony driver turned out for show day. A smart jacket and hat—often a bowler hat—are desirable. A knee rug or apron protects the clothes and looks tidy. Gloves are essential to give good grip on the reins. They should be made of dogskin and should be at least half a size too large, to allow the fingers to move freely.

Managing a Whip

● A driving whip should be held just below the ferrule.

● If a whip is to be comfortable in use, it should balance well when poised on a finger at about one-third of its length along the stick.

● A whip should be hung on a whip reel when not in use to prevent the quill at the top becoming distorted.

● A round, flat can, nailed to the wall, makes a good substitute for a whip reel.

Driving Vehicles

Vehicles for harness horses fall into two basic categories: two-wheel vehicles and four-wheel vehicles. A single horse or pony can be put to both types, but pairs of horses are used only with four-wheel vehicles—with the exceptions of the curricle and the Cape cart, for which special equipment is necessary.

It is for safety reasons that two-wheel vehicles are recommended for single horses. If the horse should turn suddenly when frightened, the vehicle will move with him. With four wheels, the undercarriage is likely to lock and the vehicle may overturn.

Vehicles should be of the correct size for the horses pulling them, particularly so with the two-wheelers. If they are too large, the shafts will press down on the tugs, putting extra weight on a horse's back. If too small, they will point upwards, and with the weight of the passengers may almost pull a horse off his feet.

The Parts of a Vehicle

Vehicles have two main parts: the carriage (gear) and the body. The carriage consists of the wheels, springs, axles, forecarriage parts, fifth wheel, perch, splinter bar and futchells.

The fifth wheel is a circle of iron which pivots on the king pin (a pin connecting the forecarriage to the body framing), shouldering the wear and providing stability. The perch, a long piece of iron, runs under the body and connects the rear axle to the forecarriage.

The splinter bar is fitted to the front of the forecarriage for attaching pair-horse or team wheeler traces. Futchells connect it to the sway bar, which steadies the forecarriage.

The body of the vehicle is the upper section—the section that carries the driver and the passengers.

Materials and Design

The materials used in vehicle construction vary from plain timber and iron to the silver, brass, silk and leather of the ornate coach. Care should be taken when fitting any vehicle that the floor is level and parallel to the ground. The shafts should never be too long, extending no more than about 15 cm (6 in.) beyond the point of the horse's shoulder. The loaded vehicle should be so well balanced that the tip of the

shafts can be lifted with one finger.

Vehicles vary enormously in design. They can, however, be divided broadly into those suitable for their owners to drive and those for professional coachmen. Of the owner-driven types, the following are basic examples.

Gigs

Gigs have two wheels and seats for two people only. They were considered the

'mini-cars' of their age. They had humble beginnings and, at first, were very roughly built. But eventually they were produced by the best coach-builders and used by the aristocracy.

Gigs varied greatly in outline. Each design was named after its builder, its owner or the place where it originated. Thus there are now the Tilbury, Dennett, Stanhope, Liverpool, Lawton, Murrieta and many more.

Gig

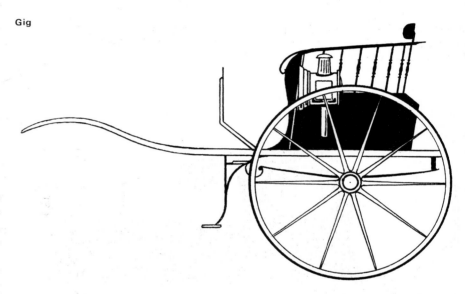

The Siamese phaeton is the lightest of phaetons for a pair or single turnout. Phaetons are four-wheeled carriages used for private driving. There are many designs, including the Mail, Demi-Mail, Park, Spider and Equirotal.

Dog Carts

Dog carts were built with either two or four wheels. Their name relates to the fact that they were designed originally for the transport of sporting dogs, which were accommodated under the seats and received ventilation from louvre boards on either side of the vehicle.

The chief feature of dog carts is that they have seats for four people sitting back to back. Two face fore, two aft, and those at the rear rest their feet on a moveable board.

Although dog carts did not altogether supersede gigs in popularity, their added passenger and luggage accommodation made them so useful that they were widely used until well into the motor age. A few of the wide variety of designs are the Alexandra (named after the Queen of England), Bedford and Malvern.

Dog Cart

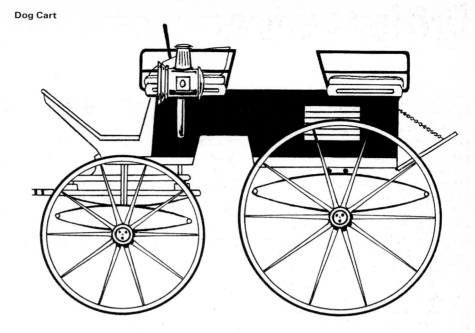

Phaeton

Phaetons

Just as gigs never had more than two wheels, phaetons were never built with fewer than four. They held a minimum of four people, sitting in pairs behind one another and facing forward. They were named after the mythical son of the sun god Helios, who lost control of his father's chariot and nearly set fire to the earth.

Originally, phaetons were built very high, but they were lowered for King George IV of England when he became portly, and then grew in popularity as vehicles for ladies to drive.

As with all vehicles, phaetons have many different outlines and names. They include mail phaetons built with the perch undercarriage of a coach; demi-mails and Stanhopes, named for the Hon. Fitzroy Stanhope; and spiders, built on arched ironwork.

Other Vehicles

The governess (tub) cart is completely enclosed and has a door at the rear. It was once used for the safe transport of children. The float is similar, though larger, and was used mostly on farms for carrying produce and livestock.

For family outings, particularly in the country, there were wagonettes, brakes, and char-a-bancs of different sizes and designs. They could be driven either by the owner or by the family coachman and with either a pair of horses or a four-in-hand. A private drag was exclusively for use by the owner-driver with four horses.

Horses, Drivers and Vehicles

- Ideally, a horse should be chosen to match his vehicle.

- A stocky cob looks better with a dog cart than with an elegant phaeton. A Hackney should not be put to such a vehicle as a float.

- Large carriages with box seats, such as landaus and broughams, were designed to be driven by professional coachmen. They are unsuitable vehicles for amateurs.

American Driving Harness

The long distances between towns in post-revolutionary America, and the condition of the roads, were probably among the reasons for the interest shown by Americans of the early nineteenth century in fast trotters and light vehicles. Certainly, by mid-century, the carriages and harness of North America had taken on a character noticeably different from that of Europe, and the American trotter was already acknowledged to be faster than any bred elsewhere.

Although the wealthier citizens of the eastern seaboard began to follow the taste of their European counterparts during the closing years of the Victorian era, popular taste continued to favour lightweight styles of harness and carriages. Equipages of the English pattern came to be classed in equestrian circles as 'heavy harness'. This term is no longer heard in that connection, but English styles of harness continue to be used with appropriate vehicles.

Whereas in Britain the family trap was most often a two-wheeler, in America the family buggy was nearly always a four-wheeler, generally built with a reach, or perch, connecting the front and rear axles. The shafts for single harness were made in one unit, both shafts being held together by a crossbar which usually had a whiffletree fastened at the centre. The shafts were attached directly to the front axle, fastened by shaft couplings, of which there were several patented types.

The pole for a pair was a drop pole, one that was not rigidly supported as in most European carriages, but was attached to the axle by means of the shaft couplings. A neck yoke was fixed across the end of the pole to hold it up and to take the place of the pole pieces or pole chains used with European carriages.

These mechanical arrangements influenced the design of harness, of course, and such was the demand at the turn of the century that there existed a great many factories turning out quantities of harness in a great variety of styles, quality and price. Some of the catalogues of these manufacturers illustrated at least a hundred different sets of single driving harness alone, not including work harness, race harness or harness made of russet leather. This enormous range has now been reduced, and the following are some of the principal styles still being made.

Buggy Harness

In American usage, the word *buggy* has come to mean any one of a group of light, four-wheeled carriages.

The bridle differs from the English pattern in having no noseband. The driving bit is usually a broken (jointed) snaffle with half-cheeks, or half-guards, and the bearing rein is of the overcheck pattern which, in cheaper makes of harness, is fastened to the driving bit. In the better grades of harness, the bearing rein is attached to its own bridoon.

This overcheck, or *Kemble Jackson check* as it was originally called, was invented for a racing trotter of that name in 1853. Its success in that particular case led to the overcheck being used eventually on all racing harness, and in time it was also adopted for ordinary driving harness and even for work harness.

The breast collar may be made of single leather, but the better makes are of folded leather and are about 64 mm (2½ in.) wide in the body. The traces are often sewn onto the collar and they may also be made of single leather, with three dart holes punched in the trace heels.

The saddle is either 64 or 76 mm (2½ or 3 in.) wide, and sometimes has a seat (a top shaped like a miniature riding saddle) and jockeys of patent leather. The skirts may be straight or made with a swell. The shaft bearer can be sewn under the jockey, or attached to a metal dee, in which case it is called a *swinging shaft bearer*. The tugs are of the open type.

Sets of single harness of this kind are made in various grades. Some have plain or single straps, others have lined or double straps, and some have folded straps.

Double or pair harness for a buggy has the same sort of bridles as are used for single harness and may have breast collars or collars and hames.

If breast collars are used, they will normally have breast-collar irons to support the neck yoke. The breast

An American double roadster harness. In America, roadster horses are fast trotters. They wear breast collars, overchecks, overcheck bridoons and half-cheek snaffle driving bits.

collars may have tugs and trace buckles, or the traces may be sewn on. Choke straps (breastplates or false martingales) are attached to the collars and pass between the horses' front legs, looping onto the girths.

The pads are usually 38 mm (1½ in.) wide and have coach pads (pad cloths or housings). The skirts have trace-bearer loops sewn on, the traces being passed through them.

Surrey Harness

For heavier carriages such as Surreys, rockaways or traps, a stronger kind of harness is used, often with collars and hames.

The hames usually have box loops with straight wire trace buckles. The traces are lined and stitched and have a single dart hole.

The saddle is 89 mm (3½ in.) wide and the most popular style has the seat,

jockeys and skirts covered with patent leather. It may have straight or swell skirts.

The bridle for Surrey harness may be similar to that for buggy harness, but more often it is made with a side-check bearing rein fastened to a bridoon and passing through gag leathers, or gag chains, attached to the crown piece. The usual driving bit used with a side-check bridle is a curb, either a Liverpool, Ashleigh or elbow bit. There will also in most cases be a noseband.

Double harness is usually made with collars and hames, somewhat heavier than those used with the average buggy harness. The traces, for instance, would be 32 to 38 mm (1¼ to 1½ in.), doubled and stitched, whereas buggy traces might be 25 to 31 mm (1 to 1½ in.) and single leather, in the cheaper grades.

The pads have 31 mm (1½ in.) skirts

and usually have housings made of leather, sometimes decorated with chain links or raised leather. The trace-bearer loops may be wavy cut to match the rest of the harness. The turnback (backstrap), as with most American light harness, is made to buckle like a martingale—that is, with the strap point turned back inside the loop. Hip straps, or trace bearers, are used with Surrey harness if there are no breechings, but in hilly districts breechings are necessary. If there are no hame tug buckles, the breeching straps are made to be attached to the centre of the girth and so pull against the choke strap. If there are hame tug buckles, the breeching is made long enough to fasten into those buckles.

The reins may be made of black or russet leather, or black with russet hand parts. The splices are usually made with a wavy cut.

Single Surrey Harness

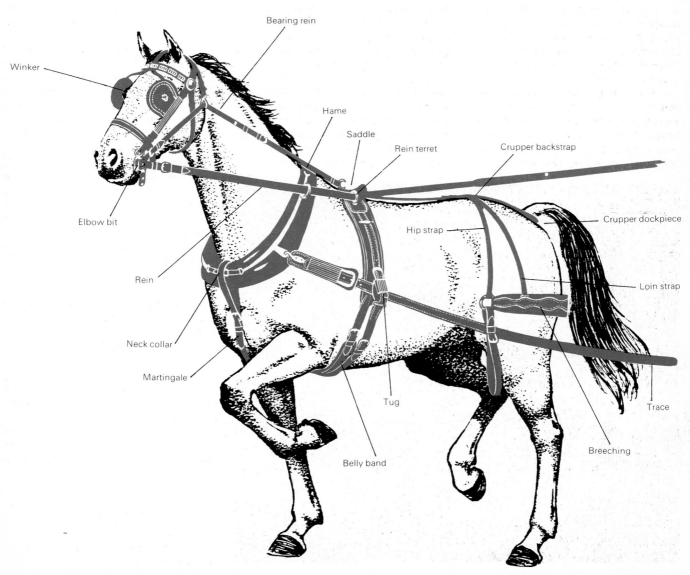

Roadster Harness

In North America, the term *roadster* is applied to a fast trotter, and many shows offer classes for roadsters in both single and double harness. Standardbreds, Morgans, and Arabians may be shown as roadsters, usually in separate classes.

Single roadster harness has a bridle with square winkers, an overcheck which must buckle into a separate bridoon and a half-cheek snaffle driving bit. A running martingale is used. The bearing rein and throatlatch are sewn round. The bridle front is made of patent leather with a narrow band of coloured leather along its centre, the whole being only about 13 mm ($\frac{1}{2}$ in.) wide. The martingale is also made of rounded leather.

The breast collar is made of folded leather, about 41 mm ($1\frac{5}{8}$ in.) wide with a wavy cut layer sewn on. This layer is an extension of the outer layer of the traces, which may be rounded or lined and double stitched. The neckstrap is also rounded and it has a loop at the centre to attach to the bearing rein hook on the saddle.

The saddle is made on a 64 mm ($2\frac{1}{2}$ in.) tree, and has straight skirts. Housings, if used, might be made of silk of a colour to match the bridle front. A breeching is always used, and it often has a wavy cut layer to match the breast collar.

The lines (reins) are made of brown leather sewn round up to the hand pieces. The bit billets are made narrow, not more than 16 mm ($\frac{5}{8}$ in.), and have a steel inner lining to give strength.

The rein terrets and bearing-rein hook are usually brass, or gilt, and the smaller buckles can be leather-covered or rubber-covered. A small monogram may be used on the winkers, rosettes or martingale.

Double roadster harness has shaped Kay collars and light hames that may be leather-covered, joined at the bottom by kidney links of dog pattern, to which the choke straps (breast-plates) are fastened. The hame tugs have box loops and a lined safe under the buckle. Traces are usually sewn round, except for the heels.

The pads are 29 to 32 mm ($1\frac{1}{8}$ to $1\frac{1}{4}$ in.) wide, are patent-leather covered and have trace-bearer loops. The cruppers are sewn to the turnbacks, or backstraps. The reins are rounded up to the handpieces and are made of brown leather.

Fine Harness

In modern American terminology, *fine harness* refers to a style developed for the show ring in 1905 as a new class for American saddle horses. In these classes, the horses are expected to perform at an animated park trot and extreme speed is penalized. Nevertheless, the harness used is based on fast-trotting harness. Arabians and Morgan horses are also shown in similar classes.

The bridle of fine harness is fitted with a cavesson trimmed with black and coloured patent leather. Otherwise it is similar to a roadster bridle.

The pad is also similar to the roadster harness but may be more deeply padded. The crupper usually buckles to the turnback. No breeching is used.

Runabout Harness

Although the runabout was originally designed as a carriage for fast trotters, the harness specified for runabout classes at shows is of the sort used for pleasure driving.

The bridle may have square, *D*-shaped or hatchet-shaped winkers, facepiece and noseband, but no bearing rein. A curb bit, either Liverpool, Ashleigh or elbow, is customary. A breast collar, made with folded leather and a straight layer and trace buckles, is used. The traces are made of doubled leather, double stitched.

The saddle is about 76 mm (3 in.) wide, with straight skirts, round or Tilbury tugs and a bellyband. The reins are made of flat russet leather. The harness buckles are generally of the West End or London wire patterns.

'Sweetheart on Parade' a great winner of fine-harness classes in the 1930s. Fine-harness horses must perform at an animated park trot. The harness is similar to that of the roadster, but it has a cavesson trimmed with patent leather, and the pad may have additional padding. Breeching is not used.

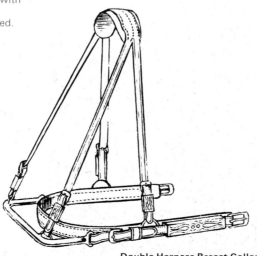

Double Harness Breast Collar

Double Roadster Harness

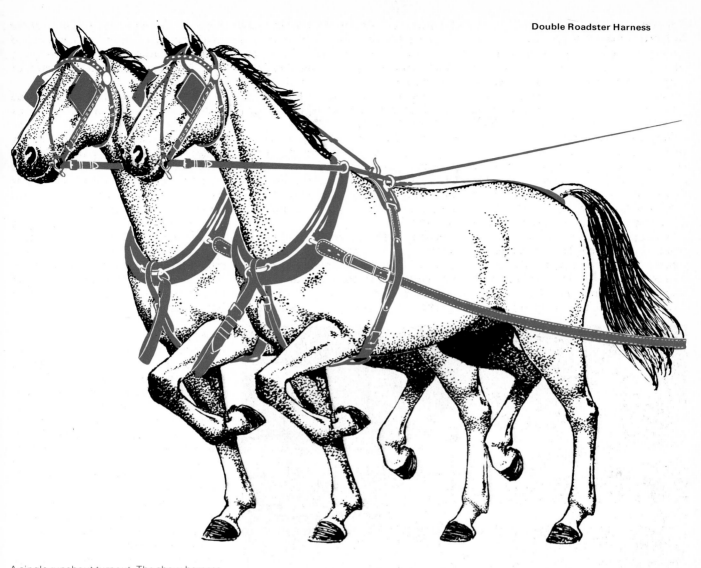

A single runabout turnout. The show harness is the same as that used for pleasure driving. It has a closed bridle with a curb bit, a breast collar and a saddle. A bearing rein is not used in modern runabout harness.

Ready-Made Harness

Some of the harness commonly used may be bought ready-made in cheaper grades. Horses and buggies are still used for everyday personal transport-ation in the Mennonite communities in several parts of the United States, and some small shops turn out standard sets of buggy harness. Pony harness of a similar type can be ready-made.

Work Harness

Horses are still used on the land in America to some extent, and ready-made harness of traditional patterns can be bought. Collars for this work harness are machine-made in a range of sizes and quality.

Magnificent teams of heavy horses are used also for publicity purposes. Harness for them is made to order to a very high standard.

Harness Racing

Harness racing may not have originated in America, but its development there as an organized sport can be traced back to the early years of the nineteenth century. Contemporary pictures show that specially-built vehicles and light harness were already in use in those days, although much trotting racing was done under saddle.

In the making of light racing vehicles, American carriage builders led the world, due in part to the availability of quantities of suitable timber. The harness was made as light, yet as strong, as possible, and was devoid of any purely decorative parts. Side-check bearing reins, snaffle driving bits and running martingales were the usual equipment. After the overdraw bearing rein, or overcheck,

was invented in 1853, it came into use more and more.

Much of the harness in use today is no longer made of leather, but almost entirely of man-made materials—often plastic-coated nylon—which do not need more than a wipe-over after use. As a result, some parts of the harness are lighter, and may be bought in a range of colours to suit individual taste or stable practice. The basic design of the harness has changed little during the past 50 years. The two-minute style, which has no breast collar, first appeared about 80 years ago and is in use again, usually with a buxton (breastplate) to secure the saddle.

Pony harness racing is now popular in North America. Usually the ponies wear leather harness in a pattern similar to that of the horse harness.

Bridle and Bits
The harness racing bridle is similar to the ordinary pattern of blinkered driving bridle. It is used without a noseband. The reins are long and have a number of hand-loops so that the driver can keep close contact with the mouth at all times. He sits on the spare ends of the reins during racing, to keep them from being caught up. The reins are passed under the breast harness straps, through terrets on the saddle and to the driver. Generally, half-spoon cheek snaffles with thin jointed mouthpieces are used.

Overcheck
The overcheck is used to keep the horse's head up. It does not induce flexion, which is the aim of the bearing rein.

Harness Racing

Bluffter

Driving snaffle

Breast harness

Terrets

Pole

Hand loops

Hobble

Hobble

Hobble hanger strap

Boots

The overcheck bit is fitted above the ordinary driving snaffle and is kept high in the mouth by a high, snug nosepiece joining the bit rings. The overcheck rein straps cross on the forehead and pass under the browband, through two keepers on the headpiece and to a *T*-shaped check hook on the saddle.

The overcheck rein is adjustable at the saddle end. It is used only for racing or during fast workouts, and is the last piece of equipment to be adjusted. The more experienced the horse, the tighter the check rein is put up.

Many horses find that they can breathe more easily if their heads are kept up, and they place their heads even higher than the overcheck requires. They move better, too, because they can achieve better balance.

Breast Harness
Light buggy breast harness is used. The breast piece is elongated at each end to form long traces that pass through loops on the saddle and are coiled tightly round the length of the shafts of the two-wheeled sulkies. They are then hooked onto the ends of the shafts.

Saddle
The saddle is fitted with a check hook and rein terrets at the top, and an extra tug pocket high up on each side, into which the ends of the shafts are driven. The girth need never be fastened tightly, because straps extending up from the girth at each side are tied round and round the shafts very tightly and then buckled. This not only keeps the saddle in place, it fixes the shafts so that they cannot move and upset the balance of horse and sulky.

Hobbles
Hobbles (hopples) were first introduced as training devices, particularly for pacers. In time, they came to be used in actual races and today at least 95 per cent of pacers race in hobbles. Many trotters are still raced free-legged.

Hobbles for pacers consist of four stiff, elongated loops. These were originally made of metal liners covered with leather, or of latigo leather covered with calf-skin. Two of these loops are fitted on the forearms, closer to the elbows than to the knees, and the other two are put on the hind legs above the hocks. The two hobbles at each side are joined with adjustable straps and are kept in place by four hobble hanger straps, with a spreader at the top of the rear ones.

At one time, similar hobbles were used on trotters, but with connecting straps that joined them diagonally. The trotting hobbles more commonly used today are put on the forearms only and are connected by a strong cord passing through a metal pulley hanging just behind the girth.

Modern hobbles are made from plastic, generally, and are much lighter and less abrasive than the old-fashioned patterns. To allow them even greater freedom of movement, vaseline or lard is rubbed onto the insides of the leg loops and on the legs.

The length of the hobbles is adjusted between the leg loops, and the spare ends are taped for safety. Experience tells the driver how long they should be for each individual horse.

At first, the horses' legs are 'rubbed up' by the hobbles and made sore. The horses are kept in work until finally the sores heal and the skin becomes hardened.

Pole
The pole is a length of wood used to prevent the horse from bearing to one side—a tendency that can be dangerous. It is hooked between the bridle and the saddle and keeps the horse moving straight.

Bluffter
Shying, too, may be dangerous during a race, so many trotters and pacers are fitted with a sheepskin noseband known as a *bluffter*. This is a thick foam-rubber roll, covered in fleece and passing not only right round the nose but up the sides of the horse's face to meet the browband, where it is tied. It obscures vision of anything below or behind the horse. A centre strap fastens to the headpiece and another strap secures the rear of the noseband.

Ear Cones
Ear cones are small hoods made of cloth. They are slipped over the ears to deaden the sound of horses coming from behind.

Trotting Shoes
The shoeing of a trotter can be of decisive importance, but this is not so much the case with pacers. Trotting shoes usually weigh about 230 gm (8 oz). Flat shoes are usually worn in front and swedge (creased or fullered) shoes behind, to give more traction. Sometimes, removable toe weights are used on the front feet of trotters.

The shoes of pacers are almost always lighter and are rounded on the inside to reduce the risk of injury from interference. Moulded plastic shoes are now available, and are popular for pacers.

Protection from Injury
Brushing, speedy cutting and other interferences are often the cause of injuries to horses driven at speed. There are many devices to guard the legs and feet against them. Most are now made of plastic materials.

The list of harness racing boots includes: coronet, scalper, speedy cut, quarter and over-reach (bell) boots for the feet, and brushing boots, shin and ankle boots and knee boots. Knee boots are usually secured by elastic suspender straps.

Harness racing equipment must be light and strong. The driver must have very sure and sensitive control of the horse.

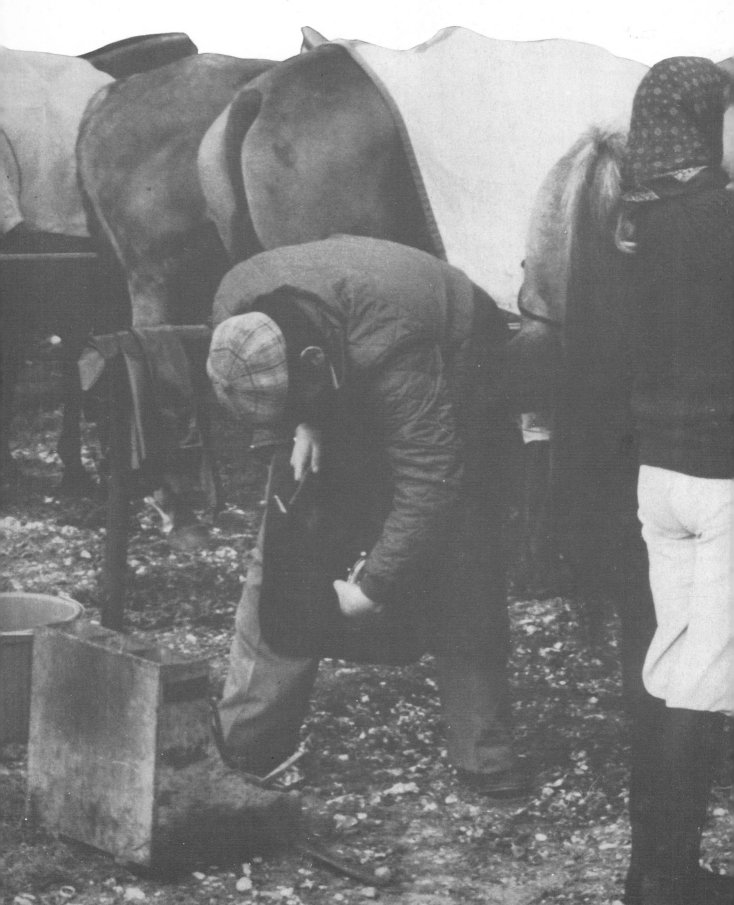

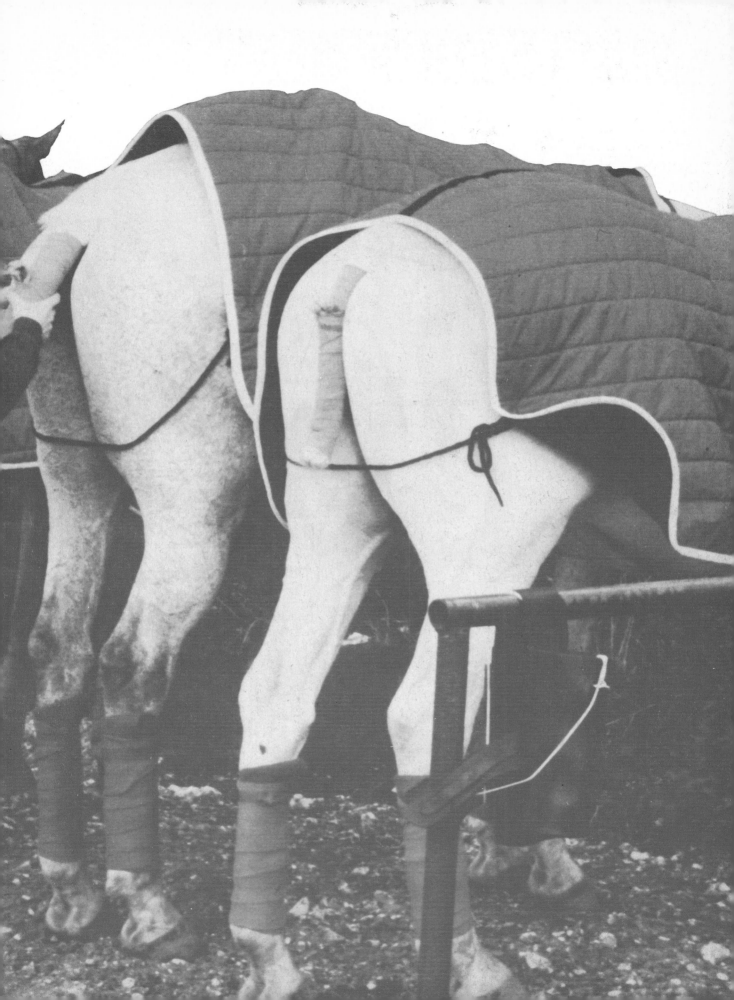

Stable Equipment

1.

The amount of equipment needed for the care and protection of the horse is usually far greater than that needed to ride or drive him. And the harder a horse is asked to work, the greater the amount of care and attention he should receive, both in and out of the stable.

One professional English horseman works by the maxim that at work his horses are treated as students—at rest they live like kings. It is a maxim that has led to success.

Equipment for the care of the horse today includes such necessary items as rugs, bandages, boots, shoes, studs, headcollars and halters, grooming tools and clippers. Then there are the stable and tackroom fittings, and all the equipment used to prevent stable vices and to provide veterinary treatment at home.

The variety of modern equipment is vast. But many of the basic principles of horse management have remained unchanged for centuries.

The Athenian Xenophon in about 400 BC made his grooms use wooden combs on the body, followed by a great deal of hand massage and a final rub with a date-palm-fibre rubber. Medieval horsemen, although they treated their horses to some of the most barbarous riding equipment, appear to have cared for their steeds in the stable in a more humane fashion. They fed and groomed them after the manner of Xenophon. The Greek horsemaster's principles are still in use today.

By the early seventeenth century, the use of grooming tools as we know them was already widespread. Horses were strapped with brushes and curry combs, straw wisps, stable rubbers and the wet hands of the groom.

Much of the standard modern equipment remains unchanged from those times. The invention of electricity has led to the development of electric clippers and the electric grooming machine, which is designed to take the hard work out of strapping.

Horse Dressed for Stable

1. Front buckle fastening
2. Roller
3. Day rug
4. Tail bandage
5. Fillet string
6. Stable bandages

Rugs

Rugs are generally used to provide protection and warmth in the stable or during travelling. Many different patterns of rugs are available, made in a variety of materials. The commonest materials are jute, wool, linen, canvas and synthetic fabrics.

Fitting

Rugs must fit properly if they are to provide adequate protection and not chafe the horse when he moves around. It is also important that they should fasten securely to prevent them slipping off and becoming torn underfoot. Before buying a rug, it is advisable to measure the horse and determine the right size. Measurements are taken from the centre of the horse's chest, where the rug will buckle, to the position the rug should reach on the quarters if it is to give adequate loin and quarters protection. This is usually about 100 mm (4 in.) from the root of the dock.

To avoid causing sores, a rug should fit comfortably and easily at the withers and should allow plenty of freedom of movement across the chest. If, in spite of all precautions, a rug does chafe the neck, a piece of sheepskin or foam sewn inside the neckpiece may provide an answer to the problem. Alternatively, a piece of thick felt tacked onto the rug lining a short distance below the withers on each side will raise the rug just enough to alleviate pressure.

Rugs for horses range in size from 1·7 to 2 m (5 ft 6 in. to 6 ft 6 in.). Those for ponies range from 1·25 to 1·6 m (4 ft to 5 ft 3 in.).

Surcingles

Many horsemen prefer to buy rugs with surcingles (webbing belts) already sewn on. They are usually 65 to 75 mm (2½ to 3 in.) wide and are fitted in pairs to secure the rug round the belly.

The front surcingle should be padded on either side of the withers and sewn into place. A loop of web is left above the spine in order to avoid constant pressure at that point. The second surcingle is fitted farther back and does not have to be fastened tightly to be effective. It may therefore be sewn on flat, without a loop.

Generally, the cheaper rugs are fitted with only one surcingle and have no wither loop. They are not to be recommended because in addition to bringing a certain amount of pressure to bear on the spine, which can cause serious spinal injury, a single surcingle is unlikely to hold a rug in position when the horse lies down or rolls.

Body Rollers

Separate body rollers are necessary when a rug is not fitted with surcingles. They should be well padded at the top, or else should be used with a foam rubber pad on either side of the withers to prevent spinal pressure.

Normally, rollers are from 100 to 125 mm (4 to 5 in.) in width, and are made from hemp web, wool web, heavy flax or leather. They have leather fittings and two straps—or three if they are to be used on stallions. Cheap rollers made of jute are not very hard wearing.

An efficient type of adjustable front fastening for a New Zealand rug. The buckle and strap may be moved lower down to widen the neck of the rug for use on a broad horse, or moved higher up to narrow it for a slim animal.

Sweat Rug

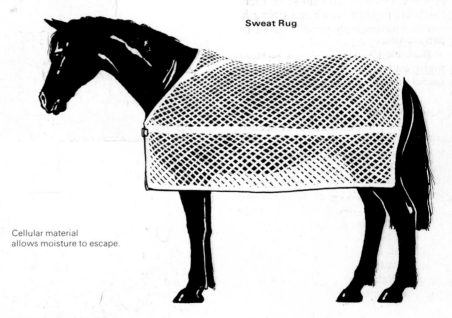

Cellular material allows moisture to escape.

Arch Rollers (Anti-Cast Rollers)

Arch rollers prevent pressure on the spine. They are sometimes called anti-cast rollers because the wither pads are joined by a tubular piece of curved metal to prevent a horse rolling and becoming cast in the stable. Some arch rollers are hinged at each side of the arch and, consequently, will fit any width of horse.

Roller and Breastgirth

It is wise to fit a breastgirth to stop a roller or unsewn surcingle from slipping back. A misplaced roller can badly upset a sensitive horse.

Breast Fastenings

The breast fastenings of rugs are usually buckles, fitted either singly or in pairs. The best are those that may be adjusted to fit a narrow or a wide neck, but these are not common. There are also some other types of fastening, such as self-adhesive tapes or the double-ring fasteners. In general, they are good and easy to maintain.

Fillet Strings

Many rugs are either sold with fillet strings (tail strings) or with eyelets to take them. These strings are made of coloured braided cotton or thin leather. They pass round the horse's quarters, a short way above the hocks and under the tail, to help prevent the rug sliding forward or flying up.

Types of Rugs

Stable Rug (Night Rug or Jute Rug)

The rug that receives the hardest wear is usually the stable rug, often known as the 'jute rug' because of the material most frequently used in its manufacture. Some of the cheaper varieties are made of lightweight jute and are only half-lined. But the best rugs are of heavy jute or finely-woven canvas and are fully-lined with blanketing. They are resistant to rotting and tearing and, provided that care is taken, can be washed regularly and will last a long time.

Various types of synthetic and quilted materials are now becoming popular for stable rugs. They are light and easy to wash, and most of them provide plenty of warmth and strength. Some are particularly good because air can circulate through them.

Because the stable rug can be used night and day, it is by far the most useful general-purpose rug.

Under-Blanket

In winter, an under-blanket is needed under the stable rug to keep the horse warm. Under-blankets are traditionally fawn, with stripes at each side.

High-quality, heavy wool blankets weighing 3 or 3·5 kg (7 or 8 lb) are expensive, but they provide greater warmth than thinner types and stand up better to stable wear.

Special, fitted under-blankets made of such materials as synthetic fleece are now available. Generally, they stay on well, and are warm and easy to wash.

Day Rugs

By day, owners who want their horses to look smart in the stable, when travelling or at shows, use woollen day rugs of the same shape and size as their stable rugs. They can be obtained in a variety of colours with matching bindings, and it is customary for the owner's initials to be shown on a rug's rear corners.

Jute is still the most common material for a night rug, although synthetic materials are gaining in popularity.

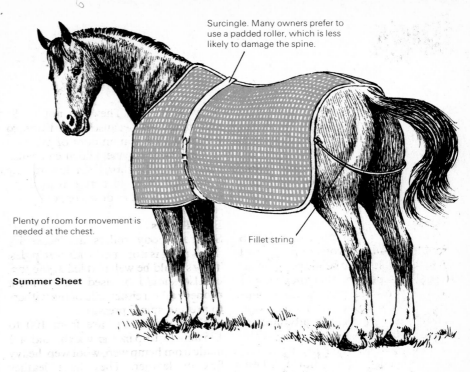

Surcingle. Many owners prefer to use a padded roller, which is less likely to damage the spine.

Plenty of room for movement is needed at the chest.

Fillet string

Summer Sheet

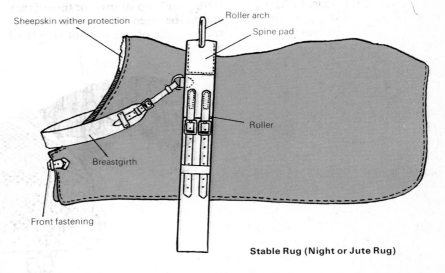

Sheepskin wither protection

Roller arch

Spine pad

Roller

Breastgirth

Front fastening

Stable Rug (Night or Jute Rug)

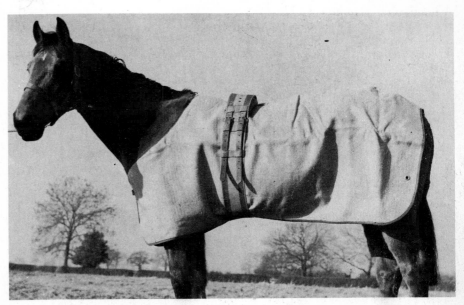

The day rug always has a braided fillet string looped round the quarters, and a roller of wool web. It may have a matching hood for warmth during travelling. The hood has eye holes, and covers the head, neck and ears.

Summer Sheet

A summer sheet made of cotton or linen is used instead of a day rug in hot weather. It protects a groomed horse against dust and the worry of flies, and is not intended to provide warmth. Summer sheets have fillet strings and surcingles or rollers.

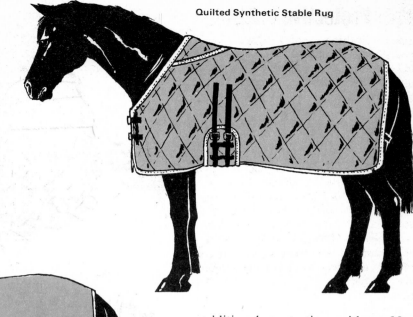

Quilted Synthetic Stable Rug

Day Rug

New Zealand Rug

The New Zealand rug is not intended to be worn in the stable, only in the field. It has very individual qualities and fastenings, and is a tough, half-lined or fully-lined rug of waterproof canvas or flax. Even a clipped horse may be turned out in a New Zealand rug in winter.

Correct fitting of the rug is very important because it must stay on day and night, often with infrequent checking. Particular care should be taken to avoid chafing at the withers, shoulders, and breast and between the hind legs.

Because the rug has to stay in place while the horse is moving around in the open, it has adjustable straps that cross between the hind legs. They should be fitted long enough not to chafe, but not so long that the horse can catch his legs in them. Some rugs have straps fastening near the forelegs, and all have one or more fastenings across the breast.

Many New Zealand rugs are fitted with a surcingle, but if this is too tight it will hinder the air flow along the back and cause condensation, followed by

chills. The best New Zealand rugs are well-enough-secured to need no surcingle.

Outdoor rugs require frequent maintenance. Leather straps must be kept supple so that they do not chafe or break, and fastening hooks must be oiled to prevent rusting. Tears in the canvas should be repaired immediately.

A waterproof hood may be used as additional protection with a New Zealand rug. It envelops the full length of the head. The hood overlaps the rug as far back as the withers, where it is fastened with either buckles or clips.

Anti-Sweat Sheet (Sweat Rug)

The anti-sweat sheet may be used on a hot horse after work, or during travelling. It is made of open cotton mesh and works on the same principle as a string vest under a shirt. The mesh creates air pockets next to the skin, providing the insulation necessary to allow the horse to cool off without becoming chilled, particularly across the loins.

In the same way, during travelling, the sheet aids in preventing a horse breaking out into a sweat and consequently losing condition. Worn in the stable, it insulates the body against the cold and the heat.

To be really effective, the sheet should be worn under a top rug or sheet, or the layer of insulating air pockets cannot be formed.

Rug Sense

- Horses that have been clipped out should wear a jute rug in cold weather.
- If a horse is turned out in a New Zealand rug, the rug must be checked at regular intervals and straightened if necessary.
- Fastenings, such as buckles, should be inspected regularly for signs of wear and tear.
- Most rugs tend to irritate the top of the horse's neck. A piece of felt or sheepskin sewn inside the rug where it rests on the neck will help to prevent this.

Other Protective Clothing

Racing clothing, apart from the normal stable clothing, may consist of a quarter sheet and breastplate, a lightweight roller and a breastcloth and hood, all of which may be made up in the owner's racing colours. Special sheets are also used for exercising at home.

Quarter Sheet (Paddock Sheet)

Usually, the quarter sheet is made of wool or of linen. It has no front fastening, but is cut off midway along the shoulder and curves slightly back towards the withers. It is kept in place with a breastplate, often of the same material as the rug. A leather strap sewn at each side of the withers takes a breastcloth.

Breastcloth

The breastcloth is made in the same material as the rug. It covers the front of the chest for warmth and runs up the neck on each side of the shoulders. It is held in place by the two buckle-and-strap attachments on the quarter sheet. The bottom of the breastcloth should be in line with the bottom of the quarter sheet.

Exercise Sheet (Galloping Sheet)

An exercise sheet is the same shape as a quarter sheet. It is placed under the saddle during work to keep the loins warm. A fillet string is fitted to prevent it flying up and frightening the horse.

Exercise sheets are usually made of wool, but a rubberized showerproof material is now available. This is more effective than wool in eliminating excessive sweating. It is also windproof and dries quickly, which is a help when it is required for use on more than one horse.

An exercise sheet will quickly slide back from under the saddle unless correctly fitted. The front corners should be folded upwards to form a triangle and then held in place by the girth and saddle panels.

Jowl Sweater

The jowl sweater is used to sweat off surplus fat from the throat area of such animals as show horses and ponies, which might otherwise have flexion problems. It is a form of hood with ear holes, and is made of felt lined with oilskin, plastic or other waterproof material.

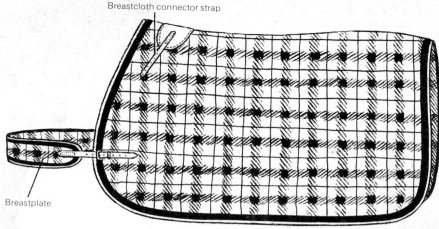

Paddock Sheet

Breastcloth connector strap

Breastplate

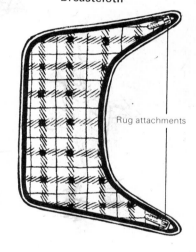

Breastcloth

Rug attachments

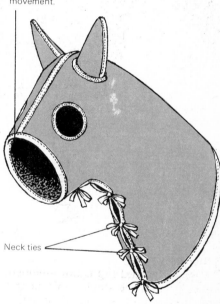

Nose hole should be wide enough to allow perfect freedom of jaw movement.

Neck ties

The popular anti-sweat sheet is used to keep a sweating horse warm as he cools off, thus preventing him from getting a chill.

Bandages

Bandages are used for protection against injury, for support, for warmth and for veterinary care. In knowledgeable hands, they can be invaluable. If they are applied wrongly, they can cause serious harm. White marks ringing the legs or dock, or lumps on the tendons, can frequently be traced to incorrect bandaging.

Bandages are rolled up tape-side inwards and applied with the main roll to the outside. They are put on from the top and rolled with equal tension as far down the leg as required. If the fetlock is to be covered, the bandage should be rolled past the joint and only covered on the way back up the leg, to allow joint movement.

Tapes, which should never be of stretch material, should be flat and tied to the outside of the leg, where they can do least damage to tendons and ligaments. They should be tied no more tightly than the rest of the bandage. They may be knotted or tied in a bow and the ends tucked in neatly. For exercising, they should be sewn or secured with adhesive tape for safety.

Almost all bandages require some form of cushioning under-protection between bandage and leg.

Gamgee

Gamgee is strong, white tissue packed into layers and rolled. It can be cut to the size required for use with any type of bandage. Gamgee may be re-used but it is not washable and soon loses its cushioning ability.

Some people use cotton wool as a cheaper substitute. But it has neither the strength nor the cushioning quality of Gamgee.

Synthetic Under-Protection

Synthetic forms of cushioning are also available. The foam varieties are good for exercising and are washable, but they do not have the smart appearance of Gamgee.

Better are the synthetic fleece types. These are also washable. The fleece side is placed onto the skin for soft cushioning, but is rolled over at the top and bottom for smartness.

Wool Bandages

Generally, wool bandages are about 125 mm (5 in.) wide. They are used with under-protection as stable or travel

Stable Bandage

Gamgee tissue

Tapes tied neatly on the outside of the leg

Coronet protection

Heel movement is allowed for if the bandage covers the heel only on the way up the leg.

Exercise Bandage

The turns of the bandage must be equally spaced and of equal pressure.

Fetlock joint protected but not restricted

bandages. They are applied to cover as much of the leg as possible, from the knees or hocks to the coronet. The tapes are tied and tucked in.

In the stable, wool bandages are used to provide warmth, comfort and support, particularly after strenuous exercise, when they should be left on for at least two hours. Used in this way, they can even prevent windgalls appearing. Also, they help to stop the legs filling when a stabled horse is not in work. Put on over soft straw or hay, they will help to dry off wet legs.

For travelling, they provide warmth, support and protection against knocks and in case of accident. In general, they

are not as secure as others but are very warm.

Flannel Bandages

Flannel bandages are the same size as wool bandages, are used for the same reasons and are put on in the same way. They are looser in texture and therefore stay on better, but it is doubtful whether they are as warm. They make good cold-water bandages, used to relieve heat and swelling.

Stockinette Bandages

Stockinette bandages are tubular woven cotton and are between 75 and 125 mm (3 and 5 in.) wide. They are used in the stable and for travel, although they are not as warm as wool. They are also used for exercise and as pressure bandages. They have the advantage of not over-tightening, but they are not very secure.

Pressure bandages are used in the stable over under-protection to give support and relieve swelling. They are put on firmly but not too tightly, and should be applied to both legs. The sound leg will have to take more strain than the unsound one and will therefore need support.

As an exercise bandage, used at work to support ligaments and tendons and protect against knocks, the stockinette bandage is useful. But it is not the best, because of its insecurity. It is worn over under-protection and is fitted from just below the knee or hock joint to just above the fetlock joint. It should provide protection but not interfere with the joints. The tapes should be sewn or secured with adhesive tape.

Newmarket Bandages

Newmarket bandages are made of crêpe or cotton with a certain degree of stretch, which should not be very great. They are between 65 and 100 mm ($2\frac{1}{2}$ and 4 in.) wide, and are used for exercising and as pressure or tail bandages.

For exercise and pressure, they are more secure than stockinette but they can rather easily be put on too tightly. If they become wet, they should be removed before they dry out or they will tighten and cause injury.

Newmarket bandages make the best tail bandages. They slip less easily than others. But they should not be put on too tightly and left overnight or for long periods at any time.

The bandages are used to keep a pulled tail neat, to keep the tail from being rubbed out, or to keep the tail out of the way, as in polo, for example. They should not be put on immediately after pulling or they can cause scabbing.

Sandown Bandages

Sandown bandages are made in two parts: fleecy wool at the beginning and stockinette at the end. They are approximately 125 mm (5 in.) wide. They may be used as stable, travel, pressure, exercise or cold-water bandages, all without under-protection.

The fleece is put on close to the leg for protection and warmth. Then the stockinette is wrapped over it to pack it more tightly and secure it.

The Sandown is an excellent all-round bandage. It stays on well and provides support with no fear of over-tightening.

Linen Bandages

Linen bandages are available in different sizes. They are used over surgical dressings after injury.

Stockinette bandages used as stable bandages over gamgee tissue to protect the horse's lower leg, and to keep him warm. This type of bandage is commonly used in the stable and for travelling. It does not over-tighten, but is not as warm as wool.

Tail Guard
The tail guard is a rectangular piece of rugging, blanket or leather, fitted with three or four straps or ties at the sides and a long strap at the top. It is fastened round the dock to prevent the horse rubbing hair from his tail—which may happen during travel or if the horse's blood is overheated or he has a skin disease.

Usually, the tail guard is fitted over a tail bandage. The straps should not be pulled too tight in case they cut off circulation. The top strap, which is fastened to the surcingle or roller, prevents the guard slipping down.

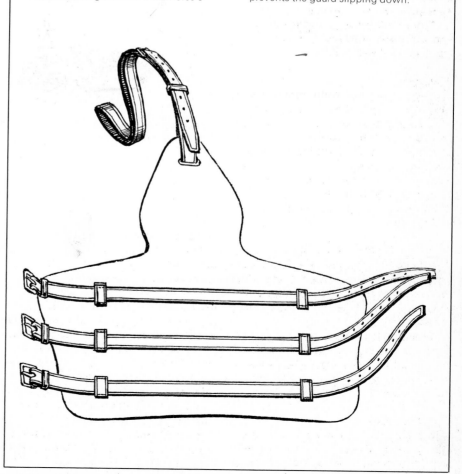

Boots

The primary purpose of boots is to protect legs against injury during work and travel. They are used also to give support, particularly to the susceptible tendons of the forelegs.

Boots give less overall support than bandages. But because they are usually made of stronger materials they afford better protection against knocks and scrapes. Injury may be caused not only by a horse's legs striking an obstacle, but also by one leg accidentally touching another.

Brushing Boots (Splint Boots)
Brushing occurs when a horse knocks the inside foreleg or hind leg, usually in the fetlock area, with the opposite leg, causing sores and eventual lameness. It may result from bad conformation and action, from faulty shoeing or from weakness or tiredness. It is particularly common in young and immature animals and these should always be schooled in light brushing boots.

Brushing boots are made of box-cloth, kersey, leather or felt. Box-cloth and kersey are soft but are difficult to clean and take a long time to dry out. Leather is strong, but it must be lined with soft material and kept supple or it will cause as many problems as it solves. Felt makes a good, soft boot but it is not as hard-wearing as leather. Padded caps, usually of leather, run down the inside of many boots to give added protection. They should be rounded at the bottom to accommodate the fetlock joint.

The boots are fitted in various ways, depending upon their design, but most have either three or four buckle and strap fastenings on the front boots and five on the hind. Hind boots are always longer.

Brushing boots may be divided into light- and heavy-duty. The former are good for everyday schooling, but stronger boots are essential for strenuous work. Light boots include ankle, French brushing, fetlock ring, scalper, quarter and Yorkshire boots. Among the heavy-duty patterns are polo, French chasing, speedicut and heel boots.

Ankle Boots
The ankle boot is the most basic and common type of brushing boot. Most ankle boots are made in kersey, leather or felt. They have a shaped and rounded padded cap of leather or kersey and protect the joint of the fetlock as well as the tendons and ligaments above it. Some leather boots are lined with foam rubber, but this can set up an irritation that produces infection.

The boots are shaped in such a way that the straps tighten above the fetlock joint. When fitting, the centre strap should be tightened first, followed by the top ones, then the bottom. The lowest strap should not be tight or it will restrict the joint and trap pieces of grit, which will cause sores.

French Brushing Boot
The French brushing boot is shorter than the ankle boot, protecting only the fetlock joint. It is made of soft, rubber-lined leather, shaped at the back to leave room for fetlock movement, and fastens with a single strap just above the joint. It protects both sides of the fetlock.

Fetlock Ring Boot (Brushing Ring)
The fetlock ring boot is a hollow, rubber ring fitting over the fetlock. This simple device is effective as a buffer against brushing, but gives no added support or protection. Often only one leg is fitted with a ring.

Scalper Boot
The scalper boot is a rubber ring with a large flap descending at one side to cover the inside of the fetlock. Care must be taken that the flap does not move away from the joint.

Quarter Boot
The quarter boot is a better and bigger version of the scalper boot. Being shaped like a French brushing boot, it offers protection to both sides of the joint and does not shift easily.

Fetlock Ring Boot

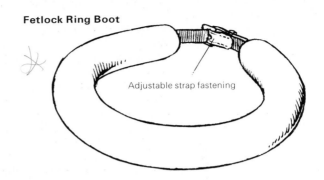

Adjustable strap fastening

Single Strap Brushing Boot

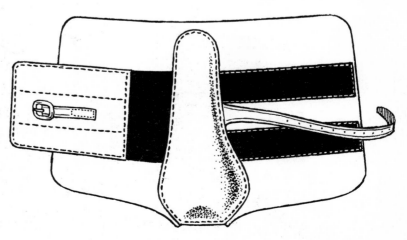

Yorkshire Boot

The Yorkshire boot is a simple rectangle of material, usually felt, with a tape sewn along the centre. The tape is tied just above the fetlock joint, and the top of the boot is then doubled down over it, providing two layers of protection.

Yorkshire Boot

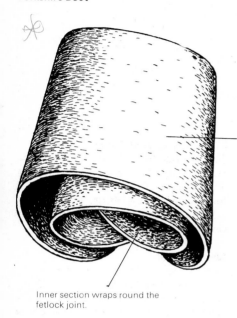

Outer section folds over the inner one, after the tapes have been tied.

Inner section wraps round the fetlock joint.

Polo Boots

There are many varieties of polo boots, but all are particularly strong and cover as much of the horse's lower leg as possible. The hind boots have a low flap for added protection. Many are made of felt and are strengthened with a cowhide lining. In some, strong elastic is built in for extra tendon support.

French Chasing Boot

As with the French brushing boot, the chasing pattern is usually made of rubber-lined leather. It is a large boot with a rounded fetlock protector at the bottom and a shin protector at the top.

Speedicut Boot (Speedy Cut Boot)

The speedicut boot is designed to prevent 'speedicutting' injuries caused when a horse hits his own leg high up above the fetlock joint. Such injuries often happen at high speed, hence the term 'speedicut'. The boot is a larger version of the ankle boot, extending high up towards the knee. It is made from either box-cloth or leather.

A pair of five-strap leather speedicut boots designed to be used on the forelegs. They are coupled with ribbed rubber over-reach boots. The safest over-reach boots do not have fastenings; however, they are difficult to put on and remove.

Speedicut Boot

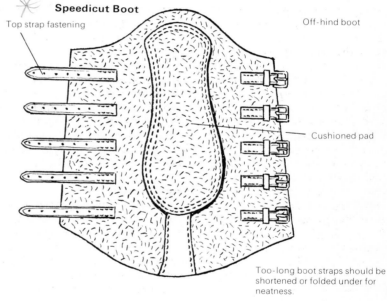

Top strap fastening

Off-hind boot

Cushioned pad

Too-long boot straps should be shortened or folded under for neatness.

Strong, slightly elasticated band

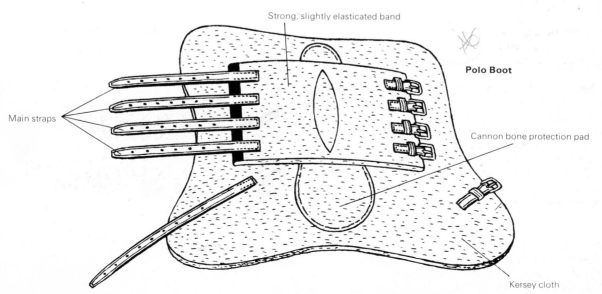

Polo Boot

Main straps

Cannon bone protection pad

Kersey cloth

Heel Boot

This boot combines protection against brushing with protection of the point of the fetlock. It is usually made of kersey. A heel boot has a rounded flap extending over the back of the fetlock and either left loose or strap fastened. If strapped, care must be taken that the joint movement is not restricted.

Heel Boot

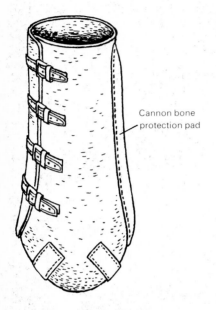

Cannon bone protection pad

Low heel prevents point of fetlock hitting the ground or being hit by toes of hind shoes.

Over-Reach Boots

Horses can do a great deal of damage to themselves by over-reaching, which is striking the back of their fore legs with their hind feet. It can happen anywhere from the coronet upwards and causes some of the more slow-healing wounds.

Over-Reach (Bell) Boot

Over-reach boots of a frequently used type are made of rubber, and are bell-shaped and ridged. They fit just below the fetlock, covering the heel and coronet. The coronary band is in particular need of protection because injury to it can lead to inflammation of the soft coffin-bone lining.

The best over-reach boots are made of pure rubber, because of its stretching ability, and have no fastenings. They are pulled on and off over the feet—sometimes a difficult operation with horses whose feet are big. Once fitted, they should not be loose and revolve around the pastern.

Some over-reach boots are split and are fastened either with laces or by

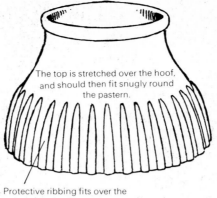

The top is stretched over the hoof, and should then fit snugly round the pastern.

Protective ribbing fits over the bulbs of the heel.

Some patterns have a plain rubber cuff at the bottom.

Rubber Over-Reach Boot

means of a vertical leather strap slotting down through metal dees along the sides of the boot. But plain boots are safer and more secure in use.

Coronet Boot

The coronet boot also protects the back of the heel and coronary band and is widely used by polo players. It is a double-strapped felt boot, usually lined with leather for strength.

Tendon Boot (Rundown)

The most dangerous form of over-reach injury occurs above the joint, when the tendon sheath or tendon is damaged. To prevent this, tendon boots are worn.

They are made of either kersey or leather, with a thick pad fitted at the back to support and protect the tendon. This pad is shaped and may put as many as three thicknesses of leather and kersey around the tendon. The boots have four or five straps.

Correctly-fitted plain kneecaps. The elasticated upper strap should be fitted firmly, but the narrow lower strap must be very loose to allow the knee to move. Plain kneecaps are generally used in the stable and for travelling. A lighter pattern—the skeleton kneecap—is less bulky for use when riding.

Kneecaps

Broken knees can ruin a horse. If a horse is in any danger of coming down on a rough surface or of knocking his knees when jumping fences, kneecaps should be fitted.

Basically, there are two types: plain and skeleton.

Plain Kneecap

This kneecap has a padded leather top with a leather strap set on elastic and buckling above the knee. Below is a semi-circle of felt, rugging or leather, with a large blocked and stuffed leather cap to enclose the knee. A lower strap is looped very loosely round the back of the leg, below the joint.

Plain Kneecap

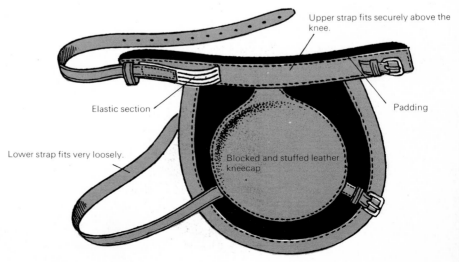

Upper strap fits securely above the knee.

Elastic section

Lower strap fits very loosely.

Padding

Blocked and stuffed leather kneecap

Skeleton Kneecap

The skeleton kneecap is similar to the plain kneecap but does not have the semi-circle of material, only the cap and straps. It is lighter and less cumbersome than the plain pattern.

Other Boots

There are several other types of boots, serving various purposes.

Travel Boots

Travel boots are used by some riders in preference to bandages. They are thick, rectangular pieces of felt, leather-backed foam or similar material, held in place by a number of straps.

The boots offer protection from below the coronet to—sometimes—well above the knee and hock joints, though most of them stop below these joints. They are quicker to put on and remove than bandages, but they provide less support. The foam-rubber types may cause irritation on long journeys.

Hock Boots

Hock boots are designed to stop a horse bumping his hocks against the back of the box whilst travelling. In the stable, they prevent capped hocks and similar injuries.

The boots are made of thick felt, rugging or leather, with a padded, blocked leather cap over the hock and the same type of fastenings as knee-caps. Again, the lower strap must be fitted very loosely.

Boots designed specifically for travelling. They must be well padded so that the top straps can be tight enough to keep the boots in position without putting pressure on the sensitive lower legs. Boots do not give as much support as bandages and are therefore not as suitable for long journeys.

Hock Boot

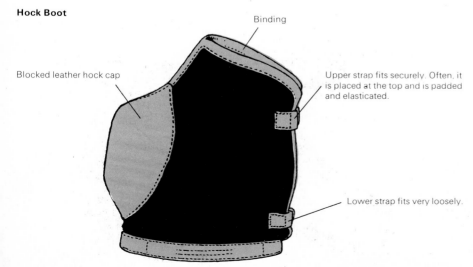

Binding

Blocked leather hock cap

Upper strap fits securely. Often, it is placed at the top and is padded and elasticated.

Lower strap fits very loosely.

Shin Boot

The shin boot is another well-padded boot. It is used purely to protect the shins against knocks and is therefore not as versatile as the French chasing boot.

Skid Boot

This boot is worn by American stock horses to protect the point of the fetlock from damage as it hits the ground during a quick turn or stop. It is made of leather, with two straps fastening above and below the fetlock. A leather cup protects the heel.

Shoes and Studs

Many types of shoes are in use to protect horses' hooves from damage and wear and, in some cases, to correct such faults as bad action. They all have at least one thing in common—they must fit correctly or the horse will not only be unable to perform to the best of his ability, but may even become permanently unsound. The foot must be evenly trimmed, and the type and weight of shoe must suit the animal that will be wearing it and the work he is required to do.

Shoes may be made of wrought iron, mild steel or aluminium alloy. Farriers often fashion new shoes from the metal of old shoes that have been removed. It takes about one and a half old shoes to make one new one.

Wrought iron contains up to three per cent slag. It is tough and fine-grained, is easily worked and makes a good shoe. Mild steel stands more wear than wrought iron.

Aluminium is very light and is used for racing shoes, called *racing plates*. Alloys are used in preference to pure aluminium because they are stronger.

Clips

It is important that the clip or clips on a shoe should be fashioned properly. A clip should be large enough to give the horse's foot purchase on the shoe and to stop the shoe moving. The best clips are low but broad and strong. Weak, tall and narrow clips can damage the sole when the shoe is lost.

Plain Stamped Shoe

The plain stamped shoe consists of an unmodified bar of iron, shaped to fit the hoof and having a single clip at the toe and stamped nail holes. Usually, as with most shoes, there are three nail holes on the inside and four on the outside.

Plain shoes are used on heavy horses and others doing slow work. They are not suitable for fast work or for light horses and ponies.

Fullered Shoe

The fullered shoe is a further modification. The groove in the ground surface gives the shoe not only lightness but a ready-made nail channel and dirt channel. In wear, the groove collects particles of grit, and as a result helps to prevent the horse slipping.

In some countries stainless steel, also, is used for racing plates. Although heavier than aluminium, it gives more wear.

The size of iron most commonly used for shoes is 19 by 9·5 mm ($\frac{3}{4}$ by $\frac{3}{8}$ in.). To measure a horse's foot for the farrier, the distance across the quarters of the sole is doubled and 25 mm (1 in.) added. The shoes may be put on hot or cold. Hot shoeing is generally preferred because the shoes tend to stay on longer; but any type of shoe can be fitted in either way.

Hand-made shoes are markedly different from those that are mass produced. Generally, hand-made shoes have a wider web, which provides more bearing surface for the weight of the horse. They also have a wider fullering (the groove round the outer edge of the ground surface of the shoe), which allows the nails to be driven home. If the nails cannot be driven far enough up the white line, the foot sometimes breaks up below. Also, the protruding nail heads wear down quickly and the shoe is lost.

Fullered shoes are the shoes most commonly used today. They are seated-out, the front shoes are pencilled and the hind toes rolled.

The term *seated-out* means that the inner edge of the bearing surface has been lightly hammered from heel to heel, to remove sharp edges. *Pencilling* is the rounding-off of the front shoe heel to minimize the risk of the hind toe catching it and tearing it off. The hind shoes are *rolled* (curved) at the toes for the same reason and to prevent injury

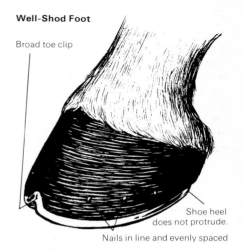

Well-Shod Foot

Broad toe clip

Shoe heel does not protrude.

Nails in line and evenly spaced

to the forelegs. The concave, fullered and seated-out shoe used for everyday work on the average riding horse should weigh in the region of between 425 and 510 gm (15 and 18 oz).

Shoe with Calkins

The calkin is a thick projection from the heel of the hind shoe; its purpose is to give a better grip on hard surfaces. Calkins should be fitted in pairs, one on each branch of a shoe. If only one is fitted, the foot will be constantly at an angle. Calkins were once widely used, and are still fitted to shoes for heavy horses. For light horses, calkins have been largely replaced by studs.

Feather-Edge Shoe (Anti-Brushing Shoe)

The feather-edge shoe helps to prevent horses damaging themselves when they brush. The inside branch of the shoe is narrower than the outside one. It has two nail holes, at either the toe or the heel.

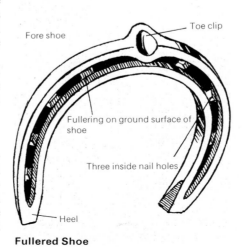

Fore shoe

Toe clip

Fullering on ground surface of shoe

Three inside nail holes

Heel

Fullered Shoe

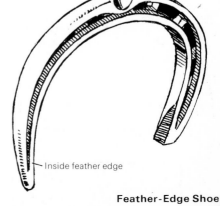

Toe clip

Inside feather edge

Feather-Edge Shoe

Concave Shoe

A development of the plain stamped is the concave shoe, the ground surface of which is narrower than the bearing surface. This prevents the shoe being sucked off in holding ground.

Three-Quarter Shoe

The three-quarter shoe is also used on horses that brush or those that need to have pressure removed from the heel. It has no inside quarter. This leaves that section of the foot unprotected and without support, but it allows ailments such as corns to be treated easily.

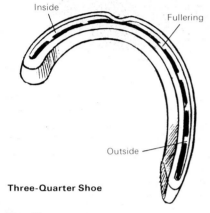

Three-Quarter Shoe

Bar Shoe

The bar shoe is more oval than usual and its heels are turned back over the frog and joined. It is used to put the frog back in work and to relieve pressure from the heels and quarters. It will also hold a leather pad over the sole after, or in case of, injury.

Cross-Bar Shoe

The cross-bar shoe is similar to the plain bar but has a thick, flat bar joining the two branches of the shoe across the frog, not too close to the heel. It gives extra support to the soles. The shoe is used particularly for competition horses and for those suffering from such ailments as laminitis and navicular.

Cross-Bar Shoe

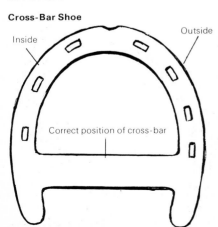

Tips

Tips are the small and light toe ends of shoes. They are used on horses at grass to stop their feet breaking up, and sometimes—because of their lightness—on racehorses during a race.

Grass Tip Shoe

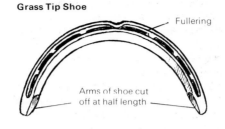

Racing Plates

Racing plates are made of very thin aluminium or alloy. They weigh about 60 to 115 gm (2 to 4 oz), and are used only during a race because they are short-wearing. The plates fitted to a horse should be an exact copy of his training shoes (which are made of mild steel) so that the hoof will not be weakened by fresh nail holes.

Pads

Plastic pads are sometimes fitted between a horse's hooves and the shoes. They are shoe-shaped and have a T-bar across the middle of the frog.

The purpose of pads is to cushion hooves and tendons against strain and to prevent injury to sensitive frogs and thin or dropped soles. They are used mostly on competition horses and on Thoroughbreds, which have a naturally lower heel than most other breeds.

A concave, fullered and seated-out hunter shoe fitted with one screw-in road stud. Some trainers feel that studs should only be used in pairs, so that the foot rests evenly on the ground, and that they should be fitted towards the front of the shoe.

Studs

Studs are inserted into the ground surfaces of shoes to give extra grip. The best are the large, screw-in varieties. They should be used in pairs to give a horizontal bearing surface.

Often, a rider possesses several types of studs. But all should have screw threads of the same diameter. When a horse is shod, the farrier makes holes of corresponding diameter in the shoes. In the front shoes, the holes should be set about 16 mm ($\frac{5}{8}$ in.) from the heels. Care should be taken with both front and hind shoes to ensure that the studs do not protrude and catch the horse's legs.

There are various types of studs, serving different purposes: blanks, which are square-ended, are used on the inside branch of a shoe to prevent injury; H-studs, which are shaped like a horizontal H, cut into the ground and are used to stop slipping and to act as shock absorbers on hard ground; pointed studs give purchase on wet ground; and road studs, square with a rounded steel centre tip, provide grip on slippery roads. Horses should not be ridden on roads when wearing sharp studs.

Immediately after work, studs should be removed with the stud spanner. The holes should be packed with grease and cotton wool so that they do not fill with dirt and grit.

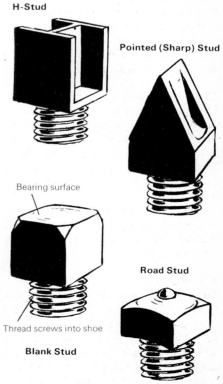

H-Stud

Pointed (Sharp) Stud

Bearing surface

Thread screws into shoe

Blank Stud

Road Stud

Halters and Headcollars

Halters and headcollars are in daily use in almost all stables. They should therefore be of the correct design and material for the job they have to do. Many styles are made—for the foal, the yearling, the in-hand show horse and even the horse that consistently pulls back, as well as for general leading, tying up and turning out.

Halters and headcollars may be made of leather, nylon, hemp or rope. In several countries, the term *headcollar* is used for the leather and nylon patterns, and *halter* for the rope and hemp. In the United States, however, they are all called *halters*. Leather is the smartest material, but unless the leather is rawhide, nylon and rope are stronger.

Newmarket Headcollar

The most basic leather headcollar is the Newmarket pattern. It consists of a headpiece that buckles either at the nearside or on both sides of the face above two metal rings. The throatlatch is attached to these rings, and they also support the cheekpieces, to which the nosepiece is fitted. There is no adjustment in either the throatlatch, which is rolled, or the nosepiece.

Three headcollar stop squares are fitted into the nosepiece. The rear one takes the headcollar shank, and the two side stops are used for pillar reins.

The headcollar is available with or without a front (browband). As with most patterns, the best quality Newmarket is adjustable at both sides, stitched in three rows, lined and fitted with brass furniture.

One variation of the Newmarket allows for vertical throatlatch adjustment. Its headpiece adjustment buckles have D-rings at the rear, to which the throatlatch is attached. If the headpiece is shortened, the throatlatch is raised. Another variation, the French pattern, has a D-ring at the nosepiece front for leading from the nose.

Albert Headcollar

The next most popular headcollar is the Albert, which is sometimes confused with the Newmarket. The Albert differs in that its throatlatch, which is adjustable, is slotted up into the loops of the front and over the headpiece. It has no metal rings on the cheekpieces. The Albert is less liable to break than the Newmarket because when the horse pulls back not only is the strain taken at the poll, but the horse tends to relax because he dislikes pressure at that point.

Headcollar Bridle

The headcollar bridle is of either the Newmarket or the Albert pattern. The headcollar stop squares on each side are fitted with adjustable buckle attachments for the bit.

Usually, the headcollar bridle is used for showing in hand. It should be of best quality, with brass fittings, and may be fancy-stitched.

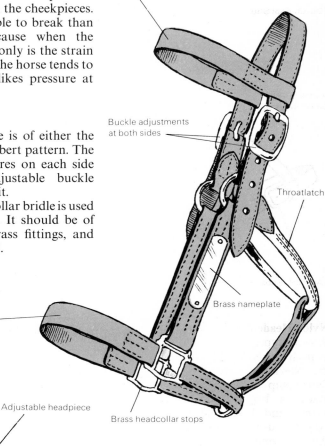

Newmarket Headcollar

Front (browband), sometimes white

Buckle adjustments at both sides

Throatlatch

Brass nameplate

Nosepiece

Brass headcollar stops

Adjustable headpiece

Rolled, non-adjustable throatlatch

Cheekpiece

Leather Yearling Headcollar

Adjustable nosepiece

Back strap

Queen's Headcollar

The Queen's headcollar is based on the Albert. It differs only in that the throatlatch is attached to metal rings at the point where the front also fastens. It is adjustable on both cheekpieces and on the throatlatch, but it is not as strong as the Albert. The Salisbury headcollar is similar to the Queen's but has no front.

Yearling Headcollar

Yearling headcollars are variations of the Newmarket. They have no fronts and are adjustable at the nosepieces. This enables the headcollar to be adjusted at intervals to fit the growing head of a yearling; many yearlings are turned out wearing headcollars.

Dutch Slip

Dutch slips are the most popular head-collars for foals. The adjustable head-pieces and cheekpieces are set through a metal ring under the foal's chin: the adjustable nosepiece also passes through the ring. Short straps at each side anchor the various parts together. A further strap hangs down from the metal ring to help in catching the foal. Dutch slips fit well and are not expensive.

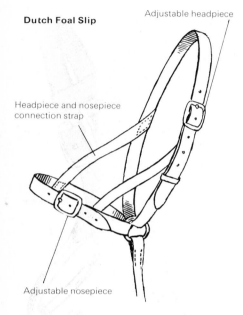

Dutch Foal Slip

Adjustable headpiece

Headpiece and nosepiece connection strap

Adjustable nosepiece

Nylon Headcollars

Various types of nylon headcollars are available, usually without fronts and in the Newmarket, Albert, yearling or Dutch slip patterns. Often, they are made in bright colours. They are strong and hard-wearing items for everyday use, but are not suitable for the show ring.

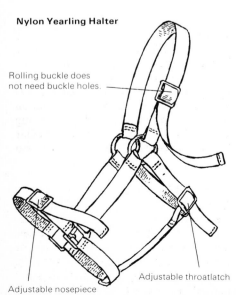

Nylon Yearling Halter

Rolling buckle does not need buckle holes.

Adjustable nosepiece

Adjustable throatlatch

Headcollar Shanks

Headcollar shanks (lead reins) should be approximately 1·5 m (5 ft) long by 20 mm ($\frac{3}{4}$ in.) in diameter. They can be made of leather, chain or hemp or jute rope.

Leather varieties may have a buckle loop and billet at the headcollar end, or a short piece of chain ending in a buckle or large spring hook. Spring hooks must be well cared for. A sprained hook can tear open a horse's nostril or lip.

Metal chain shanks are known as *rack chains*. They are particularly useful for short-racking stabled horses that might otherwise chew their shanks. If rack chains are fastened to the stable wall, they should be left to hang. If they are looped back on themselves, the horse may catch his feet.

Rope shanks are the most popular. They are soft and easily tied, but they need frequent replacement because they are soon chafed and chewed through.

Pillar Reins

Pillar reins are used in pairs to secure the horse at both sides of the head in a stall, where he is faced outwards for tacking up.

Usually, they are of leather or chain and are about 0·8 m (2 ft 6 in.) long. They have buckle attachments onto the stall posts rings, and spring hooks onto the headcollar sides.

A leather Newmarket headcollar fitted with a clip-on rope shank. This is one of the most popular patterns. The best-quality headcollars have brass furniture and are available with buffed leather browbands.

Basic Halter

The basic halter consists of a web headpiece and nosepiece front. Its rope shank forms the nosepiece rear. Such a halter is not really satisfactory because it has no throatlatch and therefore comes off easily, and the shank can over-tighten on the nose.

Yorkshire Halter

A better type of halter is the Yorkshire pattern. This is a complete ribbed hemp headpiece and nosepiece with a string throatlatch and fitted shank. It is strong, and a horse cannot easily pull it off. Consequently, it is particularly useful for horses that pull back.

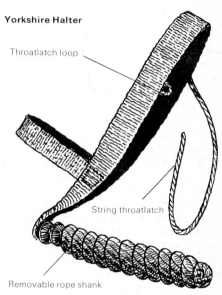

Yorkshire Halter

Throatlatch loop

String throatlatch

Removable rope shank

Grooming Equipment

Proper grooming equipment is essential in the stable. Grooming keeps the horse clean and healthy, improves his appearance and maintains him in condition.

Hygiene in the use of grooming equipment is of major importance. All items must be kept clean, and each set of brushes should be used on one horse only to guard against the spread of such skin diseases as ringworm.

Stabled horses should be quartered before exercise; that is, given a brush over, have their feet picked out and have their manes and tails dampened. On their return, they should be well strapped—given a thorough grooming—while their skin pores are open, so that they can get the most benefit from it. At night, they should receive a second cursory brushing before being rugged up. Horses at grass should have the mud removed from their coats before exercise, and the sweat removed afterwards.

Grooming tools include brushes, curry combs, mane combs, trimming scissors, sponges, hoof picks, stable rubbers, grooming pads and sweat scrapers.

Brushes are either machine-filled or hand-drawn. The bristles of machine-filled brushes are plugged into the wood base. Each tuft of bristles in a hand-drawn brush is secured, usually by wire, into a base, before a wooden top is screwed and glued into place. The dividing line between base and top is clearly discernible, and consequently it is easy to distinguish between articles of good and of lesser quality.

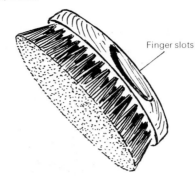

Dandy Brush

Finger slots

Body Brush

The body brush is oval and has short, closely-set bristles, softer than those of the dandy brush. Its back is either wooden or leather, which is softer on the hands; a loose band of leather or webbing fits over the back of the hand to anchor it.

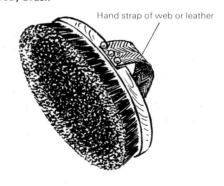

Body Brush

Hand strap of web or leather

The function of the body brush is to remove dust, dirt and sweat marks from the body and to condition the skin and muscles. It is used in conjunction with a metal curry comb—a device for cleaning it. Some people use the body brush on the tail. But many prefer to separate the tail into strands gently with the fingers to prevent the hairs coming out.

Sweat Scraper

The sweat scraper is used on a horse that has been washed down, not on one that is sweaty. It is a band of metal either shaped into a half-moon and attached to a wooden handle, or flat with a handle at each end so that the user can bend it. Usually, one metal edge is rubber-covered; this edge is used to scrape excess water from the horse's body. The sweat scraper should not be used on the bonier parts of the body, such as head and hips.

Sweat Scraper

Rubber edge is used on the horse.

Water Brush

The water brush is narrower in shape and has longer bristles than the body brush. It is used to dampen the mane and tail into place and to clean mud and dirt from the feet and legs. After use, it should be placed bristle-side down to dry, or the water will rot the wooden back.

Dandy Brush

The dandy brush is a wooden-backed brush with strong bristles, or plastic or nylon tufts. It is used to remove dried mud and sweat from the body, although sensitive or clipped-out horses sometimes object to this. It may be used on thick manes, but should never be used on tails because the stiff bristles pull out and break the hairs.

Care and Safety

● A wooden box is ideal for keeping grooming equipment tidy. Tools left lying around a stable yard can cause accidents.

● Regular checks on metal tools, such as the curry comb, ensure that rust does not take hold. Sweat scrapers should be cleaned and dried after use to prevent the rubber perishing.

● Loose hairs must be removed from the dandy brush and body brush before and after they are used.

Metal Curry Comb

The modern metal curry comb is a flat square of metal that is either attached to a wooden handle or has a webbing hand strap. Blunt teeth are set on one side of the metal to scrape clean the body brush.

The curry comb is used after every stroke of the body brush. It is pulled across the bristles of the brush, and the dirt emptied from it at intervals by tapping on the floor.

Curry Comb

Some curry combs have a hand strap instead of a handle.

Rubber Curry Comb

The rubber curry comb is a softer, oval version of the metal comb, and is always fitted with a hand strap. It is used on the horse's body to remove dried sweat, a shedding coat or mud. It is particularly useful for horses at grass, because it does not remove grease from the coat. A similar comb is made in plastic, but is not so effective in use.

Rubber Curry Comb

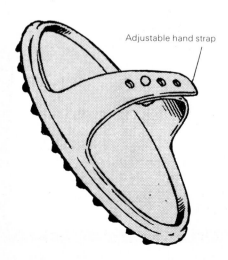

Adjustable hand strap

Mane and Tail Comb

The mane and tail comb is a strong-toothed metal comb. The large type is adequate for everyday use on the mane; but for mane and tail pulling, narrow combs are easier to handle and do a better job.

Mane and Tail Comb

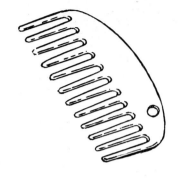

Trimming Scissors

The blades of trimming scissors are curved and the ends blunt to lessen the risk of a horse being cut or stabbed. The scissors are used for trimming whiskers and the hair from such places as the ears and fetlocks.

Hoof Pick

The hoof pick is usually about 100 mm (4 in.) long, and has a blunt cleaning hook at one end and a loop at the other so that it can be hung up. A folding hoof pick can be obtained; it is useful for carrying in the pocket when riding out. Hooves should be cleaned out at least twice a day, whether a horse lives in or out.

Hoof Pick

The end of the pick may be pointed, or it may be flattened to avoid damage to the sole and frog.

Sponges

Two sponges are needed for use in grooming a horse. They may be synthetic, but they must be strong. One is used to wipe the eyes and muzzle; the other is reserved for the sheath and dock area.

Sponge

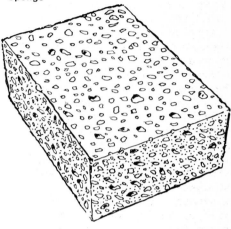

Stable Rubber

The stable rubber, a large rectangle of twill linen or some similar material, is formed into a pad and used for 'banging' the horse. This operation consists of banging hard on the muscles of the neck, shoulders and quarters. It promotes circulation and builds up muscles. The stable rubber is also used to give a final polish after grooming.

Stable Rubber

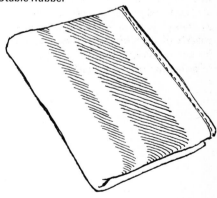

Grooming Pad

A grooming (massage or strapping) pad is a circular leather case filled with hay. It has a leather or elastic hand strap and is used for toning-up the muscles.

171

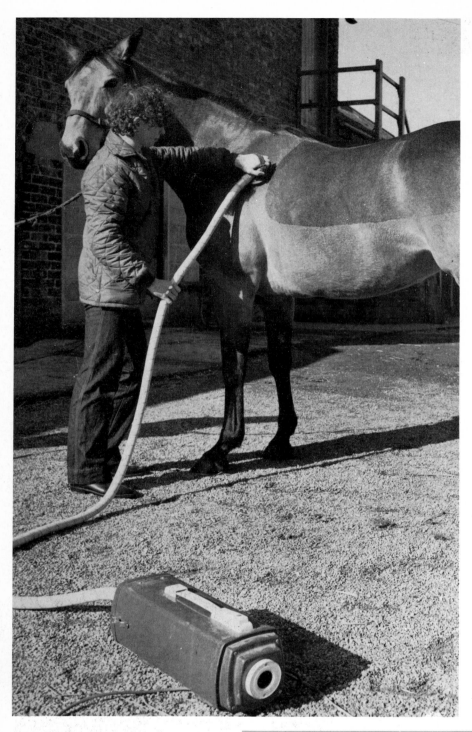

tion cleaner and works on the same principle. The machine is plugged in and left on the floor. A long, flexible tube is attached to the machine at one end and at its other end has a rubber curry comb which can be held with a hand strap. Grooming is carried out in the normal way, and dust and dirt end up in a bag in the machine. The bag has to be emptied regularly.

The revolving brush type of groomer has a motor that drives a revolving brush or polisher on a movable arm. The brush can be made to revolve at high speed in either direction, and care must be taken not to catch the mane or tail in it. As a precaution, the mane can be simply bunched into rubber bands and the tail knotted or bandaged out of the way.

The electric groomer is beneficial and stimulating to the horse's coat and skin, and does not remove grease. It should not be used to replace everyday strapping and banging of the horse. But it is perfectly efficient, is often well liked by the horse and can cut cleaning time by half.

Some electric groomers also have clipping head attachments. Consequently, they are a rather more economical buy.

A vacuum-cleaner electric grooming machine in use. The rubber curry comb attachment at the end of the flexible vacuum tube is used in the same way as usual, but the dust and dirt are sucked into the machine. Most horses enjoy the feeling once they have become used to the noise and the movement of the tube. Care should be taken to keep the electric cable away from the horse so that he cannot stand on it.

Electric Grooming Machine

Electrically-operated grooming machines are becoming popular. When they were first introduced they were expensive, and many horsemen were inclined to look upon them as aids for the lazy. But today they cost less and are more effective, and many private and professional horsemen are making use of them. There are two basic types of grooming machines: the vacuum-cleaner type and the revolving-brush type.

The vacuum-cleaner groomer is a stronger version of the household suc-

Using an Electric Groomer

● Rubber boots should be worn when using an electric groomer, particularly if the stable floor or the ground is wet.

● The grooming heads that touch the horse's skin can become dirty very quickly. They must be carefully cleaned each time the horse is groomed.

● If the horse is not used to an electric groomer, he should be introduced to it gently. Particular care must be taken when grooming the horse's head and other sensitive parts of his body.

Clipping Machines

Horses doing any work in the winter months when they normally have a heavy coat must have excess hair removed by clipping. Clipping allows a horse to work efficiently without sweating too hard or too quickly, both of which will make him blow up sooner and lose condition. A clipped horse dries faster and has less chance of breaking out (sweating) again. He is healthier and is much easier to clean.

The three basic types of machines in use today are hand-operated, wheel operated and electric. Of the three, only electric clippers are easily obtained.

Hand clippers are old-fashioned and slow. But they are quiet and cool, and some people prefer them for trimming delicate areas of the heads of touchy horses.

Wheel machines are also out of date, but can still be seen in use. They require one person to wind a wheel to generate power, while another person clips.

Electric clippers are now the only really practical pieces of equipment. They are available in two basic patterns: hand-operated clippers and hanging clippers.

Hand-Operated Electric Clippers
The hand-operated electric clipping machine is the most widely-used model. It is the cheapest and most readily transportable, and may be used wherever there is an electric power point (outlet). For safety, this should be a wall socket not a light socket.

The clippers are held in the hand. The cutting head is fitted with either body blades, which are used on all parts of the horse's body except the legs, or leg blades, which do not cut as close as body blades.

A screw fitted to the top of the cutting head adjusts the tension of the blades. If they are too tight, they strain the motor. If too loose, they will not cut correctly and may pinch the horse. Blades need regular re-sharpening.

The clippers work against the lie of the coat, which should be clean in order not to clog up the blades. The machine should be allowed to clip at its own pace; pushing strains the motor.

At intervals during a clip, the machine may become warm. Clipping should then be stopped for a while,

both to safeguard the motor and to spare the horse discomfort. The motor may be cleaned of hair and given a light oiling during this interval. After clipping, the machine should be stripped down and cleaned and oiled, before being wrapped in an oily cloth for storage.

Hanging Electric Clippers
The motor for hanging clippers is contained in a large case suspended from a roof beam. The clipper head is attached to a flexible arm.

Machines of this type are used in establishments where there are several horses requiring clipping, or which provide a service for owners without clippers. They have a stronger motor, which does not overheat easily. Because it is not in contact with the horse, any slight heat it produces will not affect him.

An added advantage is that the groom does not have to hold the weight of the motor as well as the clipper head and blades. This sometimes enables more accurate work and also cuts down the time needed to complete a clip.

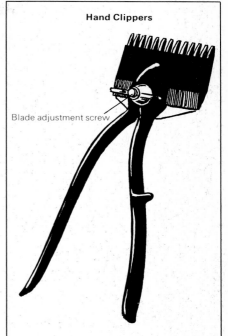

Hand Clippers

Blade adjustment screw

Hand Clippers
Hand clippers are slower and more tiring to use than their electric counterparts. But they can be handy for occasional use. They must be kept sharp and rust-free.

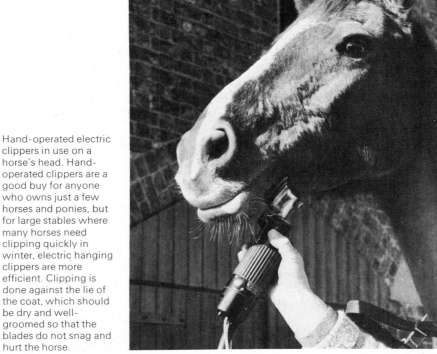

Hand-operated electric clippers in use on a horse's head. Hand-operated clippers are a good buy for anyone who owns just a few horses and ponies, but for large stables where many horses need clipping quickly in winter, electric hanging clippers are more efficient. Clipping is done against the lie of the coat, which should be dry and well-groomed so that the blades do not snag and hurt the horse.

Tack Room Fittings

Because of the increasing cost of new saddlery and harness, and of its repair, private owners as well as professionals are paying greater attention to the care and storage of their equipment. Constant improvements have been made to the methods of storing saddlery and harness neatly and securely. In particular, new types of materials are being used for the construction of tack room fittings.

Traditional fittings still abound, but the fittings that may be bought today are usually lighter and more easily transportable, and need little or no maintenance.

Proper storage of saddles is particularly important. Riding saddles must be stored in such a way that pressure is kept off the delicate trees, and support is given to the panels. The familiar long peg mounted on the tack room wall is no longer considered a satisfactory means of storage.

Bridle Brackets

The best types of bridle brackets are like small rounded arches on which headpieces can be hung. They are fitted on the tack room wall.

These brackets may be made of metal or of the same plastic-covered metal as saddle brackets. Often they have a small hook under the arch to take a martingale when the bridle is put up.

Satisfactory bridle brackets may be made by fitting round cans or their lids to the wall. They should be at least 25 mm (1 in.) deep, and no wider than about 230 mm (9 in.). Another way of making brackets is to slice a cylindrical piece of wood to the required widths.

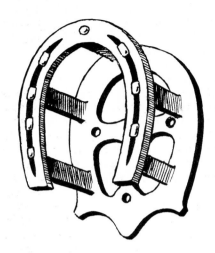

Bridle Hooks

Bridle hooks are used for hanging bridles during cleaning. They should not be used for storage.

The hooks are usually about 1 m (3 ft) long, but some extend to 1·5 m (5 ft). They are suspended from the ceiling at a convenient height for cleaning. Most such hooks are made of stainless steel or of plastic-coated metal.

Bridle hooks are ideal for hanging tack on whilst it is being cleaned. However, bridles should not be left hanging on the hooks for long because they are too narrow to keep the bridle headpiece in shape.

Saddle Brackets

Saddles have been stored on saddle brackets on the wall for a great many years. Some old-fashioned brackets were made of pieces of wood screwed together in the shape of an inverted V. These provided the correct support so long as the arms of the V descended some way down the panels.

Modern saddle brackets are similar in appearance to the old-fashioned metal varieties. They are made of strips of metal moulded to the shape of the saddle panels. Often, they are fitted with a bridle hook under the bracket arch. But many brackets are now made of metal covered with plastic; they are easy to clean, do not need to be painted and wear well.

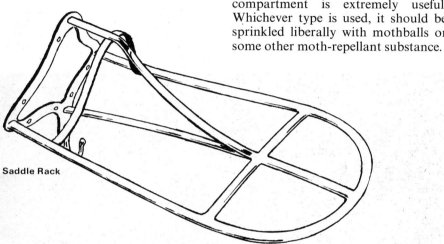

Saddle Rack

Most brackets are designed to support the normal astride saddles. But there are some for side-saddles, which have a particularly high dome at the back.

Saddle-Horses

Saddle-horses are used to combine a supporting rack for a number of saddles with storage space, often in the form of built-in drawers and cupboards. Usually, they are shaped roughly to the body of the horse and are traditionally made of polished wood. One particularly good design converts from a flat table-top into individual storage 'horses' and then into positions to hold the saddles upside-down for panel cleaning. A large set of bridle hooks holds at least four bridles for cleaning and storage.

There are now several light metal saddle-horses on the market. Some enable the saddles to be held in convenient cleaning positions. Metal saddle-horses are easily transported with the saddlery to shows and events, to help with the storage and cleaning of equipment.

Miscellany Hooks

A line of plastic-coated hooks on the wall, about 2 m (6 ft) from the ground, is ideal for storing reins, martingales, girths and similar items. Pairs of hooks set about 150 mm (6 in.) apart provide a useful means of storing bits and curb chains. Stirrup irons can also be kept in pairs on these hooks.

Rug Chests

Damp-proof, vermin-proof rug chests are vital if expensive rugs are to be kept in good condition, particularly during the summer months when they are not in constant use. Heavy, purpose-built wooden or metal chests can be bought, but a large travelling trunk may be a satisfactory substitute. A bandage compartment is extremely useful. Whichever type is used, it should be sprinkled liberally with mothballs or some other moth-repellant substance.

Boot Chest

A horse's leg boots must be stored in a ventilated box or rack. They should be cleaned and dried before being stored, or they will go flaccid and mouldy.

Stable Tool Box

The stable tool box is generally a suitcase-like container. It has two layers: the lower holds such items as cleaning materials, clippers and spare blades, scissors, a knife and screwdrivers. The upper layer contains grooming equipment and has a handle so that it may be carried from horse to horse.

Medicine Chest

No tack room is properly equipped without a medicine chest. Its contents should be thought about carefully. They should be appropriate not only to the illness or injury of the horse, but also to the injury of the rider or groom.

Harness Brackets

Driving harness brackets are made of similar materials to those used for riding tack, but they have to be purpose-built for the particular items.

Single harness needs four brackets, for saddle, reins, bridle and collar and crupper. Double harness requires two each of the following brackets: bridle, reins and crupper, pad, girth, bit, and collar and martingale.

Harness bridle brackets are larger than those used for riding bridles. Their design has to allow for winkers being stored in the correct shape.

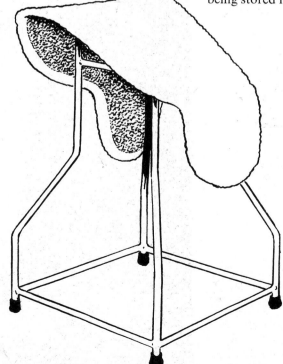

Light alloy saddle-horses are useful when tack has to be transported to shows or other competitions.

Stable Fittings

The number of fittings in a stable should be kept to a minimum to reduce the risk of the horse being injured. Some items are essential, however, and careful consideration should be given to their construction, siting and installation.

Mangers
Built-in brick and concrete mangers are traditional. Often, they are constructed across the stable corners. The manger bowl should be smooth-bottomed, wide and deep enough to prevent the horse pushing his feed onto the floor. A horizontal bar fitted at either side of the manger also helps to stop this.

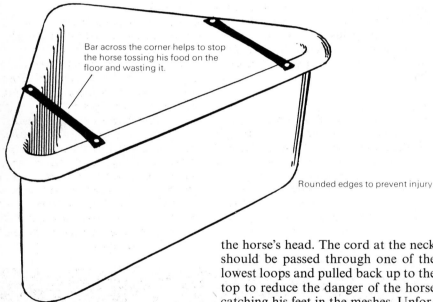

Bar across the corner helps to stop the horse tossing his food on the floor and wasting it.

Rounded edges to prevent injury

Corner Manger

The manger should be about 0·8 m (2 ft 6 in.) high. Its sides should slope away to meet the stable wall at the floor so that the horse can neither knock his knees nor become trapped.

Many owners prefer to buy metal or plastic feed bowls that can be removed and cleaned after each meal. These bowls should be large and heavy enough to remain still while the horse is eating, and they must be removed when he has finished to lessen the risk of his legs being damaged by them.

Hay Racks
Built-in hay racks are often placed too high. They not only drop hay seeds and dust into the eyes of the horse, but make him stretch his neck up and, as a result, drop his back. This puts pressure on the kidneys and encourages the horse to muscle up under his neck, rather than on top of it.

Hay racks at manger height can also be unsafe if they are constructed of iron bars that the horse can become tangled in.

Hay Nets
Hay nets are made of such materials as rope and nylon cord. Usually, rope nets are tarred to prevent them rotting when the hay is dampened, and to stop the horse chewing them.

Nets should be tied to a ring above the horse's head. The cord at the neck should be passed through one of the lowest loops and pulled back up to the top to reduce the danger of the horse catching his feet in the meshes. Unfortunately, when the net is high enough to be safe, it is also high enough to cause the same problems as the hay rack. It must, in any case, be removed when empty.

Many owners prefer to copy nature by feeding hay little and often on the floor, loose or from a boxed-in compartment fitted with a grille. It can be weighed before being fed loose just as easily as it can in a hay net.

Salt Holders
A salt holder is a small metal or plastic rack fitted to the stable wall near to the manger in order to hold a salt lick. Many owners consider salt holders an unnecessary hazard and leave salt licks in the manger.

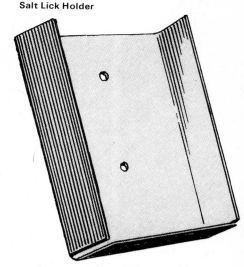

The edges must not be sharp or they will injure the horse.

Feed Scoops
Scoops made in the traditional pattern, with a handle and bowl, are convenient to use and are hard-wearing, but almost any small container will do for measuring out feed. The important point to remember is that the amount must be measured—not arrived at by guesswork.

Traditional-pattern scoops are easy to use and hard wearing. Food must be weighed out—not judged by bulk—because grain is very variable in weight.

Scoop

Water Buckets
Old-fashioned wooden and metal buckets are being replaced by lighter and more efficient plastic and rubber buckets, which will not damage the horse if he kicks them around the stable. Oak and metal buckets should never be left in with the horse, and plastic and rubber buckets should have their handles removed for safety, though they then have to be filled from other buckets. This is hygienic as well as safe, since each horse retains his own bucket. Daily cleaning, however, must not be neglected.

176

If a bucket is left in the stable, its handle should be removed for safety.

Water Bucket

mounted on a stem driven into it. Some owners tie short loops of string through them to fasten the headcollar to, so that if a horse pulls back he will break the string before the headcollar or its shank. Others staple string straight into the wall as a safe and easily renewable alternative to a ring.

Automatic Water Bowls

Automatic water bowls are excellent as long as they are boxed in well enough to avoid causing injury. They are plumbed-in and the water flow is either automatic or controlled by a spatula that the horse pushes as he drinks.

Automatic bowls provide a constant and fresh water supply. If the horse is too hot to be allowed to drink his fill, the water supply can be turned off, leaving him only what is already in the bowl and pipe.

Stable Rings

At least one ring is required in the stable for short-racking during grooming. It should be at chest height. Other rings may be fitted as necessary. In stalls, at least three rings are required, one for tying up at the manger, the other two for pillar reins.

Rings may be screwed to the wall or

Short-Rack Rings

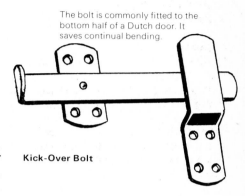

Stable Logs

Instead of tying a horse up, stable logs may be used. These rounded pieces of heavy wood or iron are attached to the ends of headcollar or halter shanks after these have been passed through stable rings. They lessen the risk of the horse getting his leg over the shank, because the shank is always taut. They also discourage a horse from pulling back.

Lights

Stable light bulbs should be protected by cages of heavy-duty wire mesh. The mesh stops horses touching a bulb and prevents wisps of straw or hay reaching the hot bulb and perhaps causing a fire.

The best light switches for use in a stable are the waterproof, round patterns that the horse finds difficult to master. Preferably, they should be fitted beyond the horse's reach.

Door Fastenings

Both halves of a Dutch door must be fitted with strong, galvanized metal stable bolts. The lower door should have two bolts, the bottom one of which may be a kick-over bolt to save bending. A small wedge placed through the bottom hole of the bolt catch will prevent the horse undoing the bolt with his teeth or shaking it loose.

The bolt is commonly fitted to the bottom half of a Dutch door. It saves continual bending.

Kick-Over Bolt

Ventilation

Generally, ventilation is provided by doors, windows and louvre boards.

The best type of door is the solid, hardwood Dutch variety, split into two so that the top half may be left open. Both halves should open outwards. A strip of metal will protect the top of the lower door from being chewed.

Windows should be high above the horse's head so that he cannot get to them and draughts cannot reach him. They should, in any case, be covered in small-mesh wire, open outwards and be hinged at the bottom. Louvre boards are safer than glass, but these too should be fitted high up the wall to minimize draughts.

A stable door must be secured with bolts that the horse cannot undo. Some horses show remarkable ingenuity in opening doors. A kick-over catch at the bottom of a stable door is safe and saves the groom continual bending to open or fasten.

Curative Equipment

Stable vices are bad habits, some of them constituting unsoundness, developed by horses through boredom, because of their temperament or because of the example of the horse next door. Some vices are inherited.

The major vices are biting; rug-tearing; crib-biting and windsucking; eating bedding, droppings and timber; pawing the door; and weaving. Most vices are injurious to the health of the horse and must therefore be prevented or cured.

Muzzles

Muzzles prevent a horse biting, crib-biting, eating droppings, bedding or timber, and rug-tearing. The problem is that they also stop the horse feeding normally.

Muzzles are held with a leather slip-head over the poll. One of the most common patterns is shaped like a leather bucket. It is ventilated with large holes, but the horse is unable to eat or drink when wearing it.

Mesh muzzles made of either wire or glass fibre allow the horse to drink. Bar muzzles, which are leather and have an open end spanned by two metal bars, allow him to drink, and to eat a little, although he may choose to eat droppings if his appetite is very depraved.

Wooden Neck Cradle

The neck cradle stops the horse tearing at his bandages or at blisters or other injuries. It is a necklace of poles, fitted with straps and placed horizontally around the horse's neck from throat to

Mesh Muzzle

Wire mesh. The facepiece may also be made from glass fibre, net or leather.

shoulders. The horse cannot even bend his neck, and is unable to bite himself.

Crib-Biting Straps

Crib-biters arch their necks, hook their top teeth onto a stable door or manger and gulp in great mouthfuls of air. Not only can this vice cause colic and loss of condition, but it can lead to wind-sucking, where the horse does the same

thing but without a door or manger. Windsucking is an unsoundness in a horse.

Crib-biting straps fasten tightly round the gullet. They prevent a horse arching his neck and inhaling large volumes of air at once. A variation, the Meyer's anti-cribbing strap, has a U-shaped loop at the bottom to fit snugly round the windpipe.

Door Bars

Crib-biters that hang onto the box door, and other horses that paw the door and damage their knees, can be thwarted by narrow iron bars being fitted above the bottom stable door. The crib-biter cannot then touch the door, and the pawing horse cannot get close enough to damage his knees.

Bars may also stop horses from weaving. Weavers shift their weight from one foreleg to the other, swaying their head and neck in rhythm. Weaving is an unsoundness. It causes great strain on the tendons, mental fatigue and loss of condition.

Wooden Side Bar

The wooden side bar has the same

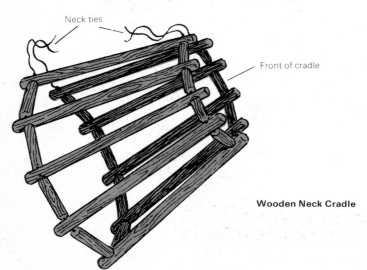

Neck ties

Front of cradle

Wooden Neck Cradle

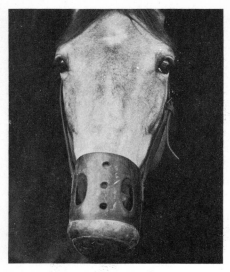

A strong leather muzzle, with good ventilation holes for the horse's nostrils and a leather sliphead. The muzzle prevents the horse from biting, eating his bedding, timber or rugs, and crib-biting. It should be remembered that it also stops him from eating and drinking!

effect in the same uncomfortable way as the neck cradle. It is a rounded pole stretched from headcollar to roller.

Clothing Protectors

Clothing protectors are designed to allow a horse to feed whilst preventing him chewing rugs or bandages. They are shaped like the rear half of a muzzle, extending a short way down below the chin. Most are made of leather, but a chain pattern acts in the same way and is more flexible.

Clothing Protector (Bib)

Headcollar attachments

Strong leather protector fits behind the chin of the horse.

Nose adjustment

Flute Bit

The mouthpiece of the flute (wind-sucking) bit has a series of holes in it. When the horse gulps in air, this mouthpiece blocks the air flow and the horse therefore receives no satisfaction from the practice.

Flute Bit

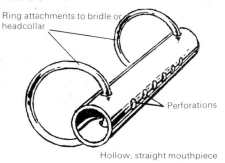

Ring attachments to bridle or headcollar

Perforations

Hollow, straight mouthpiece

Other Curative Equipment

Certain pieces of veterinary-type equipment are required also by private horsemen. Such items as the twitch have a place alongside equipment used to deal with injuries and ailments.

Leg Sprays

Leg sprays are thin pieces of circular plastic hose with fine holes all round. They are attached to a garden hose and fitted round a horse's leg. The fine spray of water hoses a filled leg with cold water without the constant attention of the groom.

Sausage Boots

The sausage boot is a means of prevention rather than of cure. It is a well-stuffed circle of leather with an adjustable strap. When placed round the pastern, its bulk prevents the horse capping his elbow by continually hitting it with his shoe when he lies down.

Twitch

The twitch (touch) is used to restrain any horse that objects to such treatment as teeth rasping or clipping. It is a wooden pole with a loop at the end made of either chain or string.

The loop is fitted round the upper lip and twisted until it is secure. The chain loop is less severe than the string because it does not have to be as tight and does not impede the horse's circulation.

Poultice Boot

Injuries and ailments to the foot and heel region are slow to heal, not least because they easily become dirty and infected. Bandages and sacks used as makeshift boots to secure dressings and poultices are easily torn off and are rarely waterproof.

Poultice boots can often be extremely helpful. They cover the foot and lower leg and fasten with straps and draw strings. Some have leather feet and canvas tops; others are made of rubber.

Poultice Boot

Adjustable leg strap

Rubber is now more commonly used than canvas for poultice boots because it is more practical.

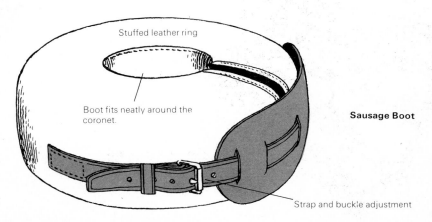

Stuffed leather ring

Boot fits neatly around the coronet.

Sausage Boot

Strap and buckle adjustment

Hats

For the past four centuries, hats and boots have been considered essential pieces of riding equipment. At first, fashion was their sole objective. Today, riders combine considerations of safety with those of style.

Men and women rode in everyday hats and shoes until the sixteenth century. By the end of that century, riding boots were made either knee-high or thigh-high, and turned over at the tops. They were fastened with buckles, buttons or laces.

Hats, however, remained soft and fashionable. By 1800, light leather boots called *jockey boots*, looking rather like modern top boots, had come into use. Short tasselled boots were popular, too.

Hats for men were either three-corned cocked varieties, or what was the first of the safety caps—the velvet jockey cap. Ladies wore either these or rather unsafe large-brimmed hats.

The black beaver top hat had been introduced by 1850. This was closely followed by the bowler and the less-tall top hat—which has been getting gradually lower ever since.

Headgear

The single most important item of equipment for a modern rider is a hard hat. It is wrong to think that protective headgear is necessary only when competing. Serious and even fatal injury can be avoided if riders wear well-fitting hard hats even out hacking.

There are five different categories of headgear available: hunting cap, bowler, top hat, skull cap (crash helmet) and polo cap.

Hunting Cap

The hunting cap is the most common. It is ideal for hacking as well as for such sports as hunting, showing, show jumping and dressage. It is light, comfortable and smart, and is generally available in black, navy or brown.

As with all headgear, it is important that the hunting cap be the correct shape, as well as size, for the head. Ideally, caps should be made-to-measure (custom made).

Made-to-measure caps are hand-made, usually from layers of gossamer and shellac. They are finished in velvet, and lined. Draw strings ensure that

Screw top ventilation button

College-cap back

Peak may be constructed to collapse on impact and help to prevent facial injuries.

Velvet Hunting Cap

there is a small space between the head and the dome of the cap.

Most riders settle for mass-produced caps. These are produced by high-impact injection to mould a thermoplastic shell. They are very strong and are finished in velveteen, lined, and fitted with draw strings and a pocket for any padding that might be necessary. They have adjustable chin straps. Before buying, the rider should make sure that these caps conform to the standards of the national safety institutions.

Generally, caps are made with flexible peaks. The reason is to avoid such injuries as broken noses during falls. They should remain in place without chin straps. It is considered incorrect to wear chin straps and they should be unnecessary. It is possible, however, to buy separate safety chin harnesses for hunting caps.

Traditionally, hunting caps were worn out hunting only by farmers, their wives and daughters, Masters and hunt servants. This 'rule' has now been relaxed so that all women and children, and some men, wear hunting caps rather than bowlers.

Top Hats

Top hats are made from gossamer and shellac and are finished in polished felt. Formerly, they were finished in hatters' silk from Holland, Germany and France, but this is virtually unobtainable today. Although they are expensive, it is possible to reblock them if they are damaged.

The hats are made in various heights: the highest is used by men in scarlet for hunting, the lowest is used for dressage and for showing. For

side-saddle riding, low hats are used with a veil.

The tallest varieties are the safest. They leave plenty of cushioning space between the head and the top of the hat, which concertinas in a fall.

There is continuing discussion over the wearing of top hats when hunting. Many riders say that they are useless either in a fall or in high winds, because they come off. If they fit well, this should not happen. But if a rider is concerned about losing his hat, a hat guard (a string of braid attached to the back of the hat and then to the inside of the collar) may be worn.

Top Hat

Bowler Hats

Bowler hats have changed little over the years. They are made from a mixture of rabbit fur, gossamer and shellac. Invariably, they are black. Because of their construction, they are almost impossible to repair if crushed.

They are correct hunting dress for women other than farmers' wives, and men other than farmers, Masters and hunt servants, and those followers wearing scarlet.

Bowler Hat

Skull Caps

Skull caps are the strongest and most protective headgear. They are made from a tough shell of glass fibre and are padded with foam rubber. A draw-string harness fits inside to hold the cap securely on the head, and there is an adjustable chin strap fitted to a tough chin protector.

The skull cap is the safest riding hat and is becoming increasingly popular with safety-conscious riders. It is lightweight and fitted with an anti-concussion harness fixed firmly round the head. The cap should protect the head, even if the crown cracks in a fall. Silk, or synthetic colours are worn over the cap. Jockeys push the flexible peak up away from the face, but cross-country riders usually wear it horizontal.

Skull caps have no peak, for safety reasons. Usually, they are worn with silks (caps), which are coloured coverings with slightly stiffened peaks. These are drawn tightly to hold them in place. Jockeys raise the peaks away from the top of the skull caps. Other users keep the peaks horizontal.

Skull caps are used in racing and in all types of cross-country competitions. They are compulsory for all racing-stable employees in Britain.

Crash Helmet

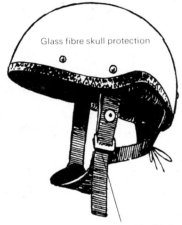

Glass fibre skull protection

Adjustable chin harness

Polo Hats

Most polo headgear today is of the polo cap rather than the traditional 'pigsticker' helmet type. The caps are made of three-ply cork, laminated into three layers for strength. They have a college cap back and a peaked front, and are fitted with adjustable chin straps, draw strings, anti-concussion tapes and rubber crown pads.

Polo Helmet

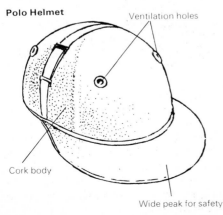

Ventilation holes

Cork body

Wide peak for safety

Hints on Hats

- Hard hats should always be checked after a fall to ensure that the shell has not been damaged.

- The rider's hair should be arranged neatly when wearing a hard hat—a hair net is often used for this purpose.

- It is important that a hard hat fits well. It should stay on of its own accord even if the rider falls.

Boots

Tall leather boots are the best footwear for almost all types of riding. They are shaped to fit the leg and foot snugly and give the highest degree of support. They protect the leg from kicks by horses and from knocks against tree trunks, gateposts and other obstacles. In addition they are the warmest and the smartest boots that can be bought.

Riding boots are made from various grades of leather, including box calf, which is one of the least expensive, and Bordeaux leather, one of the most expensive. Bordeaux is treated to a protracted vegetable tannage to become waxed calf, and is the only type of leather that requires boning rather than ordinary polishing.

If possible, it is best to have boots made-to-measure (custom made), a craft in which few firms specialize. Although such boots are expensive, the buyer is at least assured of a perfect fit. Fit is very important: too-large boots provide little support, and can even be responsible for sprained and broken ankles.

Should the rider have what boot manufacturers consider the average shape and size of leg, ready-made boots may fit well. If they are a good fit except in one or two places, they can sometimes be altered to fit more tightly or even expanded.

There are four main types of tall leather boots: butcher boots, top boots, race boots and polo boots. There are also short, ankle-length boots—used by children wearing jodhpurs and, for everyday riding out, by adults wearing chaps or leggings to prevent chafing. Most of these are jodphur boots.

Butcher Boots
Butcher boots are the most common of the tall varieties. They are plain, full-length hunting boots fitted with garters. Usually, butcher boots are black, but sometimes they are made from brown leather. These boots have shaped legs and feet, leather soles, a square heel and garters of matching colour. Correctly, all garters should be fastened on the inside of the knee. Any spare strap should be trimmed close to the buckle, not tucked in.

Butcher boots are available made-to-measure or ready-made. Manu-facturers of ready-made boots place

increasing emphasis on producing as many different widths and heights of fitting as possible.

In Germany, particularly, boots are being made to assist riders in various equestrian sports. Boots designed for the leg position required in dressage are being produced by at least one major company. They have a synthetic whalebone support at the back, and are honed on the inner leg to enable the rider to give clearer leg aids. The leg of the boot is fashioned at such an angle to the foot that walking in them is very difficult. But they give a good leg position for the rider and also wrinkle less around the ankle than most butcher boots.

Butcher boots are considered correct dress at all times for women. Men may wear them when they are not wearing scarlet coats.

Garter. Always fastened at the front, and the spare end trimmed

Butcher Boot

Jodhpur Boots
Invariably, jodhpur boots are made of leather and have leather soles and heels of the same style and height as butcher boots. They may be either black or brown, with elastic sides or strap and buckle fastenings. The elastic-sided design is probably safer for children, who might trap buckles in the stirrup irons.

Jodhpur Boot

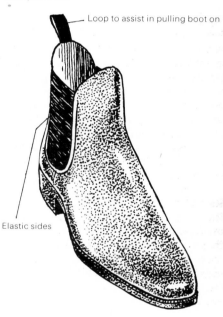

Loop to assist in pulling boot on

Elastic sides

Jodhpur boots give good support to the feet and ankles, but not to the calves. Generally, children wear them only for competition work until they are in their teens, when they change to butcher boots.

Rubber Riding Boots
When tall rubber riding boots first appeared on the market, they were little different from the rubber or synthetic waterproof boots used for gardening and similar occupations. But their design and finish have improved so much that, in some cases, they are hard to distinguish from leather at first glance.

Rubber boots do not give as much security or warmth as leather, however good the design. They are also rather light, are garterless and draw the feet in warm weather.

Rubber and Leather Boots

A new type of tall boot has a rubber top and leather foot. These boots allow the foot to breathe better, and give slightly more support to the ankle. But the calf is still left with little protection.

Polo Boots

Polo boots are brown butcher boots made of special vegetable-tanned polo brown calf. They are brown because, traditionally, players found black polish more difficult to clean off their white breeches than brown.

At one time, all polo boots were laced at the front of the ankle so that there were no buckles to catch another horse or rider when riding off. Now, they are generally left plain.

Top Boots

Top boots are identical to black butcher boots except that they have contrasting mahogany tops and white garters. The fashion of wearing top boots originated with the cavaliers in seventeenth-century Britain who used to turn down the tops of their boots to display the coloured linings.

Top boots are now worn by men in any situation in which they also wear scarlet coats.

Race Boots

Race boots are also black with mahogany tops, but they are lighter than any other boots. Most are simply made of a very light leather, such as pigskin. But some are made of fabric—and have to be held up with elastic bands.

Boot Jack

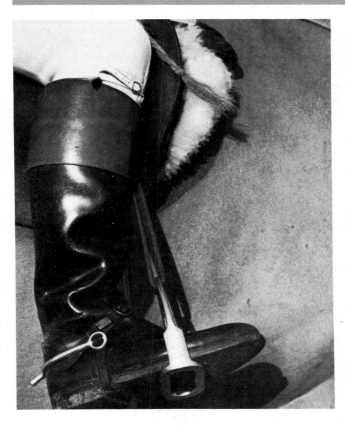

Footwear: Choice and Care

- Boots with full soles are safer than those with half soles, which may catch in the stirrup iron.

- Well-cared-for boots will last for a long time. Leather boots should be polished after use, and re-heeled and soled regularly.

- It is not essential to wear riding boots, as sturdy lace-up shoes are adequate for daily riding. Shoes with buckles or pronounced heels must never be worn as they can easily catch in the stirrup iron and trap the rider's foot.

Leather top boots worn only with white breeches by members of the field. Garters should also be white. Boots are measured to reach the small of the knee, just below the two top buttons of the breeches.

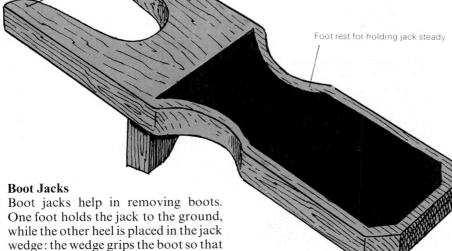

Heel grip

Foot rest for holding jack steady

Boot Jacks

Boot jacks help in removing boots. One foot holds the jack to the ground, while the other heel is placed in the jack wedge: the wedge grips the boot so that the rider can pull the foot out easily.

Boot Trees

All tall leather boots should have boot trees put in them immediately after use or they will sag at the ankles. Usually, trees are of wood, formed of a number of shaped pieces and slotted together inside the boots, but there are also trees made of plastic or metal. In an emergency, rolled newspapers are better than nothing.

Boot Hooks

Boot hooks help the rider to pull on tall leather boots. They have a handle of bone, ivory, wood or metal surmounting a metal hook. The hooks are used in pairs, and are slotted into two cloth loops inside the boots. A dusting of French chalk helps in the sometimes difficult operation of putting a tight boot on.

Quick Reference

The selection of equestrian equipment is not governed by any infallible rules. It depends not only on the rider's knowledge, skill and preferences, but also on the work the horse is to do and the nature of the horse himself. The horse is a complex and individual animal, and what suits one horse and brings out the best in him may be completely wrong for another and may even bring out the worst.

Ideally, every horse and pony should be happy and responsive in a simple snaffle bridle and cavesson noseband. Unfortunately, this does not happen in practice, and to suggest that every rider should equip his horse in this way would be foolhardy to say the least.

What all this means is that it is not possible to lay down hard and fast rules to govern the choice of equipment. Once that is understood, however, there are some guidelines to assist the rider in making a selection. Certain pieces of equipment are used primarily—though rarely solely—for particular sports and other activities. There are also pieces of equipment that have been found through experience to be suitable for the horse and the rider in particular types of event. But almost always there are alternatives that need to be considered.

The rider needs to know what items of equipment are really necessary for the sport he is taking part in. He also needs to know what is best for his own horse. When these two considerations can be balanced, the task of choosing and using equipment becomes relatively straightforward.

Show Jumping

Show jumping is the world's most popular equestrian sport not only for riders but also for the public. Each year, more and more young riders start on the bottom rung of the show jumping ladder. And each year, more new names are added to the list of well-known international riders.

One accusation sometimes levelled at show jumpers—particularly in the lower echelons of the sport—is that they use too much equipment and too-severe equipment. If this is true, and if riders find that there is a need for excessive use of severe equipment,

the cause can only lie in bad or insufficient training. One undesirable result of this is bad publicity for what should be a superb sport.

A well-trained horse needs no more gadgets to clear a round of show jumps than he does for any other jumping activity. However, in the small indoor arenas used particularly during the winter months, absolute control of the horse is necessary, and each rider must make an individual assessment of what equipment is needed to achieve this.

HORSE
Bridle
must be selected to suit the
  horse 32–53
preferably with rubber-covered or
  laced reins 62–63

Saddle
jumping saddle 74–75
Extras
bandages 160–161 or
boots 162–164
breastgirth 108
  and martingale 60–61
breastplate 108
  and martingale splits 61
numnah 104–105
pads 167
studs 167
surcingle 80

RIDER
Headgear
hunting cap 182
Footwear
top boots or butcher boots 184
spurs 109

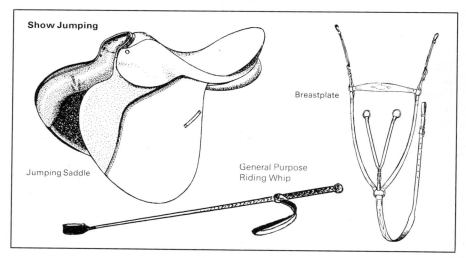

Show Jumping

Jumping Saddle

Breastplate

General Purpose Riding Whip

Eventing

Three-day events are the all-round test of the skills of horse and rider. They are the ultimate trial of obedience, courage, speed, endurance and fitness—and they have been likened to the tetrathlon as an athletic equivalent.

The dressage phase on the first day tests obedience and suppleness. The speed and endurance phase on the second day involves riding on roads and tracks, a steeplechase course and arduous cross-country work. And the show jumping phase on the final day demonstrates just how fit horse and rider are after their previous days' exertions.

Each of these phases calls for different equipment for horse and

rider. In one-day and two-day events there are fewer phases—but they are coupled usually with even faster changes of clothing and equipment.

Dressage Phase

HORSE
Bridle
for FEI tests, German
double bridle 38–41
  otherwise, double bridle 38–41
  or simple snaffle 32–35
Saddle
dressage saddle 76–77
Extras
breastplate 108
Lonsdale girth 77
numnah 104–105
stirrup irons, heavy 102
studs 167

RIDER
Headgear
top hat (with tails) or hunting
  cap   182
Footwear
butcher boots   184
spurs   109

Speed and Endurance Phase

HORSE
Bridle
must be selected to suit the
  horse   32–53
preferably with rubber-covered or
  laced reins   62–63
Saddle
cross-country saddle   80–81
Extras
bandages   160–161 or
boots   162–164
breastgirth   108
  and martingale   60–61
breastplate   108
  and martingale splits   61
numnah   104–105
studs   167
surcingle   80

RIDER
Headgear
skull cap and silk   183
Footwear
butcher boots or top boots   184–185
spurs   109

Show Jumping Phase

See SHOW JUMPING

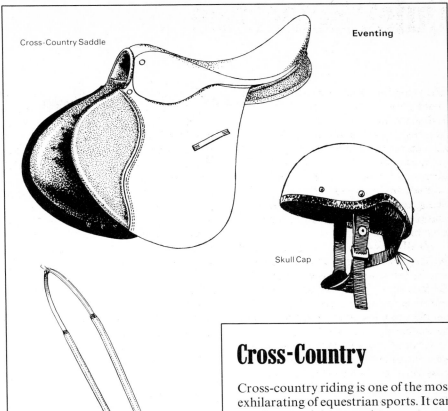

Cross-Country Saddle

Eventing

Skull Cap

Rubber-Covered Reins

Cross-Country

Cross-country riding is one of the most exhilarating of equestrian sports. It can also be one of the most dangerous, and all the equipment used must be well-fitted, secure and chosen in the interests of safety.

Cross-country riding includes such universal events as hunter trials and the newer team chasing events. Both of these are timed, and are ridden at speed over natural fixed fences.

HORSE
Bridle
must be selected to suit the
  horse   32–53
preferably with rubber-covered or
  laced reins   62–63
Saddle
cross-country saddle   80–81
  or steeplechase saddle   84
Extras
bandages   160–161
  or boots   162–164
breastgirth   108
  and martingale   60–61
breastplate   108
  and martingale splits   61
numnah   104–105
studs   167
surcingle   80

RIDER
Headgear
skull cap and silk   183
  or hunting cap   182
Footwear
butcher boots or top boots   184
spurs   109

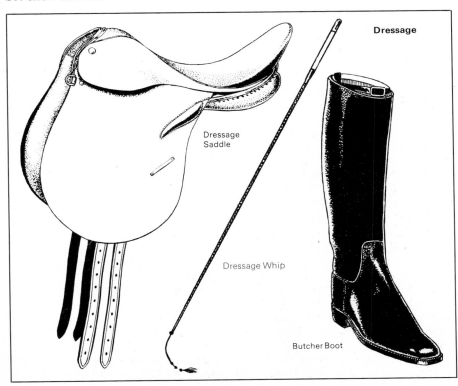

Dressage

Dressage Saddle

Dressage Whip

Butcher Boot

Showing

Showing is the competitive display of the horse and pony, and it is therefore instrumental in keeping up good standards of conformation and manners.

There are various classes of showing according to type or breed—and height—either under saddle or in hand. While a horse's conformation cannot, of course, be altered in order to secure him a place in the final line-up, good training and good equipment both contribute to success.

Some of the various show classes call for their own specific types of equipment. The following are the basic items required, however, for showing under saddle.

HORSE
Bridle
plain double bridle   38–41
snaffle bridle for working hunter
   classes, if necessary   32–35
Saddle
show saddle   82–83 or
dressage saddle   76–77
Extras
none

RIDER
Headgear
bowler or hunting cap   182
Footwear
butcher boots   184
blunt spurs   109

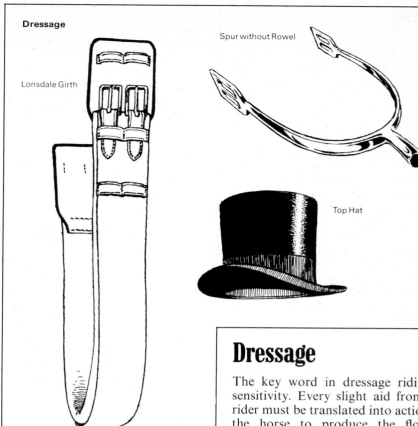

Dressage

Lonsdale Girth

Spur without Rowel

Top Hat

Dressage

The key word in dressage riding is sensitivity. Every slight aid from the rider must be translated into action by the horse to produce the flowing sequence of movements that earns high marks in the dressage arena.

The equipment for dressage is kept to the minimum. At novice standards, only the simple snaffle bridle is worn. Later, the snaffle is replaced by the double bridle when greater degrees of precision and collection are required in advanced tests. The saddles used in dressage remain the same, of course. The aim is to reduce the bulk between rider and horse, and thereby to heighten sensitivity.

HORSE
Bridle
double bridle   38–41
   or snaffle   32–35
simple, one-piece noseband   56–57
Saddle
dressage saddle   76–77
Extras
breastplate   108
Lonsdale girth   77
numnah (if essential)   104–105
stirrup irons, heavy   102
studs   167

RIDER
dressage whip
Headgear
top hat (with tails) or hunting
   cap   182
Footwear
butcher boots   184
spurs without rowels   109

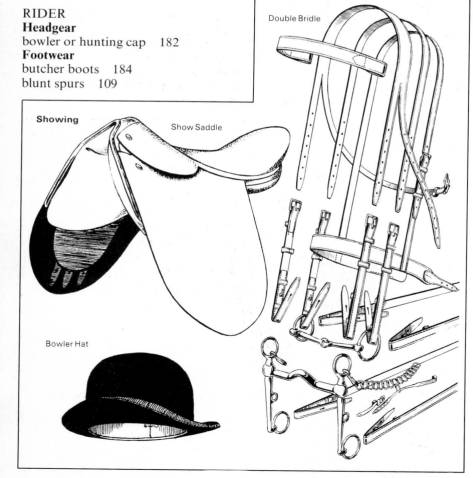

Showing

Show Saddle

Double Bridle

Bowler Hat

Racing

The two major types of horse racing are flat racing and steeplechasing. Flat racing is the most costly as well as being the best-known and most popular internationally. But steeplechasing is becoming increasingly popular in some countries.

To say that the equipment needed for flat racing is minimal is an understatement. In a sport where weight is supremely important, the quantity and weight of equipment must be honed down rigorously.

In steeplechasing—and therefore in its amateur counterpart of point-to-pointing—there is a little more leeway. Riders must have security over the fences, which will in any case sort out the field in a way that does not happen on the flat.

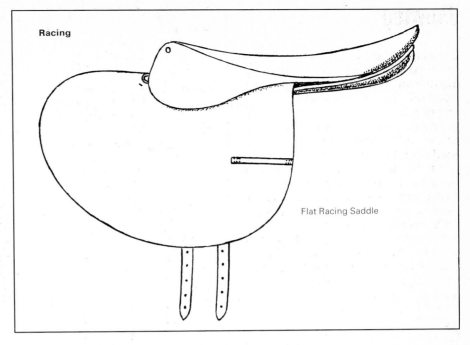

Racing

Flat Racing Saddle

HORSE
Bridle
snaffle—D-cheek or wire-ring   32–35
with cavesson, sheepskin-covered or
  Kineton noseband   56–59
rubber-covered reins   62–63
other bridles   53
Saddle
flat racing saddle   84–85
steeplechase saddle   84
Extras
Australian cheeker   54–55
blinkers   55
breastgirth   108
flat race webs   101
girths, web or elastic   99
Irish martingale   61
saddlecloth   106–107
surcingle   80
weightcloth   106–107

RIDER
Headgear
skull cap and silk   183
Footwear
race boots   185

Hunting

Traditionally, hunting is the great sport for riders. Young devotees are inspired by tales of their predecessors' gallant feats while following hounds. And although the sport receives threats from many quarters, the hunting folk of today still try as much as possible to keep to the traditions of their forbears.

Certain equipment is *de rigeur* in the hunting field, and some is strictly taboo—such as the wearing of coloured show-style browbands. The theme is: the plainer the better, coupled with complete control of the horse in the interests of safety in the field.

HORSE
Bridle
double bridle, traditionally   38–41
otherwise, to suit the horse   32–53
preferably with rubber-covered or
  laced reins   62–63
Saddle
hunting saddle, traditionally   86–87
otherwise, general purpose
  saddle   72–73
  or cross-country saddle   80–81

Extras
boots   162–164
breastplate   108
martingale splits   61
numnah   104–105
studs   167
surcingle   80

RIDER
hunting crop
Headgear
top hat or hunting cap or
  bowler   182–183
Footwear
top boots or butcher boots   184–185
spurs   109

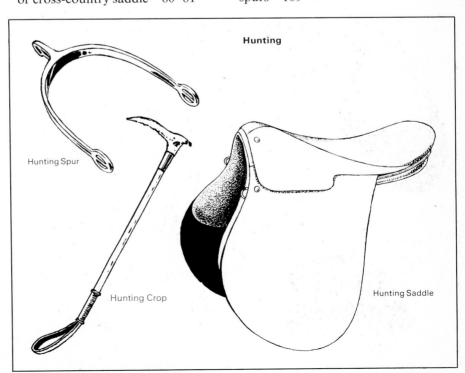

Hunting

Hunting Spur

Hunting Crop

Hunting Saddle

Driving

Competitive and pleasure driving are experiencing a revival in many countries. What was once merely a means of conveyance—until super-seded by the steam engine and the automobile—has now become an absorbing equestrian sport in its own right.

The fairly new branch of combined driving—the equivalent of the ridden horse trial—has brought great thrills and spills to the sport, particularly on the 'marathon' cross-country phase.

The number of showing turnouts, both heavy and light, is increasing annually. And harness racing is becoming more and more popular outside its traditional home, the United States.

Driving equipment is generally a matter of personal preference. However, it must, of course, suit the type and number of horses being driven.

One-Ear Bridle

Western Stirrup

Western Riding

Western riding has a style all its own—and so has its equipment. Today, the Western style is used not only by working cowboys in the United States and Canada, and in Central and South America, but by many other people, too, who appreciate it. This is particularly the case in countries where long-distance competitive riding is on the increase. Many of its *aficionados* say that the Western saddle and the seat position it forces the rider to adopt are much more comfortable on a long ride than their 'English' counterparts.

The multitude of different pieces of Western equipment are used not only in the show ring and for rodeos and other competitive work, but for every-day ranch work.

Breaking

The gentle art of horse-breaking begins the moment the first light slip is placed on the young foal's head. From then on, all handling and all equipment should be aimed at bringing the horse into training as gently as possible.

The slip makes way for a yearling headcollar, which in turn is replaced by a cavesson headcollar and then a breaking bridle and bit. A breaking roller paves the way for the saddle. And lungeing and long-reining prepare the horse for a rider.

Each stage on the long road of breaking has its appropriate pieces of equipment. These have been tested by experience. If any of them is missing, the task of the trainer is made harder.

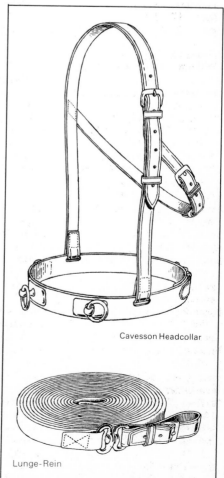

Cavesson Headcollar

Lunge-Rein

Tandem Harness

Index

Entries in italics refer to illustrations.